TORFAEN LIB
WITHDRAWN

Book No. 1609520

Anarchism and Moral Philosophy

Also by Benjamin Franks

REBEL ALLIANCES: The Means and Ends of Contemporary British Anarchisms

Anarchism and Moral Philosophy

Edited by

Benjamin Franks
University of Glasgow, Dumfries, UK

Matthew Wilson
Loughborough University, UK

palgrave
macmillan

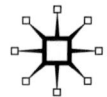

Selection and editorial matter © Benjamin Franks and Matthew Wilson 2010
Chapters © their individual authors 2010

All rights reserved. No reproduction, copy or transmission of this publication may be made without written permission.

No portion of this publication may be reproduced, copied or transmitted save with written permission or in accordance with the provisions of the Copyright, Designs and Patents Act 1988, or under the terms of any licence permitting limited copying issued by the Copyright Licensing Agency, Saffron House, 6-10 Kirby Street, London EC1N 8TS.

Any person who does any unauthorized act in relation to this publication may be liable to criminal prosecution and civil claims for damages.

The authors have asserted their rights to be identified as the authors of this work in accordance with the Copyright, Designs and Patents Act 1988.

First published 2010 by
PALGRAVE MACMILLAN

Palgrave Macmillan in the UK is an imprint of Macmillan Publishers Limited, registered in England, company number 785998, of Houndmills, Basingstoke, Hampshire RG21 6XS.

Palgrave Macmillan in the US is a division of St Martin's Press LLC, 175 Fifth Avenue, New York, NY 10010.

Palgrave Macmillan is the global academic imprint of the above companies and has companies and representatives throughout the world.

Palgrave® and Macmillan® are registered trademarks in the United States, the United Kingdom, Europe and other countries.

ISBN-13: 978–0–230–58066–4 hardback

This book is printed on paper suitable for recycling and made from fully managed and sustained forest sources. Logging, pulping and manufacturing processes are expected to conform to the environmental regulations of the country of origin.

A catalogue record for this book is available from the British Library.

A catalog record for this book is available from the Library of Congress.

10 9 8 7 6 5 4 3 2 1
19 18 17 16 15 14 13 12 11 10

Printed and bound in Great Britain by
CPI Antony Rowe, Chippenham and Eastbourne

TORFAEN COUNTY BOROUGH	
BWRDEISTREF SIROL TORFAEN	
01609520	
HJ	17-Feb-2011
335.83	£55.00

Contents

Notes on Contributors   vii

1 Introduction: Anarchism and Moral Philosophy   1
   Benjamin Franks

Part I Philosophical Anarchism

2 In Defence of Philosophical Anarchism   13
   Paul McLaughlin

3 Kicking Against the Pricks: Anarchist Perfectionism and the Conditions of Independence   33
   Samuel Clark

4 Anarchist Philosophy: Past, Problems and Prospects   45
   Nathan Jun

Part II Anarchism, Property and Autonomy

5 Autonomy, Taxation and Ownership: An Anarchist Critique of Kant's Theory of Property   69
   Kory DeClark

6 The Ethical Foundations of Proudhon's Republican Anarchism   86
   Alex Prichard

7 Freedom Pressed: Anarchism, Liberty and Conflict   113
   Matthew Wilson

Part III Alternative Anarchist Ethics

8 Anarchism and the Virtues   135
   Benjamin Franks

9 Green Anarchy: Deep Ecology and Primitivism   161
   Elisa Aaltola

10	Listening, Caring, Becoming: Anarchism as an Ethics of Direct Relationships *Jamie Heckert*	186
11	A Well-Being Out of Nihilism: On the Affinities Between Nietzsche and Anarchist Thought *Jones Irwin*	208
12	Are Postanarchists Right to Call Classical Anarchisms 'Humanist'? *Thomas Swann*	226

Index   243

Notes on Contributors

Elisa Aaltola has been a research fellow in philosophy for a number of years, both in Finland and the UK. She is currently a lecturer in philosophy at the University of Eastern Finland. The emphasis of her research is on animal and environmental philosophies.

Samuel Clark is Lecturer in Philosophy at Lancaster University, and the author of *Living Without Domination* (2007), and of articles in journals including *Res Publica* and *Philosophy*. He works on the nature and conditions of human flourishing.

Kory DeClark is a graduate student working in political philosophy at the University of Southern California.

Benjamin Franks is Lecturer of Social and Political Philosophy at Glasgow University, Dumfries. His work on anarchisms has appeared in *Anarchist Studies*, *Capital and Class* and the *Journal of Political Ideologies*. He is the author of *Rebel Alliances: The Means and Ends of Contemporary British Anarchisms* (2006).

Jamie Heckert holds a PhD in sociology from the University of Edinburgh. He is the editor of a special issue of *Sexualities* on anarchism and sexuality (2010). He is a contributor to a number of scholarly volumes on anarchist theory, research methodologies and intimate relationships. He currently lives in Poole, England.

Jones Irwin completed his PhD in philosophy at University of Warwick in 1998 and he has taught at University College Dublin, University of Warwick and University of Limerick. Since 2001, he has been a lecturer in philosophy at St. Patrick's College, Dublin City University, where he is Co-Director of the MA in Human Development and Ed.D programmes. He is also Visiting Fellow at University of Warwick, Centre for Philosophy, Literature and the Arts, for 2008–2010.

Nathan Jun is Assistant Professor of Philosophy at Midwestern State University in Wichita Falls, Texas (USA). He is co-editor (with Shane Wahl) of *New Perspectives on Anarchism* (2009) and (with Dan Smith) of *Deleuze and Ethics* (forthcoming).

Paul McLaughlin is a research fellow in the Department of Philosophy, University of Tartu, Estonia. He is the author of *Anarchism and Authority* (2007) and *Mikhail Bakunin: The Philosophical Basis of His Anarchism* (2002).

Alex Prichard is an ESRC Postdoctoral Fellow at the Department of Politics, University of Bristol. He gained his PhD from Loughborough University in 2008 and is founder and secretary of the Anarchist Studies Network. He has published widely on anarchism and international relations. He is currently working on a manuscript on the international political theory of Pierre-Joseph Proudhon and is co-editing a volume on twentieth-century libertarian socialism.

Thomas Swann is currently a postgraduate student at Radboud University, Nijmegen, where he specialises in anarchist and socialist political philosophy. As a political activist, he is also involved in a number of left-wing collectives in the Netherlands.

Matthew Wilson is currently completing his PhD at Loughborough University, which explores the problems of freedom, diversity and conflict in anarchist thought and practice. He is also involved in various forms of political activism, in particular, with the anarchist cycling collective, Bicycology.

1
Introduction: Anarchism and Moral Philosophy

Benjamin Franks

Alongside the growth of avowedly anarchist and anarchically influenced contemporary movements, such as anti-capitalist networks, radical environmentalist groups and grassroots community campaigns, there has been renewed academic interest in anarchist thought and practice. Significant volumes have appeared discussing anarchism from a range of anthropological, sociological, historical and political theoretical perspectives. However, instances of interest by philosophers have been much rarer and occur more intermittently, despite the scholarly studies by George Crowder (1991), Paul McLaughlin (2002, 2007) and Samuel Clark (2007).

This book has three main goals: The first goal is to expand on, and clarify, the distinctive interpretations of anarchism from different, and often rival, schools in order to initiate meaningful and productive dialogue. The second goal is to bring in perspectives from contemporary activists into academia in order to contest the sterile division between the two. Either side of the academic/activist divide is replete with stereotypes. Academics are viewed as over-privileged obscurantists who function to justify, and thereby maintain, existing social divisions, while activists are irrational hotheads with little of interest to say for the serious scholar: these caricatures of (and from) both sides are damaging to dialogue and meaningful effective action.

The third goal is to encourage further research into the relevance of anarchist approaches to contemporary philosophical fields of enquiry. Because of shortage of space there is little discussion in this book of the applicability of anarchism to fields such as pedagogy and feminist philosophy (areas where there are at least small canons of existing texts) or medical and research ethics, aesthetics and jurisprudence (where there are, at present, significant lacunae).

While this collection demonstrates that there is considerable original contemporary research by (largely) younger university workers, some of the concerns have parallels with discussions and debates in earlier anarchist and unaligned socialist periodicals. Examples drawn from past anarchist periodicals highlight that key concepts and core social problems are stable features of the various constellations of anarchism. The archives of popular anarchist newspapers and magazines (some of which had readerships in their tens of thousands) provide an underutilised resource to assist in the understanding of debates that developed anarchism prior to its suppression by, among other things, 70 years of Leninist hegemony. While some are written in a populist discourse with a number of *enthymemes* (unstated assumptions shared by writer and audience), they, like many contemporary libertarian texts, rarely display the disordered characteristics often mis-associated with anarchism – a perception of irrationalism that is so strong that even critical commentators feel that it is necessary to offer correctives (see Tverdek, 2001: 405; Knowles, 2002: 249).

The view that anarchism is intellectually unsophisticated is often evinced in certain anarchist's reductive rejection of any moral consideration. As discussed elsewhere (Franks, 2006: 95–6), there has been a peripheral, but oft-highlighted, section of anarchists who rejects any ethical consideration, as either irrelevant or oppressive. Irrelevant because changes in society are the result of historical laws that lie outside human control, where morality is simply a product of particular determining economic forces, a position associated with Leninist readings of Karl Marx (in particular, Marx, 1992: 425–6), as illustrated in the (then) independent and libertarian-aligned socialist paper *The Call*: 'Law, education, philosophy [...] are organised and interpreted to maintain capitalist exploitation of the workers' (Fairchild, 1916: 2). Philosophical concepts in general are merely epiphenomenon of real, economic change. Oppressive because their implementation requires restrictions on individuals' instincts of freedom and requires the coercive institutions of the state, Patriarch or Church (Bakunin, 1970). Similarly, *The Egoist* (1914a: 2), often associated with Max Stirner, argued in its first edition that universal codes are simply an excuse for the state, who can justify its existence by claiming to act to ensure that such principles are applied to all. Dora Marsden (1914: 341), one of *The Egoist*'s more committed Stirnerites, launched an attack on non-egoist anarchists for wishing to impose ethico-political norms onto others, and thus being simply statists.

Alongside Stirner, *The Egoist* also promoted the work of Benjamin Tucker, and the economic-individualism that academic political philosophy usually associates with anarchism. Since the 1970s social philosophy has frequently portrayed anarchism simply as an offshoot of Nozickian right-libertarianism, and thus subsumes 'anarchism' into Murray Rothbard's 'anarcho-capitalism' or ultra-liberalism (see for instance Freeman, 2001: 124 and many of the papers in Long and Machan's (2008) collection). This book is aimed at re-shaping this partial or, as some chapters here argue, inaccurate account of anarchism and replacing it with a more sophisticated, richer and potentially more subversive and interesting set of canons, principles and arguments.

Because Anglo-American philosophical accounts of anarchism have portrayed anarchism as largely synonymous with the most individualistic forms of anti-redistributive, classical liberalism, these philosophical arguments have had little relevance to anarchist movements and traditions that are largely anti-capitalist and critical of hierarchies of power including, but not exclusively, economic power. As a result, when philosophers discuss anarchism, they either appear as being disengaged from contemporary debates or risk talking across other interested parties. In order to re-focus debate and analysis towards these more common, but more philosophically overlooked, anarchisms, this book deliberately excludes chapters premised on an 'anarcho-capitalist' *Anschauung* (framed-view) of anarchism.

In part, the identification, or perhaps misidentification, of anarchism has been the product of the dominant analytical approach to political philosophy in general and categorisation of anarchism in particular. The chapters in the first section of the book explore and assess the analytical account of anarchism. McLaughlin's contribution, 'In Defence of Philosophical Anarchism' (Chapter 2), following Robert Paul Wolff's (1976) *In Defence of Anarchism*, refers to this Anglo-American academic version as 'philosophical anarchism'. Philosophical anarchism concentrates its analysis on the legitimacy (and limits) of political authority and promotes the protection of the rational, independent sovereign subject. McLaughlin recognises in this philosophical account of anarchism is widely assumed by many activists and academics (in a rare example of agreement) to be largely co-extensive with free-market social theories and the latter's corresponding acceptance or acquiescence to inequalities of distribution. Activists as a result have little positive to say about this dominant analytical version of anarchism.

However, McLaughlin, with reference to Alan Carter's 'analytical anarchism', argues that contrary to this received opinion, an analytically rigorous anarchism can be engaged in resisting illegitimate authority. McLaughlin's version of philosophical anarchism distinguishes it from anarcho-capitalism. He further argues that the analytical techniques philosophical anarchism privileges offer a more suitable set of theoretical tools than those associated with poststructural theorists or political activists. Samuel Clark (Chapter 3) and Kory DeClark (Chapter 5) also embrace the dominant analytical traditions and similarly contest the association with anarcho-capitalism, but in distinctive ways. Clark, in his contribution, argues that a key inspirational feature of philosophical anarchism is that its implied perfectionism provides a desirable, guiding account of the good.

Clark's contribution unusually endorses the position ascribed to anarchists by analytical political philosophers, such as Jonathan Wolff (2006: 30), that there is a biologically determined way for humans to flourish. This account of anarchism is usually rejected by others with an interest in anarchism. However, unlike Wolff, and in accord with contemporary anarchists like Class War, Clark suggests that coercion is not antipathetic to anarchism. For Clark we need coercion to flourish, in order to practise the virtue of independence. In effect, we need pricks to kick against, although Clark acknowledges he is unhappy with this and suggests there may ultimately be ways to get around it.

Nathan Jun (Chapter 4) also considers the analytic philosophical definition of anarchism. However, he considers the description based on a rejection of coercive authority to be inadequate. Jun develops the anarchist account of legitimate versus illegitimate authority to distinguish what forms of social relationship are incompatible with a commitment to anti-hierarchical practice. Like Clark, Jun articulates the positive vision of anarchism as one that promotes the possibility for the development of myriad, irreducible individual and collective attributes, rather than just the negative account of 'anti-coercion'. However, Jun is critical of the analytical tradition's liberal presuppositions. The agent of change is not the abstract, independent and rational agent, but a fluid, interdependent being.

Similarly, Jun is critical of the association of anarchism with support for free-market property relationships, a point developed in the second section of the book, dealing with central political-philosophical concerns of property rights and autonomy. DeClark's critique (Chapter 5) illustrates that acceptance of Kantian principles of autonomy does not, contrary to right-libertarian and anarcho-capitalist arguments, commit one to a position of support for private property. In its place DeClark proposes that notions of *possession* derived from Pierre-Joseph Proudhon, as opposed to *property*, are more consistent with genuine autonomy and thus have more in common with the egalitarian principles of the majority of anarchist groups, both past and present.

Alex Prichard's chapter (Chapter 6) outlines Proudhon's contribution to questions of normative and applied issues of citizenship and property rights. Importantly, Prichard's chapter highlights the impact of Enlightenment thought, in particular Immanuel Kant's rationalism and Auguste Comte's naturalism, on the development of a theory of meta-ethics that lies at the base of Proudhon's distinctive form of Republicanism. Prichard consequently highlights how major philosophical works have impacted on the development of anarchist theory and practice.

As Prichard and Jun demonstrate, key anarchist schools of thought have developed as a result of their critical adoption of rationalist and naturalist moral theory. By contrast, Matthew Wilson (Chapter 7) is critical of anarchists' failure to ask difficult moral questions, such as those arising from the problems of conflicting freedoms. Drawing on critiques of liberalism's understanding of freedom, and the related concept of value neutrality, he suggests that anarchism is vulnerable to similar problems: value neutrality is an impossible goal, and when values or freedoms conflict, it is not simply the state that is capable of oppression. Freedom can never be absolute, even in an anarchist society. Anarchists need to ask how they themselves would respond to such conflicts. Wilson concludes that a more overt recognition of the limits of freedom and a similarly explicit acknowledgement of values other than freedom are essential, if anarchism is to be both viable and credible.

The final section examines alternative ethical approaches to anarchism. Benjamin Franks (Chapter 8) argues that the standard Kantian, philosophical accounts of anarchism are insufficient as they misrepresent past and current anarchist movements and thinkers and are inadequate at dealing with complex issues of agency and responses to oppressive inequalities of power. In their stead, Franks proposes that anarchism is most consistent with a practice-based virtue theory, based on the work of Alasdair MacIntyre. Franks deals with objections to this virtue account of anarchism based on anarchism's apparent rejection of law (*nomos*) and teleology. There are anticipations of MacIntyrean criticisms of Enlightenment ethics in popular nineteenth-century anarchist thought. Sheffield's *The Anarchist* (1895b: 3) condemns capitalism for destroying humane social practice and argues that the task of anarchism is to develop new co-operative ventures that allow for the freer and fuller development of the individual, for the benefit of all.

Elisa Aaltola (Chapter 9) provides a timely examination of the impact of anarchism on environmental ethics. Aaltola too eschews the philosophical, liberal version for one which emphasises a collectivist account of the individual and a commitment to contesting hierarchical power-relations. These principles, she argues, find anarchism sharing ever greater sympathy with environmental ethical theory.

Aaltola examines the two main competing versions of environmental theory that claim greatest allegiance to anarchism: Arne Naess's deep ecology and primitivism (especially, but not exclusively, the version associated with John Zerzan), to assess which is the most coherent and consistent with anarchism. In carrying out this evaluation, Aaltola uses the criticisms raised against deep ecology and primitivism by a third variant of anarchist-inspired ecologism – Murray Bookchin's social ecology. The argument concludes that both deep ecology and primitivism offer some powerful criticisms against modernist assumptions concerning our everyday relationship to non-human animals and the wider environment, but it also illustrates that there are significant ontological, normative and political weaknesses in both.

The adoption of anarchist principles and sensibilities into day-to-day practices is the subject of Jamie Heckert's more practitioner-orientated contribution (Chapter 10). While distinctive in its less scholastically philosophical language, Heckert's chapter argues against realist meta-ethics and political behaviours based on a priori claims to knowledge. Instead, Heckert proposes a localised, micro-political moral sensibility that prioritises the polyvocal and rejects representationalism – the paternalistic claim to be able to speak on behalf of others. Heckert highlights the structural difficulties that prevent the development of meaningful, productive discourses and immanent value-rich social relationships and suggests practical strategies for overcoming these limitations. Anticipations of Heckert's approach can be found in some of the earliest British anarchist writings. *The Anarchist* (1895a: 3) reflects favourably on a meeting with rival socialist groups, like the Independent Labour Party, whose 'tolerant spirit' allowed for meaningful debate and sharing of information, in contrast with those groups, like the Social Democratic Federation, whose refusal to enter into dialogue made mutual aid impossible.

Heckert acknowledges that the stress on the micro- rather than macro-political draws upon the work of poststructuralist theorists like Gilles Deleuze and Felix Guattari and poststructuralist-influenced anarchists (postanarchists) like Todd May. While Heckert's discourse and examples are highly contemporary, the identification of anarchism as existing within everyday relationships goes back to the nineteenth century. *The Alarm*, a working-class anarchist periodical, in its first issue explained how anarchy is the development of 'the principles of liberty, love [solidarity] and toleration' and rejection of domination and wage-relationships in 'everyday life' (1896: 4).

The intersection of contemporary continental philosophy on anarchist ethics is examined in the final two chapters by Jones Irwin (Chapter 11) and Thomas Swann (Chapter 12). Irwin discusses the parallels and differences between Friedrich Nietzsche's deconstruction of ethical systems and anarchism's scepticism of claims to authority. Irwin draws on Bakunin's critique of authority as the basis for the comparison, but even popular anarchist texts shared the critique of morality. *The Call* (1916: 1), when it was an independent revolutionary socialist newspaper, was critical of 'professional theologians and moralists [...] whose business is to construe the religious and ethical motives for trade wars [and...] Zeppelin attacks [on civilians]'. The identification of how groups and institutions construct moral discourses to legitimate their authority and pacify opposition is shared by anarchists and Nietzsche. A further similarity between Nietzsche and the anarchists is their desire not to remain as merely nihilists, but develop a transformative ethics. It was not just writers in *The Egoist* that sought in overtly Nietzschean fashion the 'transvaluation of all values' (Mowrer, 1914: 8); other recent works have also excavated the often-overlooked impact of Nietzsche not just on Stirnerite egoism, but on many others, from the likes of anarchist communists like Guy Aldred (2004) and Emma Goldman (Starcross, 2004) to the libertarian socialist movement in general (Sheehan, 2003; Colston, 2004). Irwin, however, identifies precisely the affinities between Nietzsche's *Genealogy of Morals* and anarchist critiques of the construction of legitimising discourses by powerful institutions; he also explores the discontinuities and ruptures between the two.

Irwin explains that there are significant distinctions between Nietzsche's moral critique and an anarchist meta-ethics. Irwin concentrates his critique on Nietzsche's metaphysical mysticism with regard to concepts such as 'eternal return' and the 'Will to Power'. In addition Irwin also examines weaknesses in anarchism's meta-ethical approach as it often descends into the type of systematic thought which prevents the transvaluation of values. Despite these differences, Irwin argues that Nietzsche's meta-ethics not only can provide a necessary conceptual frame to understanding key classical anarchist thinkers but can also assist in the development of new anarchist approaches, such as those associated with 'postanarchism'.

The final contribution comes from Thomas Swann, and appropriately, with allusion to Nietzsche, brings us full circle. Swann critically evaluates the supposed distinction between a humanist classical anarchist ethics, based on a particular fixed concept of moral agency, and postanarchist moral theory which claims to transcend such reliance on an unknowable and restrictive metaphysical entity. Swann highlights the different forms essentialism takes within the distinctive versions of anarchist ethics, from those resting on utilitarian, Kantian or Aristotelian moral principles. Yet, Swann argues that despite the humanist limitations of these approaches, postanarchism also has an essentialism, though of a different form.

A single edited book alone is not going to produce sweeping changes within Anglo-American philosophy departments. Current academic institutions are unlikely to embrace, any time soon, an anarchist sensibility and begin to engage differently with other educational, economic and cultural groups external to the academy or comprehensively reappraise their internal social relations and thus radically alter their hierarchical pedagogies and curricula. Nonetheless, it is hoped that this book will make a small impact on raising the profile of the classical anarchist canon within philosophy departments, raise awareness of the limitations as well as the strengths of standard analytical descriptions and analyses of anarchism and highlight some of the developments in contemporary libertarian thinking. In addition, the book has already succeeded in a minor way with two ambitions: first, bringing together both academics who identify with rival (and often hostile) philosophical schools of thought. Second, this book has also enabled dialogue between another set of antagonistic groupings: academics and activists. All concerned – militants and scholars from competing traditions – were willing to share their wisdom and were open to challenge and critique. Contributors therefore exhibited the virtues associated with both anarchism and philosophy.

The support this project has been shown suggests that there is significant interest in further examination and application of anarchist theory and practice to the methods and problematics of philosophy, and vice versa. In particular we are grateful to the large number of paper-givers at the initial Anarchist Studies Network (Specialist Group of the Political Studies Association) conference which, because of the interest shown, had a major strand on 'anarchism and moral philosophy', and from which the majority of the contributions for this book were drawn. We are grateful to the conference organisers Ruth Kinna, Dave Berry and the aforementioned Alex Prichard for their willingness to accommodate so many philosophers. Special mention must also be made to Costas Athanasopoulos for his assistance in setting up the conference panels and sharing our enthusiasm for this theme.

On behalf of the editors I would like to thank not just the contributors for their hard work and patience in the construction of this book but the team of specialist readers who helped with specialist blind review of the chapters: Drs Stuart Hanscomb, Mike Hannis, Ralph Jessop, Sean Johnston, David Lamb, Paul Smith and Annette Thompson. Thanks also to Priyanka Gibbons of Palgrave for the editorial assistance, Joeljones Alexander for his careful proof-reading and to the Carnegie Trust for the grant that assisted in the writing of the introduction. In addition, a big 'thank you' too for Steven Gillespie for his technical know-how and Lesley Stevenson for her warm encouragement.

Bibliography

Alarm: For Your Liberty and Others, The (1896), I (i), Sunday 26 July 1896.
G. Aldred (2004) 'Friedrich Nietzsche' in G. Moore (ed.) *I am Not a Man, I am Dynamite!: Friedrich Nietzsche and the Anarchist Tradition* (New York: Autonomedia).
Anarchist: Communist and Revolutionary, The (1895a), II (iv), Sunday 20 January 1895.
Anarchist: Communist and Revolutionary, The (1895b), II (v), Sunday 24 February 1895.
Call: An Organ of International Socialism, The (1916), II, Thursday 9 March 1916.
M. Bakunin (1970) *God and the State* (New York: Dover).
S. Clark (2007) *Living Without Domination: The Possibility of an Anarchist Utopia* (Aldershot: Ashgate).
Class War (1992) *Unfinished Business: The Politics of Class War* (Edinburgh: AK Press).
D. Colston (2004) 'Nietzsche and the libertarian movement' in G. Moore (ed.) *I am Not a Man, I am Dynamite!: Friedrich Nietzsche and the Anarchist Tradition* (New York: Autonomedia).
G. Crowder (1991) Classical Anarchism: The Political Thought of Godwin, Proudhon, Bakunin and Kropotkin (Oxford: Clarendon).
Egoist: An Individualist Review, The (1914a) I (i), Thursday 1 January, 1914.
E. Fairchild (1916) 'War and class war' in *The Call: An Organ of International Socialism* III, Thursday 23 March 1916.
B. Franks (2006) *Rebel Alliances: The Means and Ends of Contemporary British Anarchisms* (Edinburgh: AK).
S. Freeman (2001) 'Illiberal libertarians: Why libertarianism is not a liberal view', *Philosophy and Public Affairs*, XXX (ii): 105–51.
D. Knowles (2002) *Political Philosophy* (London: Routledge).
P. Kropotkin (1992) *Ethics: Origin and Development* (Montreal, Canada: Black Rose).
R. Long and T. Machan (eds) (2008) *Anarchism/Minarchism: Is a Government Part of a Free Country?* (Aldershot: Ashgate).
D. Marsden (1914), 'The illusion of anarchism' in *The Egoist* I (xviii), Thursday 15 September 1914.

K. Marx (1992) 'Preface (to *A Contribution to the Critique of Political Economy*)' in *Early Writings* (Harmondsworth: Penguin).

P. McLaughlin (2002) *Mikhail Bakunin: The Philosophical Basis of His Theory of Anarchy* (New York: Algora).

—— (2007) *Anarchism and Authority: A Philosophical Introduction to Classical Anarchism* (Aldershot: Ashgate).

E. Mowrer (1914) 'France to-day: A group of thinkers' in *The Egoist* I (i), Thursday 1 January 1914.

S. Sheehan (2003) *Anarchism* (London: Reaktion).

L. Starcross (2004) 'Nietzsche was an anarchist: Reconstructing Emma Goldman's Nietzsche lectures' in G. Moore (ed.) *I am Not a Man, I am Dynamite!: Friedrich Nietzsche and the Anarchist Tradition* (New York: Autonomedia).

E. Tverdek (2001) 'Review of Alan Carter's *A Radical Green Political Theory*', *Ethics*, CXI (ii): 403–5.

J. Wolff (2006) *An Introduction to Political Philosophy*, rev. edn (Oxford: Oxford University Press).

R. P. Wolff (1976) *In Defence of Anarchism* (New York: Harper Torchbooks).

Part I
Philosophical Anarchism

2
In Defence of Philosophical Anarchism

Paul McLaughlin

There are certain widespread assumptions in anarchist circles about philosophical anarchism: about what it is and what is wrong with it. My purpose in this chapter is to call these assumptions into question and to present a defence of what I describe as *weak but engaged* philosophical anarchism. Accordingly, I borrow my title (in slightly revised form) from one of the most influential works in the modest canon of philosophical anarchism: Robert Paul Wolff's *In Defence of Anarchism* (1976). This short essay has enjoyed significant academic attention (among political and legal philosophers), but is widely reviled in anarchist circles. While I oppose Wolff's *strong but disengaged* brand of philosophical anarchism, my reasons for this are somewhat untypical of his anarchist opponents, and we will examine their objections in due course, as well as my own.

2.1 The history of philosophical anarchism

What is philosophical anarchism? There are at least three understandings of this position, associated with three key aspects of the anarchist tradition. It is worth noting that these understandings, which we will clarify now, are often confused – that they are often conflated such that it is not entirely clear what position (or what aspect of the anarchist tradition) is under discussion.

The first, *classical* understanding of philosophical anarchism qua 'fundamental critique of the idea of authority' (Miller, 1984: 15) is associated with the early emergence of anarchism in Europe in the late eighteenth century up until approximately the middle of the nineteenth century. It is generally associated with the ideas of William Godwin (often referred to as 'the father of philosophical anarchism'), Max Stirner (arguably the most extreme proponent of philosophical anarchism in the classical sense) and Pierre-Joseph Proudhon (with whom anarchism began to take revolutionary shape). All three of these thinkers undertook inquiries into the fundamental socio-political question of the *legitimacy* of authority and, in so doing, distinguished themselves from their liberal counterparts, who were content to locate the *limits* of authority. Thus, they took up and extended (to all forms of authority) Jean-Jacques Rousseau's radical project, expressed when he wrote, 'I mean to inquire if, in the civil order, there can be *any* sure and legitimate rule of administration, men being taken as they are and laws as they might be' (Rousseau, 1986: 181; emphasis added). This project is clearly distinct from the project of Wilhelm von Humboldt and other liberals, who considered 'the prime question of political philosophy' to concern 'the proper aims and *limits* of state agency' (Humboldt, 1996: 1–3; emphasis added).

On different philosophical grounds – utilitarian, egoistic or socialist – the early philosophical anarchists tended to reject authority in rather absolute (if quite sophisticated) fashion. Moreover, they tended to confine themselves to philosophical reflection, with only Proudhon being inclined to put his inconsistent philosophy into inconsistent practice. (Stirner's anti-philosophical sentiments could not have been any more philosophical, as Marx was to point out.) Proudhon, in fact, is the major transitional figure in the subsequent development of revolutionary anarchism – the philosopher who provided the practical impetus as well as the theoretical apparatus for Mikhail Bakunin and those who followed him in the anarchist movement proper. Thus, there have been two main criticisms of philosophical anarchism in the classical sense: first, at the theoretical level, that it is absolutist (demanding an absurd rejection of *all* authority); and, second, at the practical level, that it is quietistic (doing nothing to challenge authority). Since these objections have persisted through the history of philosophical anarchism, we will come back to them below.

There is also a second, *cultural* (and rather antiquated) understanding of philosophical anarchism qua 'native American anarchism' (Reichert, 1967: 857). This is associated with the distinctive brand of anarchism that emerged in the late nineteenth and early twentieth centuries in the United States. It was, it seems, 'as American a contribution as pragmatism' (Yarros, 1936: 470). The most notable advocate of philosophical anarchism in this sense was Benjamin Tucker whose ideas developed under the influence of Josiah Warren and other radical American individualists, as well as Proudhon, who provides the somewhat tenuous link here with classical philosophical anarchism. An especially odd feature of this form of 'philosophical' anarchism is that it exhibits little philosophical content, beyond a basic ideological commitment to individual freedom in a free market. As David Miller observes, 'the crucial ingredient of [such] individualist anarchism is a certain (ideological) vision of man and society, not a philosophical standpoint' (Miller, 1984: 31). Why, then, was this form of anarchism known as 'philosophical anarchism' for so long, at least in the United States? One is inclined to postulate that 'philosophical anarchism' was a flag of convenience, a rather impressive-looking flag that distinguished certain 'native' American anarchists from 'outside forces' (European and immigrant opponents) within the anarchist tradition. Thus, while European anarchists after Proudhon were supposedly socialist, revolutionary, violent and even atheistic, 'philosophically minded' (i.e., seemingly, more intelligent and less belligerent) American anarchists were individualist, reformist, pacifist and even religious (or quasi-religious). It can be said, therefore, that philosophical anarchism in this second sense was a product of ideological and cultural conflict.

Activist anarchists typically condemn this brand of anarchism for its excessive individualism, irrational faith in the market as an instrument of liberation and general quietism in the face of social injustice. But it may be noted that these objections are usually ideologically motivated (or unsupported by argumentation in the context of the debate between social and individualist anarchists) and do not tell us much of philosophical interest in themselves.

The *contemporary* understanding of philosophical anarchism qua academic anarchism is associated with the work of Robert Paul Wolff and others from the 1970s to the present. Academic anarchism developed in something of a golden age of analytic political philosophy. This period is, for the most part, associated with the justice theories of John Rawls, Robert Nozick and others. However, Wolff's work on legitimacy theory also had a lasting impact on political philosophy. On the one hand, it inspired highly sophisticated defences of political authority by philosophers such as Joseph Raz; on the other hand, it led to highly sophisticated reformulations of the anarchist case by philosophers such as A. John Simmons.

Wolff argued, quite simply and strongly, that the authority of the state – its 'right to command, and correlatively, to be obeyed' – is 'genuinely incompatible' with our duty of autonomy – our duty to make 'the final decisions about what [we] should do' in each and every case (Wolff, 1976: 4, 71, 15). Thus, the very notion of legitimate political authority is 'inherently incoherent' (Wolff, 1969: 602) and 'philosophical anarchism would seem to be the only reasonable political belief for an enlightened man' (Wolff, 1976: 19).

The first point to be made about Wolff's (1976: 72) anarchist conclusion is that he is dissatisfied with it: 'I confess myself unhappy with the conclusion that I must simply leave off the search for legitimate collective authority.' In addition he is unwilling to accept it: 'I am unwilling to accept as final the negative results of our search for a political order which harmonises authority and autonomy' (78). The reason for this might be that the rather conventional and non-anarchist contractual argument for legitimacy retains some appeal for Wolff, who writes, for example, that 'A contractual democracy is legitimate, to be sure, for it is founded upon the citizen's promise to obey its commands. Indeed, any state is legitimate which is founded upon such a promise' (69). This position seems to contradict Wolff's anarchist claims and even suggests that he is no anarchist at all (Frankfurt, 1973). However, leaving aside Wolff's doubts about his anarchist conclusions and his taste for traditional contractual arguments, we interpret him here (consistently) as an anarchist of the strong variety who believes that, if legitimate political authority is not logically impossible, it is 'at least extremely difficult and unlikely for any government to stand close enough to fulfilling the truth conditions for attributing rightful (or de jure) authority for us to call it a "legitimate" government' (Martin, 1974: 141).

What should be stated in Wolff's favour is that he put the problem of legitimacy firmly back on the map of mainstream political philosophy and that he handled this problem with a welcome degree of sophistication. However, his defence of philosophical anarchism is open to a number of objections. First and foremost, Wolff's moral theory is highly questionable, not least because, as he himself acknowledges, he makes no attempt to argue for it: 'I have been forced to *assume* a number of very important propositions about the nature, sources, and limits of moral obligation. To put it bluntly, I have simply taken for granted an entire ethical theory' (Wolff, 1976: viii). More specifically, the notion that we have a duty of autonomy has been called into question by Raz, for example, who argues that we have good reason (on complex instrumental grounds) to give up full autonomy and obey political authorities (at least of some kinds in some instances). Another philosophical problem is that it is unclear why Wolff (with other proponents of philosophical anarchism in the contemporary sense) pays attention only to issues of political, state or governmental authority. This would appear to demonstrate the inadequacy of Wolff's anarchism (and of contemporary philosophical anarchism overall) relative to classical philosophical anarchism, which offered a highly comprehensive critique of authority.

Activists typically regard Wolff's supposed anarchism with suspicion. Its apparent abstraction and academic tone place it outside the mainstream tradition of anarchism (at least in much of the twentieth century), as does its professed indifference to matters of practical concern. Wolff's 'pure theory' of anarchism, as he himself admits, has nothing to say about 'the material, social, and psychological conditions under which anarchism might be a feasible mode of social organization' (Wolff, 1976: viii). This has led some to question his anarchist credentials (or the anarchist bona fides of academic philosophical anarchism). Thus, Wolff is criticised by many ('real') anarchists for his abstraction and his disengagement. His abstract treatment of autonomy and authority allows him to come down absolutely on the side of the former and absolutely against the latter. It is partly as a result of such a strong anarchist position that Wolff can have nothing of practical interest to say to anarchists. But *should* he have any such thing to say? And should he *do* anything about his anarchist conclusions?

These questions raise an important moral issue: when we recognise an immoral state of affairs, do we have an obligation to act to remedy it? Most anarchists believe that we do. Indeed, Wolff himself may believe it. But (1) it is not obvious that we have such an obligation (i.e., an argument to this effect is required); and (2) the question of whether we have such an obligation is separate (or logically independent) from the question that points to the immoral state of affairs. Put simply, the question of our duty to obey is distinct from the question of our duty to act, and Wolff would appear to be aware of this distinction (treating only the former question and leaving the latter aside, at least in the book *In Defence of Anarchism*).

An argument for illegitimacy, then, does not establish any obligation to act. The latter must be demonstrated by those who attack contemporary philosophical anarchists for their quietism. In any case, on Wolff's own principles, it may be very difficult to demonstrate this obligation. The principle of moral autonomy, as Wolff formulates it, requires that we act – when we act – on the basis of our own decisions, not on the basis of the authoritative commands of others. However, it does not require that we act in any particular instance, or, indeed, that we act at all. It is consistent with Wolff's principles that we respond to an immoral state of affairs in a completely passive way. The important question, therefore, is whether there is something wrong with these principles. As we have seen, instrumentalist objections have been made on behalf of the state. However, mainstream social anarchists probably ought to focus on the individualism of Wolff's position, before presenting their own case for an obligation to act. What this case looks like remains to be seen, but the point to be emphasised here is that it is Wolff's individualism (his basic moral position) and absolutism (the extremity of his anarchist view) that are most questionable, not his quietism (or his lack of an *additional* argument for an obligation to act).

Of course, Wolff is not the only academic anarchist. Another important representative of contemporary philosophical anarchism is Simmons. He manages to avoid Wolff's absolutism while offering a more sophisticated and compelling defence of philosophical anarchism – of, in Simmons's words, the view that 'There are no morally legitimate states.' The main difference between Wolff and Simmons is that Wolff's anarchism, as Simmons interprets it, is a priori, whereas his own is a posteriori. Wolff argues 'that there *can be* no morally legitimate states (that the concept of the legitimate state is "vacuous"), thus rejecting the possibility of legitimacy on a priori grounds'. Simmons, by contrast, denies 'on *empirical* grounds that legitimate states exist', arguing 'that, given present political conventions and practices, there are no good reasons for believing that citizens have political obligations or governments *de jure* political authority. Moral principles understood in their most plausible forms simply will not yield these conclusions.' As Simmons notes, assuming that the a posteriori philosophical anarchist's argument holds, there is still the possibility of 'a new ground of political obligation (a previously unarticulated moral principle)' (Simmons, 1987: 269–70). But it is not really the anarchist's task to discover such a principle; the burden of proof here lies with the supporter of the state. In any case, the only moral principle which Simmons thinks suitable (and towards which even Wolff seemed sympathetic) is the voluntaristic principle of consent. And, *as a matter of fact*, no existing or known state satisfies this principle. Simmons writes, therefore, 'Because I subscribe to political voluntarism...and because I believe no actual states satisfy the requirements of this voluntarism, I also believe that no existing states are legitimate (simpliciter)' (Simmons, 1999: 769).

So, Simmons' version of philosophical anarchism leaves open the possibility of a legitimate state, but denies that there is such a state. Crucially, however, while there is no legitimate state, there are justifiable states. That is to say, while there is no state that satisfies the principle of consent – and there is therefore no 'special moral bond' between citizens and the state – there are states that act in just ways and that deserve 'support'. As Simmons puts it, philosophical anarchism 'is compatible with the view that government may be necessary and that certain types of governments ought to be supported' (Simmons, 1987: 269). This is an argument that most anarchists would reject. It is certainly foreign to traditional anarchist thinking to claim that a state is illegitimate but justified. However, 'foreignness' does not make it a bad argument. What could be claimed against Simmons, however, is that all existing or known states are unjustified on practical grounds (that they are unnecessary, unjust and undeserving of our support). Indeed, one might find such instrumental arguments more convincing than Simmons's fundamental voluntaristic argument concerning legitimacy: that is, one might not accept consent as the moral measure of legitimacy. And here, once again, the mainstream social anarchist could attack the basic individualism of Simmons's position. Quite how this would be done – or quite what the moral basis of social anarchism might be – remains in question. But the important thing to observe is that contemporary philosophical anarchism is associated with individualistic anarchism, as indeed were the American anarchists at the turn of the twentieth century and even (somewhat more contentiously) the classical philosophical anarchists. Thus, notwithstanding the differences that we have highlighted in the history of philosophical anarchism – between (firstly) the comprehensive critique of authority (secondly) the ideological rejection of government and (thirdly) the academic attack on state legitimacy – a certain shared individualism would seem to distinguish philosophical anarchism as a whole from the mainstream tradition of social anarchism – the non-philosophical tradition in name and (to a significant degree) in fact.

2.2 Towards an adequate understanding of philosophical anarchism

A vital question must be asked at this point: should philosophical anarchism be identified with individualistic anarchism? Or, expressed rather differently, is there a necessary connection between philosophical anarchism and individualistic anarchism? I think not. In my view, the connection between philosophical anarchism and individualistic anarchism – as strong as it may appear – is wholly contingent. In the first place, one can demonstrate this by pointing to counter-evidence or to evidence of less-than-individualistic philosophical anarchism. Proudhon is no individualist (at least not in the one-sided sense that opponents of philosophical anarchism have in mind). Godwin is a complicated case (whose social utilitarianism and socialist ideals merit serious consideration in this context). But even if there were no factual evidence of a disjunction between philosophical anarchism and individualistic anarchism, a necessary connection would remain to be proven. And it seems highly improbable that a philosophical anarchism could not be socialistic, unless one simply assumes that only individualism can be philosophically supported (or supported by means of argumentation) and that socialistic principles are, by their very nature, unphilosophical (or unamenable to argumentation).

The basic point is that a philosophical anarchism is simply an anarchism established on philosophical grounds, or maintained on the basis of argument. It might be individualistic or socialistic, strong or weak – depending on the outcome of a series of arguments, not on whether it is labelled 'philosophical'. No position has a monopoly on this label; nor should any position shun it for the fear that it would otherwise be thought too abstract or disengaged. And it should be stated bluntly: this is not a matter of mere labels; it is a matter of (1) pragmatic and (2) moral concern. One might well argue, accordingly, that a philosophical anarchism is (1) more likely to work (to convince others and gain adherents) and (2) less likely to alienate (those on whom it might otherwise be imposed in morally insupportable fashion, at least by anarchist standards).

The as-yet-unconvinced anarchist may admit that philosophical anarchism is only contingently related to individualistic anarchism; he or she may admit that a philosophical anarchism could be a socialistic anarchism, very much closer to the mainstream of the anarchist tradition. But the persistent doubt concerns the relationship between philosophical anarchism and engaged anarchism, or between intellectual labour ('argumentation') and revolutionary activism ('social change'). Contemporary philosophical anarchists like Simmons continue to encourage such doubts by characterising philosophical anarchism in the following way: 'What is distinctive about philosophical anarchism is that its judgement of state illegitimacy...does not translate into any immediate requirement of opposition to illegitimate states. This is what leads many to contrast philosophical anarchism with political anarchism.' My own point is that there can be *no* such 'immediate requirement' – without, that is, an argument for an obligation to act. Simmons himself is aware of this issue (of the distinction between arguments for political obligations and arguments concerning 'general moral reasons for acting'), but he still entertains the notion of (in his terms) a 'strong' anarchism according to which 'a state's illegitimacy further *entails* a moral obligation or duty to oppose and, so far as it is within our power, eliminate the state' (Simmons, 1996: 22–3, 28; emphasis added).

In this context, then, Peter Marshall writes, 'Philosophical anarchism has often been despised by militants, although clearly any action executed without thought is just an arbitrary jerk. All anarchists are philosophical in a general sense, but it is usual to call those thinkers philosophical anarchists who have reached anarchist conclusions in their search for universal principles without engaging in any practical activity' (Marshall, 1993: 7). Marshall may be right about the usual use of terms here, but there is absolutely no reason in principle why a philosophical anarchist should not engage in practical activity (beyond the activity of thought itself). Again, any connection here (and there is such a connection in the history of anarchism, with obvious counterexamples like Proudhon) is wholly contingent. In any case, without wishing to make it sound as though I am simply making a lame self-justificatory claim on behalf of intellectuals, an additional point needs to be made. Anarchists are frequently guilty of underestimating 'the power of ideas' (or, at any rate, those more or less intelligently formulated) and ignoring the fact that, as Isaiah Berlin puts it, 'philosophical concepts nurtured in the stillness of a professor's study [can] destroy a civilization.' This point can, of course, be overstated: ideas are not sufficient in themselves (in isolation from social and economic factors) to transform society. But, as Berlin continues, 'It is only a very vulgar historical materialism that denies the power of ideas, and says that ideals are mere material interests in disguise' (Berlin, 1998: 192–3). Unfortunately, many anarchists down the years have been infected with such vulgar Marxist notions. To restate our point, then, anarchists often fail to recognise the degree to which to think (in a critically reflective manner) is to act (to engage with the world). Thinking is not disengagement, even if it is insufficient engagement.

Returning to the quote from Marshall, one might be struck by his assertion that 'All anarchists are philosophical in a general sense.' Is this true? I claim that it is false, unless one has the loosest and least informative definition of philosophy in mind. Thus, all those anarchists who – inspired by a sense of 'wonder' about the world in which we live – seek some sort of socio-political 'wisdom' might be considered 'philosophical'. But, in fact, it is not 'wonder' and 'wisdom' that distinguish philosophy from other intellectual pursuits. Science, religion and even art might be similarly characterised. Such characterisations are utterly unhelpful. Needless to say, we need to exercise caution in our attempt to define philosophy.

These attempts invariably offend all manner of philosophers who do things in another (older, newer and 'better') way. Indeed, the very attempt to define philosophy might be thought antiquated and hopeless. Nevertheless, at the risk of unnecessary provocation, I contend that philosophy is an *argumentative process* about anything and everything. Consequently, philosophy is not distinguished by its subject matter (though certain subjects – such as the nature of argumentation itself – are of special interest to philosophers) but by its argumentative mode of thought. This does not mean that non-philosophers do not argue in pursuit of their intellectual goals, but that argumentation does not distinguish their pursuits. Likewise, it does not mean that philosophers do not employ non-argumentative modes of thought in pursuit of their intellectual goals, but that these modes do not distinguish their pursuits. Thus, as natural scientists engage in argumentation (about, for example, the outcome of experimental research), so philosophers engage in observation and experimentation (generally to the degree that it informs their argument). A further distinguishing feature of the argumentative process that is philosophy is its quest for *conceptual clarity*. The basic components of argumentation are concepts, and philosophical argumentation can only hope to advance to the extent that such clarity is achieved (or to the extent that we know what our concepts mean, *that we know what we are talking about*).

Clearly, this is a very crude account of philosophy. It may seem old-fashioned (given 'post-analytic' developments in philosophy, for example) and biased (favouring certain philosophical traditions over 'less argumentative' – say, more speculative, systematic or 'edifying' – traditions). I cannot hope to respond to these metaphilosophical objections here. In any event, our broad characterisation of philosophy would satisfy most philosophical anarchists, and it also describes much of what other types of philosophers actually do (often incompetently) even when they describe their intellectual pursuits in different terms.

Many anarchists display very little conceptual clarity and argumentation. These are unphilosophical anarchists: anarchists, put simply, who refuse to tell us what it is exactly that they are talking about (e.g., 'authority', 'the state', 'coercion' and 'freedom') or provide us with any arguments in support of their case (the revolutionary transformation of society in the direction of 'anarchy'). To take a relatively random example, Albert Meltzer offers the following anarchist 'analysis' in a work ironically entitled *Anarchism: Arguments For and Against* (a work in which there is little resembling an argument): 'Duties imposed as obligations or ideals, such as patriotism, duty to the state, worship of God, submission to higher classes or authorities, respect for inherited privileges, are lies.' We are neither told what such duties involve nor why they are 'lies', that is, Meltzer practises neither conceptual clarification nor moral argumentation. His is a resolutely unphilosophical expression of anarchism. However, to those philosophers like me who might take issue with this, Meltzer has a convenient response: 'bourgeois academics borrow the name "Anarchism" to give expression to their own liberal principles.... With the bankruptcy of Marxism now universally recognised, Anarchism has become fair game for those eager to climb on the academic gravy train.' On Meltzer's extremely dated account, 'real' anarchism – which takes shape in action, not ideas – is 'based on the class struggle' (Meltzer, 2000: 19, 22). And intellectuals are, as Meltzer makes abundantly clear, on the wrong side of this struggle.

At this point, we ought to consider philosophical anarchism of the non-classical, non-individualistic and non-academic type, or philosophical anarchism that does not belong to the three familiar traditions that we described earlier. (Of course, certain expressions of anarchism from within these traditions meet our philosophical requirements, notwithstanding our objections to them. Simmons's anarchism is a good example; so too, perhaps, is Godwin's.) What would a conceptually clear and rigorously argued anarchism (from outside these traditions) look like? Here we can cite the example of Alan Carter – not necessarily to endorse his substantive claims, but to draw attention to his philosophical approach. Carter is impressed by the fact that Marxist theory after G. A. Cohen 'has evolved into a form that can hold its own within the anglophone tradition of analytical philosophy' and wonders whether anarchist theory could evolve to the same point. One possible way to find out, Carter believes, is to develop an anarchist theory 'in response to what is currently the most sophisticated version of Marxist theory – Cohen's' (Carter, 2000: 230). This is not such an unusual procedure in anarchist intellectual history; after all, Bakunin developed his anarchist views in response to Marx's.

Carter begins by defining anarchism (interestingly but contentiously) as 'the [normative] opposition to certain substantive political inequalities, combined with the [empirical] belief that the state inevitably embodies, generates, and/or preserves those inequalities' (Carter, 2000: 232). So defined, anarchism is opposed to the Marxist account of revolution (which is marked by its statism or vanguardism). Anarchists are, in fact, fundamentally opposed to the Marxist 'theory of historical change'. The question, then, is what are their reasons for opposing it? Do they have an alternative theory (that can explain the consequences of statist revolutions, for example)? Inspired by Cohen's work, Carter thinks that an alternative but similarly analytical theory can be developed along anarchist lines. He also thinks that this theory exposes the main weakness of the Marxist theory.

By way of an explanation of the latter theory, and following Cohen's interpretation, Carter (2000: 237) writes the following:

> central to Marx's theory of history is the development of the forces of production [comprising labour-power and the means of production]. These economic forces explain the nature of the economic relations [that is, the relations that effectively control, or are presupposed by, the productive forces], which in turn explain the nature of the political relations.

Political relations, according to Carter (2000: 235), are 'relations of, or presupposing, effective control of the defensive forces'. But Carter argues that there is a crucial omission from this Marxist theory: it only includes and only attempts to explain the complex relation between, economic forces, economic relations and political relations. Hence, it omits those political forces implied by Carter's definition of political relations, forces that are of particular concern to anarchists and which have to be included in a satisfactory theory of historical change. These political forces, or 'forces of coercion', comprise political labour-power (that supplied by the police, army and so on for payment) and the means of coercion (weapons, prisons and so on). Once this fourth factor is taken into account, Carter believes that he is in a position to propose an alternative, anarchist theory of history. Thus, once political forces receive theoretical attention, the 'direction of explanation' – formerly 'from the economic to the political' – is reversed and a characteristically anarchist theory (which prioritises the political) emerges. In place of Cohen's Marxist 'techno-primacy' theory, then, Carter proposes his 'state-primacy theory' (Carter, 2000: 233–47).

Without going into the complexities of this theory here, what it essentially boils down to is the following claim: 'political relations select economic relations that develop economic forces that enable the development of the political forces – these political forces stabilizing economic relations that provide them with the surplus they require.' Such a theory has, according to Carter, the potential to be 'at least as effective as Marxist theory in explaining technological, economic, and political developments'. But it is superior to Marxist theory in at least one respect: 'by drawing attention to the tremendous power that the state can exert,' it can predict 'accurately the outcome of statist and vanguardist revolutions' (Carter, 2000: 247, 250). And, as indicated already, this is a basic requirement of a successful anarchist theory.

We are not in a position here to evaluate Carter's apparently elegant theory. But it might be said that his is a rather idiosyncratic approach to anarchism. His explanatory theory of historical development is the product of reading anarchism through analytical Marxism; but it is quite distinct from the kind of normative theory of legitimacy that has formed the core of philosophical anarchism until now. Perhaps this will prove advantageous in the long run, but it seems premature to abandon the traditional concerns of anarchism without determining whether they are open to sophisticated philosophical treatment. Nevertheless, such reservations aside, Carter does offer a (1) conceptually clear and (2) rigorously argued contribution to contemporary anarchist theory; his 'analytical anarchism' is a genuine philosophical anarchism and represents a major advance in its field.

2.3 Weak but engaged philosophical anarchism

Having cited a significant example of contemporary philosophical anarchism (in our terms), I would like to comment rather generally in this last section on my own account of philosophical anarchism. (A fuller [though older] account can be found elsewhere (McLaughlin, 2007). What follows is essentially a [slightly revised] summary of the fuller account.) Mine is a 'weak' but 'engaged' philosophical anarchism. Accordingly, I need to say something about (1) philosophical anarchism as such, (2) the strength of my philosophical anarchism and (3) my additional argument for engagement.

As I have already argued, a philosophical anarchism is simply a philosophical or argumentative expression of anarchism. Such an expression – if it (as a *process* of argumentation) is to go anywhere – demands conceptual clarity (or, put simply, that we know what we are talking about). And the first concept that we need to clarify is the concept of anarchism itself, which is widely contested. Anarchism is often associated with anti-statism (the belief that a society without the state is both desirable and possible) and anti-authoritarianism (the a priori rejection of all authority). While the first conception of anarchism is inadequate (since anarchists are historically interested in a more fundamental problem than the problem of state legitimacy, namely, the problem of authority, and its legitimacy, in general), the second conception is simply false (since anarchists do not – for good reason – rule out the possibility of any legitimate authority). Anarchists, then, are fundamentally interested in the problem of authority; in fact, though they do not claim that it is necessarily illegitimate, they are doubtful about its legitimacy in each and every case. As such, anarchism can be defined as *scepticism towards authority*. It can be so defined in the etymological sense of scepticism (which denotes a process of inquiry or examination), if not in any more specific philosophical sense (and this is an issue which I will not pursue here).

Now, it might be that anarchist scepticism is motivated by a particular moral commitment (to the values of freedom, equality, community or some combination of these). We might doubt that all forms of authority satisfy our values. (And as we saw a short while ago, Carter holds this to be true of anarchism: he believes that anarchists are (at a fundamental normative level) political egalitarians who (on empirical grounds) doubt that the state, above all, satisfies their values.) But this is not necessarily the case. As Simmons explains (with reference only to the state), certain anarchists do not make 'any prior commitment to particular values (which the state is seen as violating). That is, some anarchisms are driven by a general scepticism about the possibility of providing any argument that shows some or all existing states to be legitimate – a scepticism perhaps taken to be justified simply by the systematic failure of political philosophy to this point to produce any good argument of this sort' (Simmons, 1996: 20). Anarchist scepticism can therefore be motivated by a plurality of moral commitments or by no particular moral commitment. And it is this very fact that frustrates all attempts to find a unifying or even a definitive anarchist ethic (such as political equality (Carter, 2000), positive freedom (Crowder, 1991) or communal individuality (Ritter, 1980)).

This brings us to the second concept that philosophical anarchists are bound to clarify: the concept of authority, which is, after all, their central concern. Authority is a form of *social power* (indeed, of *normative power*) which involves (1) the *right* of one party to exercise social control over another party by means, principally, of authoritative directives and (2) the correlative *duty* of the latter party to follow these directives. Authority comes in at least two general forms: practical authority (or authority in matters of conduct) and theoretical authority (or authority in matters of belief). Practical authority involves the right of one party (say, a parent or a policeman) to issue directives such as commands that another party (say, a child or an ordinary citizen) has a duty to obey. Theoretical authority (more controversially) involves the right of one party (say, a teacher or a priest) to issue directives such as 'teachings' that another party (say, a student or a parishioner) has a duty to accept.

Perhaps the most interesting aspect of authoritative relations from a philosophical point of view (quite apart from how these relations might be described and explained, say, sociologically) concerns the practical reasoning of those who are subject to authority. How does authority figure in their reasoning? A number of philosophers have sought to answer this question. Basically, they have endeavoured to show that authority does not require that its subjects 'surrender their judgement': that it is not, as it were, wholly at odds with reason. Instead, authoritative utterances provide them with (according to H. L. A. Hart) *content-independent* reasons and (according to Raz) *exclusionary* reasons for action or (arguably) belief. Thus, notwithstanding the realm and limits of specific authorities, it is *who* issues an authoritative directive ('the authority') that counts for the subject, not *what* the directive entails (its content). However, this feature of authority is not unique to it, since promises, for example, are similarly content-independent. But promises, by contrast with authoritative utterances, are not binding on others. So, how can the bindingness of authority be explained?

It has been argued that authoritative utterances also provide the subject of authority with exclusionary reasons for action or belief. On this account, authoritative utterances do not provide additional 'ordinary' reasons to be factored in by the subject in the course of his or her deliberation (about a course of action, for example), reasons which may sway a decision one way or another. Rather, they provide reasons that 'exclude and replace' some ordinary reasons that figure in the subject's reasoning (without requiring that it be surrendered altogether). Combining these two features of authority, then, Leslie Green proposes the following definition of authority: '*A* has authority over *B* if and only if the fact that *A* requires *B* to φ (i) gives *B* a content-independent reason to φ and (ii) excludes some of *B*'s reasons for not-φ-ing' (Green, 1990: 42).

Anarchists do not deny that there are such relations: relations in which one party has not only the capacity but also the (recognised) right to issue content-independent and binding directives, directives that another party is duty-bound to follow. In other words, anarchists are not oblivious to de facto authority. But the obvious questions that follow concern the morality of such relations. On the one hand, then, we may ask whether a party should have (or be recognised as having) an authoritative right; this is the question of *legitimacy*. On the other hand, we may ask whether there is (or whether we should recognise) a correlative duty; this is the question of *obligation*. These questions are inseparable since (a) legitimate authorities impose obligations while (b) obligations are only owed to legitimate authorities. Thus, to demonstrate legitimacy is to demonstrate obligation and vice versa.

Having clarified the two central concepts of philosophical anarchism – anarchism and authority – we are in a position to anticipate the main lines of philosophical anarchist argumentation. Philosophical anarchists are fundamentally concerned with the legitimacy of authority. Many anarchists, indeed, hold that there are legitimate forms of authority, and no anarchist can (at least as anarchism and authority are conceived here) reasonably deny this a priori. (Having said that, an a posteriori rejection of all authority is consistent with our anarchism, even if it represents it in its most extreme and abstract form.) What kinds of authority are legitimate, according to (some) philosophical anarchists? And what are the (stated) grounds for their legitimacy? Perhaps a single, representative example will suffice for now: parental authority. The practical authority of the parent over the child might be legitimated on pragmatic grounds. In other words, the parent may possess a legitimate right to issue commands that the child is obliged to obey because the absence of such a right (of command) is demonstrably unfavourable to the well-being of the child itself or of a larger social group (depending on whether the individual person or the community is considered fundamentally considerable). However, such instrumentalist reasoning might be rejected by other philosophical anarchists who are committed to, for instance, the non-instrumentalist principle of consent. On this argument, only those authoritative relations entered into knowingly and voluntarily are legitimate, and the child has not consented because it is incapable of doing so. But even in this case, there may be an argument for justifiable domination of the child (i.e., a justifiable non-consensual relation where consent cannot be given, as in the case of non-human animals).

Whatever direction this debate might take, the point is that philosophical anarchists have not prejudged the issue. The debate is live, even for philosophical anarchists. And this is simply evidence that philosophical anarchists are not 'anti-authoritarians'. They doubt the legitimacy of parental authority, but they do not reject it a priori. Curiously, this may also be said of their characteristic (though non-definitive) anti-statism. That is to say, although philosophical anarchists reject all known arguments for the legitimacy of the state's authority (and our political obligations to the state), they (1) are not in a position to do so a priori and (2) cannot rule out the possibility of a 'previously unarticulated' argument for its legitimacy (as improbable as such an argument may be). But, as it stands, anarchists deny that conventional instrumental and non-instrumental arguments for the legitimacy of the state's authority succeed. Hence, they deny, for instance, that the state's authority is founded on explicit, implicit or hypothetical consent. Certain anarchists believe that consent would legitimate the state's authority, but argue that no known or existing state has been or would be consented to. Other anarchists argue that even if the state had been consented to, its demonstrable consequences would still render it illegitimate on, say, utilitarian grounds. Thus, a utilitarian anarchist argument can be offered against voluntarism that also applies to statist utilitarianism. In the latter instance, the anarchist may try to demonstrate that anarchy generates greater social utility and is therefore preferable to statehood. So the debate goes on, embracing various instrumental, voluntaristic and (other) deontological arguments for and against the state, none of which (to date) works according to the philosophical anarchist. And this reminds us again that anarchism cannot be defined with reference to a particular moral commitment, but only with reference to its scepticism, to its basic doubt about the legitimacy of authority.

Such is my own conception of philosophical anarchism in broad outline. I described my philosophical anarchism as weak, and one might wonder what the strength of anarchism implies. Here I must distinguish my use of strength-terms from that of Simmons. According to Simmons, 'How strong an anarchist position is will depend on how weighty or imperative the obligation to oppose the state is taken to be.' For the weak anarchist, though there may be 'independent grounds' for practically opposing the state, it does not follow from the state's illegitimacy that it ought to be opposed or that one ought to act against it. For the strong anarchist, on the other hand, the state's illegitimacy 'further entails' an obligation to oppose or act against it (Simmons, 1996: 22). On this account, strong anarchism would be a mistaken position since, as I argued above, there can be no such entailment: an argument for illegitimacy is no argument for an obligation to act. When I speak of strong and weak philosophical anarchism, I am simply distinguishing between the anarchism which rejects all authority (though not, as we have said, on a priori grounds) and that which recognises the legitimacy of certain forms of authority (though, again, only on the basis of argument: the 'weak anarchist' is still a 'strong sceptic', merely one who draws less extreme conclusions). My 'weakness' owes to my acceptance of the case, both instrumental and non-instrumental, for 'operative authority' or authority that is 'exercised in freely formed groups', especially in cooperatives formed by people with common ends who share the functions of their group and exercise authority themselves directly (De George,

1985: 80–90). This is not just an ideal case of authority, but a real and realisable one (in at least some and perhaps many cases). In any event, it seems to me that a weak anarchism is not only theoretically defensible, but, practically, more workable than the strong anarchism of Stirner's or Wolff's kind.

Finally, we arrive at a difficult issue to which we have already referred. This is the issue of engagement (rather than strength). I described my philosophical anarchism as an engaged anarchism, so one might reasonably question my argument for engagement or an obligation to act. As stated previously, this requires a separate argument from the argument for illegitimacy (or the anarchist argument *per se*), and, for my own part, I confess that my additional argument for engagement is weaker than any argument I might offer for anarchism. Moreover, the modest and tentative argument I offer is not universally applicable: it is an argument concerning intellectual labourers such as myself. But I do not rule out the existence of a stronger argument and a universal argument for engagement. So, once again, why do I think that the philosophical anarchist should ('on independent grounds') do something about his or her anarchism or, in general, 'come to the act'? My argument is an intuitive argument from (1) privilege and (2) public service.

A commonly held intuition has it that 'doing philosophy is not digging ditches', and perhaps this intuition is morally significant. Whether a dualism of intellectual labour and real labour is really sustainable as an explanatory tool, it does seem that philosophers are in a privileged position (and not necessarily in a reductive economic sense). Thus, while intellectual labour may be valuable labour, and while philosophy does require application and talent, there is something in the nature of such labour which places the philosopher in a position of privilege vis-à-vis many non-philosophers. It might simply be that the philosopher has the opportunity to perform satisfying work, in some sense, while the 'ditch-digger' engages in 'alienating' labour, for example. Perhaps the philosopher has earned or merits this privilege while the ditch-digger does not. But this does not alter the fact of privilege. And one might be inclined to argue (intuitively) that privilege comes with certain responsibilities – or, at any rate, that the privilege of intellectual labour entails an obligation to act for the greater good (to 'return to the cave', as Plato imagined it).

The argument from privilege might be supported by a second intuition about public service. This is especially applicable to those who work for state universities, as I do. While anarchists often dismiss such work as effective support for the state or wonder how those who oppose the state can work 'for it', the point here is, of course, that public education is exactly that: education of the public, paid for by the public. Now, we might have doubts about the state's role in public education, but that is not the main issue here. In principle, the state university worker is a public employee, paid to work in the public service. Thus, I might educate by teaching, researching and writing. But it might be felt that this is inadequate public service – or that public education requires more than the development of private philosophical credentials. It might also be argued that public education involves more than merely providing a service (more or less reluctantly) on demand; perhaps it requires going 'to the people' to share and even apply the fruit of intellectual labour. This intuition has been (and continues to be) taken seriously by many public intellectuals, who regard activism as part of their public service, as an obligation entailed by the nature of their work.

As an argument for engagement, then, I would wish to advance such an intuitive argument from privilege and public service, though it requires a great deal of refinement. However, even if this argument shows a certain promise, it does not tell us *what kind* of action is required of us or *how much* action is required. But we should not really expect it to do so. Such specifics are always matters of judgement and circumstance; they are not matters of principle.

2.4 Conclusion

In this chapter, I have argued (1) that intellectual labour is necessary and desirable, (2) that three distinct historical understandings of philosophical anarchism should be distinguished, (3) that philosophical anarchism is best understood as the argumentative expression of the anarchist case, (4) that there are more and less adequate contemporary philosophical anarchisms in our sense and (5) that philosophical anarchism is defensible in a weak but engaged form. Overall, I have attempted to break down some of the barriers between 'political anarchism' and 'philosophical anarchism', as these have been understood to date. In other words, I have tried – hopefully with a modicum of success – to show how 'philosophical anarchism' can be radicalised as 'political anarchism' is intellectualised. And even if this project fails to advance the anarchist cause, it should at least help us understand anarchism a little better.

Bibliography

I. Berlin (1998) *The Proper Study of Mankind: An Anthology of Essays*, eds H. Hardy and R. Hausheer (London: Pimlico).

A. Carter (2000) 'Analytical anarchism: Some conceptual foundations', *Political Theory*, XXVIII, 230–53.
G. Crowder (1991) *Classical Anarchism: The Political Thought of Godwin, Proudhon, Bakunin, and Kropotkin* (Oxford: Oxford University Press).
R. T. De George (1985) *The Nature and Limits of Authority* (Lawrence: University Press of Kansas).
H. G. Frankfurt (1973) 'The anarchism of Robert Paul Wolff', *Political Theory*, I, 405–14.
L. Green (1990) *The Authority of the State* (Oxford: Clarendon Press).
W. von Humboldt (1996) *The Sphere and Duties of Government*, trans. Joseph Coulthard (Bristol: Thoemmes Press).
P. Marshall (1993) *Demanding the Impossible: A History of Anarchism*, rev. edn (London: Fontana).
R. Martin (1974) 'Wolff's defence of philosophical anarchism', *The Philosophical Quarterly*, XXIV, 140–9.
P. McLaughlin (2007) *Anarchism and Authority: A Philosophical Introduction to Classical Anarchism* (Aldershot: Ashgate).
A. Meltzer (2000) *Anarchism: Arguments For and Against* (Edinburgh: AK Press).
D. Miller (1984) *Anarchism* (London: Dent).
W. O. Reichert (1967) 'Toward a new understanding of anarchism', *The Western Political Quarterly*, XX, 856–65.
A. Ritter (1980) *Anarchism: A Theoretical Analysis* (Cambridge: Cambridge University Press).
J.-J. Rousseau (1986) *The Social Contract and Discourses*, ed. G. D. H. Cole (London: Everyman).
A. J. Simmons (1987) 'The anarchist position: A reply to Klosko and Senor', *Philosophy and Public Affairs*, XVI, 269–79.
—— (1996) 'Philosophical anarchism' in J. T. Sanders and J. Narveson (eds) *For and Against the State: New Philosophical Readings* (Lanham: Rowman and Littlefield).
—— (1999) 'Justification and legitimacy', *Ethics*, CIX, 739–71.
R. P. Wolff (1969) 'On violence', *Journal of Philosophy*, LXVI, 601–16.
—— (1976) *In Defence of Anarchism* (New York: Harper Torchbooks).
V. S. Yarros (1936) 'Philosophical anarchism: Its rise, decline, and eclipse', *The American Journal of Sociology*, XLI, 470–83.

3
Kicking Against the Pricks: Anarchist Perfectionism and the Conditions of Independence

Samuel Clark

The distinguished moral philosopher Philippa Foot begins her recent book *Natural Goodness* with the following story:

> Wittgenstein [in an Oxford philosophy seminar, probably in the 1940s] interrupted a speaker who had realised that he was about to say something that, although it seemed compelling, was clearly ridiculous, and was trying (as we all do in such circumstances) to say something sensible instead. 'No,' said Wittgenstein. 'Say what you *want* to say. Be *crude* and then we shall get on.'
>
> (Foot, 2001: 1)

The crude thing I want to say is that a free, non-dominating society cultivates flourishing, independent individuals; that such individuals in turn support a free, non-dominating society; and that this is the best reason for advocating such a society. The most appealing thing about the imagined anarchist utopia is the people it would make possible, and who would make it possible: 'O brave new world / That has such people in't' (Shakespeare, 1951: 24).

Call this position *anarchist perfectionism*. In this chapter, I raise some worries for anarchist perfectionism, despite my desire to support it. In Section 1, I describe perfectionism in general; in Section 2, I use some biographical examples to question the link between anarchic society and the development of flourishing individuals; in Section 3, I conclude by suggesting some possible ways forward.

3.1 Perfectionism

Perfectionism is one answer to the fundamental moral and political question, How should one live? It addresses that question by offering a theory of the *nature* and *significance* of the Good, where the Good is understood as whatever distinguishes better states of the world from worse ones: it is whatever is the correct answer to the axiological question, *What has intrinsic value?* Philosophers who can (more or less controversially) be identified as perfectionists include Aristotle, Aquinas, William Godwin, Karl Marx, John Stuart Mill, Friedrich Nietzsche and T. H. Green (Hurka, 1993).

The perfectionist's claim about the *nature* of the Good is that it is human flourishing, where *flourishing* is understood as the full development and successful performance of certain ways of functioning and being which are of central importance to human life. An individual human's life goes best, or is most successful, or is blessed, when she exemplifies and expresses human and individual potential to the full: for instance, when she is healthy, creative and independent (if those are the central human ways of functioning and being; for the moment, I mean only to give an illustrative example). The world is best when all the individuals within it have such lives (or when it is as close as is possible to that condition). The contrast here is with theories which make other claims about the Good. A hedonist, for example, identifies the Good (or welfare, well-being, the good life) with pleasure and the absence of pain (Griffin, 1986: Part I; Feldman, 2004). An anti-welfarist, for another example, rejects the hedonist's and the perfectionist's shared identification of the Good with what makes a life go best: that is, they deny that the Good is (wholly) a condition or activity of individuals.

The perfectionist's claim about the *significance* of the Good is that it is the primary and independently defined ethical concept. The other basic ethical concept, the Right, is derivative from it: the right thing to do is to promote the Good. That is, the contrast here is that the perfectionist, like the utilitarian, is a teleologist as opposed to a deontologist (Rawls, 1999: §6). The teleologist claims that there are no *independently* or *absolutely* right and wrong actions (or right and wrong policies, rules, attitudes): everything right or wrong is so because of its consequences, as measured by the Good. If murder is wrong, it is wrong because of what it does to individuals, not because there is any rule independent of that criterion, whether rooted in divine command, natural law or the self-legislation of rational agents.

The right thing to do is to promote the Good. I mean *promote* here to be wider than the notion usually used in descriptions of utilitarianism, *maximise*. The right form of promotion of the Good, for the perfectionist, may in some circumstances be to maximise overall or average human flourishing. In other circumstances, it may, for instance, be to bring everyone up to a minimum absolute level of flourishing; to defend what good there is; to attempt to exemplify the struggle for self-development in one's own life; or to focus on the development of one's children. I do not mean to make any particular claims here about which circumstances are proper to any of these kinds of promotion.

Perfectionism, then, is an ethical theory at the same level of generality as the three main competitors in normative ethics: utilitarianism, Kantianism and virtue theory. It is distinct from all three, but overlaps with utilitarianism in being teleological, and with virtue theory in denying that flourishing consists (solely) in mental states or in the satisfaction of preferences. For the perfectionist, there are things which are good for us, whether or not we want or enjoy them, and those things are, especially, conditions and activities which fit us as the kind of creature we are.

Within this general account, we can distinguish political from moral perfectionism. *Political* perfectionism is a theory of practical justification, and particularly of the justification of social action. It claims that the goal which justifies and makes sense of our joint actions – politics in the widest sense – is the promotion of human flourishing. A useful contrast here is with the common liberal claim that the only legitimate coercive social action is that which enforces neutral rules to govern interaction between people with differing conceptions of the good (e.g., Locke, 1988; Rawls, 1999). For perfectionists, social action (potentially including state action) is properly directed at promoting the Good, and not merely at protecting individuals in their pursuit of whatever they desire or whatever they believe to be good.

Moral perfectionism is the more fundamental part of the theory. It claims that the Good is human flourishing, and it goes on to describe the particular ways of functioning and being which constitute that flourishing, typically by identifying certain physical, social, aesthetic, emotional, intellectual and/or reflexive capacities. Some of these capacities might also be picked out as virtues by a virtue theorist, but the perfectionist's net is wider: the flourishing human life is likely to include good health, for instance, but few think that good health is a moral virtue, or that illness is a vice.

The perfectionist's list of central human capacities is unified and explained by an account of natural human development and of the distortions to which it can be subject. This is a further contrast with some virtue theories, which ground virtue in social practices rather than in human nature (e.g., MacIntyre, 1985; but see also MacIntyre, 1999 for a change of view). This focus on the proper development of human nature makes explicit a further element of perfectionism as I am using the term: the perfectionist understands humans as animals located in a natural world governed by causal laws, and therefore as subject to the demands of an unchosen reality. What is Good for us is not entirely up to us, because we do not choose our own natures. Like it or not, we are *Homo sapiens* – sociable, talkative, tool-using east-African plains apes – and that has unavoidable consequences. In particular, it has consequences for the nature, and the necessary and sufficient conditions, of human flourishing.

Summing up: just as we might say that the good life for an oak is to grow from acorn to spreading, ancient tree – rather than, for example, being shaped into a stunted bonsai – so, the perfectionist says that the good life for a human is to grow into a flourishing adult – rather than, for example, being tyrannised into a tamed slave. This fact about the good life for humans – about the Good – is what justifies and makes sense of individual and social action: the right thing to do – the Right – is to promote that Good. Both the oak and the human, as living things in an unchosen and recalcitrant world, need certain favourable conditions, if their flourishing is to be possible. This natural background makes sense of the perfectionist's metaphors of growth, flourishing, corruption and stuntedness.

Two obvious questions follow for the perfectionist: first, *Which* capacities are the ones central to human life, the development and use of which constitute flourishing? What does a flourishing adult human possess and do? Second, *How* are we to promote human flourishing? What are its conditions? What nourishment or cultivation do we need to grow successfully and to avoid enslavement and the other corruptions of human life? With my general account of perfectionism and these questions in mind, I now move on to consider *anarchist* perfectionism in particular.

3.2 Anarchist perfectionism

For contrast, here is a possible perfectionist position addressing my two questions: Which capacities constitute flourishing? The monkish virtues of silence, ignorance, obedience and self-abnegation. How are they to be promoted? Through comprehensive surveillance, state violence and deliberate structuring of the physical and social environment for purposes of control. This vision of a monastic utopia is a perfectionist view, but very obviously not an anarchist one. My suggested anarchist perfectionism, by contrast, answers my two questions as follows.

First, Which capacities? A complete account of human flourishing would include a huge range of capacities – emotional, aesthetic, intellectual, social... I have no complete list. I want to concentrate on one bundle of capacities which has been important in the anarchist tradition. It is the opposite of the monkish virtues: *independence*. I understand independence not as a single virtue, but as a collection of personal and social capacities. They are, first, a developed private judgement about what one should do, which is resistant to bias and to ideological and other distortions. This is, for instance, one of the central features of Godwin's imagined future humans, against the example of which he criticises current arrangements (Godwin, 1976; Clark, 2007: Chapter 1). Second, the capacity for self-government. That is, one's developed judgement is actually motivating – one is not *akratic* or constrained. Again, for instance, the possibility of such motivating judgement is one of Godwin's main philosophical problems (Godwin, 1976: Part I). Third, the capacity and physical/social resources to resist domination and to avoid dependence. At minimum, one requires food and water, and a secure place to live, if one is not to be vulnerable to domination, but one might potentially need far more, depending on the extant threats and temptations. Part of the enduring fascination to anarchists of acephalous peoples like the Nuer, I suggest, is that they are not naïve about the possibility of domination: they have developed complex social tactics for pre-empting and resisting domination, from mockery to mediation to non-cooperation to migration (Clark, 2007: 109–38).

I want to make three further comments about the concept of independence as used here. First, it is analogous to the concept of positive freedom: where negative freedom is the mere absence of coercion, positive freedom requires actually having the capacities and resources, including the capacity of self-command, to do what one really chooses to do (Berlin, 1969; van Parijs, 1995). Similarly, independence requires actually controlling one's own life according to one's own decisions, and therefore requires personal and social resources against domination. In fact, this may be more than an analogy: independence can be understood as a particular kind of freedom. Specifically, it is that kind of freedom concerned with individuals' control over their own lives, rather than, for instance, with the freedom of communities. Second, independence is a contingent personal and social achievement: some people are lucky enough to have enjoyed the conditions of development of independence; there is nothing odd about the fact that humans start out wholly dependent on others and have to be gradually nurtured into independence. Third, this developmental account of independence fits with the teleological nature of perfectionism as set out in Section 3.1: for the teleologist, to have independence is contingently to have gained the fragile blessing of an element of human flourishing. So, the moral significance of independence is that it is part of the Good which we ought to promote. There would be little sense in promoting independence if one could not fail to be independent. I shall offer some concrete examples of the independence I intend in a moment, when I go on to discuss Frederick Douglass and John Stuart Mill.

Summing up my anarchist answer to the first question for the perfectionist: part of the Good – part of human flourishing – which we ought to promote is independence, understood as a gradually and contingently achieved bundle of personal and social capacities. The second question then becomes: How are we to promote independence? What are its conditions of development?

This is where I stop being able to endorse the crude but appealing thought with which I began. I introduced anarchist perfectionism as the claim that a free, non-dominating society cultivates flourishing, independent individuals; that such individuals in turn support a free, non-dominating society; and that this is the best reason for advocating such a society. Recasting that in the light of what I have said since: the anarchist perfectionist claims that the right thing to do is to promote the Good; that the Good is human flourishing, understood as the full development and successful use of certain capacities which are of central importance to human life; that independence is one important part of that flourishing; and that the condition of development of independence is a free, non-dominating society. It is the last clause of this description which I now want to challenge.

First, the anarchist condition is neither necessary nor sufficient for the development of independence. It is not sufficient because one might live in a free, non-dominating society, but lack the appropriate stimuli or objects for the development of independence. Human capacities develop through repeated *use*. One might have nothing to practise judgement or resistance on, and therefore never develop those capacities, just as one would never develop a sophisticated musical ear without music to listen to. So, if independence includes a capacity for motivating independent judgement and the capacity and resource to resist domination and dependence, it appears that we need episodes of having to make and act on hard decisions in the face of distorting pressures, and of resisting attempts at domination, if we are to develop independence through practice. The person who *can* make such decisions and engage in such resistance is the person who has *had to*: living in an anarchist utopia of freedom and non-domination might leave one's independence stunted. The anarchic utopian citizen is revealed as a lotus-eater without character or goals, which must be shaped by choice and resistance:

> Let us alone. What pleasure can we have
> To war with evil? Is there any peace
> In ever climbing up the climbing wave?
> All things have rest, and ripen toward the grave
> In silence; ripen, fall and cease:
> Give us long rest or death, dark death, or dreamful ease.
>
> (Tennyson, 1953: 52)

If independence is part of flourishing, then the anarchic citizen is not flourishing.

The anarchist condition is not necessary for the development of independence, either, because some of our best examples of the development of independence are examples of resistance to tyranny and enslavement. Consider Frederick Douglass, for instance: Douglass was born a slave in Maryland in 1818 and escaped to the North in 1838 to become an important anti-slavery activist and to write an autobiography, *Narrative of the Life of Frederick Douglass, an American Slave* (Douglass, 1982). *Narrative* is an account of Douglass's growth into a free man in the face of oppression and violence, and its central dramas of development are two acts of resistance: first, Douglass learns to read and to write despite the attempts of his owners, Hugh and Sophia Auld, to stop him (Douglass, 1982: Chapters VI and VII). Second, Douglass fights back against the slave-breaker Mr Covey (Douglass, 1982: Chapter X). Both of these episodes, Douglass makes it clear, were turning points in his development. Reading opened 'the pathway from slavery to freedom' (Douglass, 1982: 78). Physical victory over Covey

> was the turning-point in my career as a slave. It rekindled the few expiring embers of freedom, and revived within me a sense of my own manhood. It recalled the departed self-confidence, and inspired me again with a determination to be free.
>
> (Douglass, 1982: 113)

Douglass's story dramatises the thought that one of the appropriate objects of the capacities of independence is something to resist: that *we need some pricks to kick against* (the allusion is to Acts 9:5). That is, not only is the anarchist condition not necessary for the development of independence, the conditions it excludes – domination, in particular – might be necessary for that development. Anarchic society not only is not *enough* for the development of independence, it may be altogether *wrong* for that development: not just a barren soil but a poisoned one.

My second reason for contesting the anarchist perfectionist claim that the condition of development of independence is a free, non-dominating society is that I have come to be suspicious of too-quick generalisations about the nature and conditions of the good life. Human development is complex and various, and if we are to understand it, I think we would do better to examine the development, successes and failures of particular human lives – Douglass's life, for instance – before rushing to generalise. This does not mean that there is nothing to say about the ecology of human flourishing: it does mean that we should be cautious. The way into investigating the good life which I am pursuing here (and in other work) is via autobiographies, because the individual detail of a self-understood life moves general theories closer to the complexities of real flourishing.

Consider another example: John Stuart Mill's self-emancipation from his father James Mill and from his hothouse education as the utilitarian messiah. Mill's is a familiar story told in his *Autobiography* (Mill, 1981): educated at home; Greek at age 3, Latin at 8, writing articles on political economy for national newspapers before he was in his teens; editing his father's vast textbook of associationist psychology; deliberate and ferocious honing of his analytical and rhetorical skills; and all designed to make him the best possible advocate of Jeremy Bentham's and James Mill's Greatest Happiness Principle. As Mill describes it, the pivotal transformation in which he breaks free is his 'mental crisis' (Mill, 1981: Chapter 5). The crisis is 'a drowsy, stifled, unimpassioned grief' (Mill, 1981: 139, quoting Samuel Taylor Coleridge's 'Dejection: An Ode') in which Mill finds no pleasure in his books, music and activism. It is triggered by a sudden moment of self-perception – an 'irrepressible self-consciousness' (Mill, 1981: 139) – that even if he achieves all of his life-goals, he will not be happy. Mill's recovery from his crisis is also a matter of changes in perception. First, control of the risky habits of self-analysis and self-consciousness: 'the habit of analysis has a tendency to wear away the feelings' (141); 'ask yourself whether you are happy, and you cease to be so' (147). Second, development of finer aesthetic and emotional perceptions, especially the perception of poetry and the 'pleasure of sympathy with human beings' (143). Third, a revealing and destructive analysis of the Benthamism in which he had been schooled (Mill, 1969).

Mill's crisis, then, is partly a transformation of perception, and especially a move from inwardly to outwardly directed perception; partly the discovery of proper objects for developed perceptual capacities (Wordsworth's poetry, for instance); partly the use of analytic tools drilled into him by his father to subvert his father's teaching. What does this tell us about the cultivation of independence in general? Apart from the negative point already made that it is a complex process, what Mill's story suggests is that the development of independence can involve a range of other human capacities – perception including self-perception, analytic skill. Most importantly here, it suggests that resistance to an unequal personal relationship can be a significant part of development. As I suggested above in the discussion of Douglass, perhaps domination and resistance to it are necessary conditions of the cultivation of independence.

The question I have been considering is: How are we to promote independence? The crude but appealing anarchist perfectionist answer is that independence is cultivated by a free, non-dominating society: an anarchist utopia. I have now raised several problems for that claim. First, an anarchist society provides neither necessary nor sufficient conditions for the development of independence. Its conditions are not sufficient for the development of independence because human capacities are developed by practice, and a citizen of the anarchic utopia might lack appropriate objects for such practice. Its conditions are not necessary because some of our best examples of the development of independence – Douglass and Mill – are out of resistance to domination, not in its absence. In discussing the examples of Douglass and Mill, I moved from the weaker claim that the absence of domination is not a necessary condition of the development of independence to the stronger (and more worrying) suggestion that perhaps domination and resistance are necessary conditions of that development. Independence involves the capacity to resist domination; capacities are developed by use; so, we need some domination against which to practise.

The consequence of these arguments, if they are sound, is that the development and the exercise of capacities of independence come apart. The society of free, undominated people exercising their independence is not necessarily the best environment for the cultivation of that independence: anarchist perfectionism fails.

3.3 Conclusion

A final summing up: I started from a tempting theory, anarchist perfectionism. In Section 3.1, I described perfectionism in general as an account of the nature and significance of the Good: the Right is the promotion of the Good understood as human flourishing. In Section 3.2, I offered anarchist perfectionist answers to two obvious questions: Which capacities constitute human flourishing? and How are we to promote that flourishing? I concentrated on independence as the bundle of capacities the anarchist perfectionist is concerned to promote, and then raised some problems for the anarchist perfectionist answer to the second question, *How?* In making my argument, I had two ideas in the background. First, the Aristotelian claim that human capacities are developed by practice on their proper objects. Second, the view that one good way to investigate human flourishing is to consider the developmental details of individual lives, especially as recorded in autobiographies (this is a project I am also pursuing in other work).

I admit to disappointment with my tentative conclusion that anarchist perfectionism fails, at least in the simple form in which I have presented it here. I would have preferred it to be true. The challenge of this unwelcome conclusion is that we have to find a path forward, and I will close by suggesting some possibilities.

One possibility is that we could give up on the idea that an anarchist society would cultivate independent individuals and admit that this failure makes that utopia less attractive. Or, we could take this failure as a sign that we should focus on other capacities. Perhaps independence is a temporary expedient: a revolutionary virtue, but not characteristic of the citizens of utopia. Perhaps those distant citizens will focus on other capacities, other forms of self-development towards flourishing: the pleasure of sympathy, creativity as satisfying work. Perhaps, more radically, we should accept that we do not know what the citizens of an anarchic utopia would be like. The problem with that last suggestion, though, is that it apparently leaves us without reason to promote such a utopia, at least if we hold on to the teleological and welfarist idea that what justifies social action is what it does to individuals.

Finally, two paths which I find more attractive. First, I have suggested that the development of independence – human development in general – is a complex and various process, best investigated by studying the lived details of individual lives. Perhaps, then, we can find examples of the cultivation of independence in situations *without* domination which can stand comparison with Douglass and Mill. That is not impossible, although right now, situations free of domination are rare. Second, Mill imagined that the real diversity of opinion he so valued might eventually, with the growth of knowledge, have to be replaced by skilled devil's advocates, against whom developing individuals could practise their argumentative skills and come to know the truth as living thought rather than as dead dogma (Mill, 1977: Chapter 2). Similarly, we might imagine an education by *playful practice* of capacities. Perhaps an anarchic society would need to provide invented opportunities for choice and resistance, especially in its children's lives; perhaps anarchic children would make such opportunities for themselves. Pulling these last two suggestions together might suggest an anarchist perfectionist pedagogy drawing on anarchist educational experiment and theory (e.g., Neill, 1968; Ward, 1973). We could build an account of gradual human flourishing, including the development of independence, which recognises our nature as creatures who need to practise using our capacities, and which directs that account to promoting our flourishing. That possibility, speculative though it is, is perhaps worth the disappointing failure of the too-simple anarchist perfectionism with which I began.

Bibliography

Aristotle (1999) *Nicomachean Ethics*, 2nd edn (Indianapolis: Hackett).
I. Berlin (1969) 'Two concepts of liberty' in *Four Essays on Liberty* (Oxford: Oxford University Press).
S. Clark (2007) *Living Without Domination* (Aldershot: Ashgate).
F. Douglass (1982) *Narrative of the Life of Frederick Douglass, an American Slave: Written by Himself*, ed. Houston A. Baker Jr (Harmondsworth: Penguin).
F. Feldman (2004) *Pleasure and the Good Life: Concerning the Nature, Varieties, and Plausibility of Hedonism* (Oxford: Clarendon Press).
P. Foot (2001) *Natural Goodness* (Oxford: Clarendon Press).
W. Godwin (1976) *Enquiry Concerning Political Justice and Its Influence on Modern Morals and Happiness*, ed. Isaac Kramnick (Harmondsworth: Penguin).
J. Griffin (1986) *Well-Being: Its Meaning, Measurement, and Moral Importance* (Oxford: Clarendon Press).
T. Hurka (1993) *Perfectionism* (Oxford: Oxford University Press).
J. Locke (1988) 'An essay concerning the true original, extent, and end of civil government' [The Second Treatise] in P. Laslett (ed.) *Two Treatises of Government* (Cambridge: Cambridge University Press).
A. MacIntyre (1985) *After Virtue: A Study in Moral Theory*, 2nd edn (London: Duckworth).
—— (1999) *Dependent Rational Animals: Why Human Beings Need the Virtues* (London: Duckworth).
J. S. Mill (1969) 'Bentham' in John M. Robson (ed.) *Collected Works of John Stuart Mill*, vol. 10: *Essays on Ethics, Religion and Society* (Toronto, Canada: University of Toronto Press), 75–115.

—— (1977) *On Liberty* in John M. Robson (ed.) *Collected Works of John Stuart Mill*, vol. 18: *Essays on Politics and Society* 1 (Toronto, Canada: University of Toronto Press), 213–310.

—— (1981) *Autobiography* in John M. Robson and Jack Stillinger (eds) *Collected Works of John Stuart Mill*, vol. 1: *Autobiography and Literary Essays* (Toronto, Canada: University of Toronto Press), 1–290.

A. S. Neill (1968) *Summerhill: A Radical Approach to Child-Rearing* (London: Penguin).

R. Nozick (1975) *Anarchy, State, and Utopia* (Oxford: Blackwell).

P. van Parijs (1995) *Real Freedom for All: What (if Anything) Can Justify Capitalism?* (Oxford: Clarendon Press).

J. Rawls (1999) *A Theory of Justice*, rev. edn (Oxford: Oxford University Press).

W. Shakespeare (1951) *The Tempest* in P. Alexander (ed.) *William Shakespeare: The Complete Works* (London: Collins), 1–26.

A. Tennyson (1953) 'The Lotos-Eaters' in T. Herbert Warren (ed.) *Tennyson: Poems and Plays* revised and enlarged by Frederick Page (Oxford: Oxford University Press), 51–3.

C. Ward (1973) *Anarchy in Action* (London: Freedom Press).

4
Anarchist Philosophy: Past, Problems and Prospects

Nathan Jun

This chapter is concerned with three specific questions. First, has there ever been a distinctive and independent 'anarchist' political philosophy, or is anarchism better viewed as a minor sect of another political philosophy – for example, socialism or liberalism – which cannot claim any critical and conceptual resources of its own? Second, if there has been such a distinctive and independent philosophy, what are its defining characteristics? Third, whether there is a distinctive and independent anarchist political philosophy or not, *should* there be?

The answers to these questions depend crucially on how one understands the nature and purpose of political philosophy, to say nothing of how one defines 'distinctive' and 'independent'. As I will argue, anarchism does qualify as a distinctive and independent political philosophy – one that emerged historically as a unique *tertia via* (third way) between liberalism and Marxism replete with novel philosophical concepts and ideas. At the same time, however, it must be admitted that anarchist thinkers seldom articulated and developed these ideas with the level of rigour and precision characteristic of other political philosophers, and few made any forays into systematic philosophy.

Although there are specific and justifiable reasons for this – some historical and contingent, some philosophical and conceptual – the omission of anarchism from standard canons of political philosophy has much to do with its perceived theoretical and systematic underdevelopment. I will discuss this issue in brief detail. Lastly, I will argue that recent developments in, and refinements of, anarchist philosophy are beneficial for the contemporary anarchist movement, though much work remains to be done.

4.1 What is political philosophy?

Political philosophy, writes Todd May (1994: 1), 'is a project perpetually haunted by crisis... because it inhabits that shifting space between what is and what ought to be'. Unlike moral philosophy (which May, following Kant, identifies with the study of 'what ought to be') and metaphysics (which he identifies with the study of 'what is'), 'the work of political philosophy is dictated by the tension between the two, rather than by one of the poles' (1; cf. Kant, 1965). It is not really possible, he thinks, to study 'what ought to be' without also studying 'what is', and vice versa (2). This is because all moral theories depend to a greater or lesser extent on descriptive analyses (whether metaphysical or otherwise), whereas all metaphysical theories depend on 'the normativity inhabiting the epistemology that provides [their] foundation' (2). Nevertheless, 'political philosophy... has only discussed the ought *given what is*', thus 'as the social configuration shifts, so must the philosophical approach' (2). The idea that political theories are constituted by a tension between 'what is' and 'what ought to be' underlies May's three-fold taxonomy of political philosophy. The danger of this taxonomy is that it confuses political philosophy with politics and, in so doing, divests political philosophy of any distinctive *raison d'etre*. Despite this flaw, May's taxonomy – as well as his approach to political theory more generally – is helpful for understanding anarchism in itself and in relation to other political philosophies.

The first type of political philosophy, which he calls 'formal political philosophy', aims at discovering 'the nature, or at least the important characteristics, of a just society' (May, 1994: 4). It does this by attaching itself to one or the other of the two 'poles' mentioned above (is versus ought, descriptive versus normative) and builds its analysis upon this attachment (4). Most classical political philosophy can be seen as operating in this way. For example, Aristotle, Aquinas, Thomas Hobbes and John Locke all attempt to determine 'what ought to be' on the basis of certain descriptive assumptions about human nature.

The same is true, May thinks, of much contemporary Anglo-American political philosophy. For example, John Rawls' *A Theory of Justice* (1971) is founded on a variety of descriptive assumptions, most importantly the notion that human beings are by nature rationally self-interested. As May points out, 'By utilizing the maximin principle of decision theory in a situation (the original position) of ignorance about one's eventual place in society, Rawls tries to provide the principles which all rational beings would choose as the cornerstone of [a just] society' (4). Like his classical forebears, Rawls begins with an account of what is allegedly the case (i.e., human beings are rationally self-interested) and on this basis produces an account of what ought to be the case.

Formal political philosophy can also hew to the 'is' pole (i.e., to empirical or descriptive claims about the way the world actually is). Of particular interest here are certain Marxist theories that espouse strict historical determinism. If history is necessary, as such theories suggest, then the moral responsibilities of individuals are 'negated, if not severely diminished' (May, 1994: 6). This, in turn, implies that normative considerations are at best of secondary importance. In their place, these theories offer a description of society and proceed to demonstrate by means of dialectical analyses how society will naturally evolve. In Georg Lukács' *History and Class Consciousness* (1971), to cite just one example, bourgeois capitalism automatically introduces commodification (or 'reification') across society that, in turn, produces revolutionary class consciousness among the proletariat. As proletariat consciousness grows it will eventually 'overcome reification by overthrowing the capitalist order' and replacing it with a communist society (May, 1994: 6; cf. Lukács, 1971: 161–6).

The second type of political philosophy is what May calls 'strategic political philosophy' (1994: 7). Unlike the formal, which relies on one or the other pole of political philosophy, the strategic involves 'an immersion into the tension between the two' (7). For example, whereas the formal philosophy of Rawls employs normative analyses to determine what a just society would be like, strategic philosophy employs analyses of context, including historical and social conditions, in order to answer the question famously raised by Lenin, that is, 'what is to be done?' According to May, although formal political philosophies seek to formulate conceptions of justice, they generally avoid devising concrete strategies for the realisation of justice in society. Occasionally they provide critiques of extant political institutions or sketch out hypothetical 'alternatives' that might be implemented in the future, but they seldom explain how we are to realise such alternatives in practice (a task that is instead left to activists, politicians or policy analysts).

Strategic political philosophy sometimes produces normative critiques which are in turn levelled against real historical, social and cultural institutions. This is especially true of socialists and other 'progressives' of the early nineteenth century who criticised capitalism on squarely moral grounds. More often, however, such moral critique is simply assumed or otherwise taken for granted within strategic political philosophy. Arguably there are some instances, say, in the case of Niccolò Machiavelli, where normative critique is ignored altogether. Barring these limited exceptions, given that this or that institution is unjust, the predominant question for the strategic philosopher becomes 'what are we going to do about it?' As May notes by way of summary:

Strategic political philosophy recognises that history and social conditions unfold not of necessity but are mutable and perhaps even regressive at times. However, neither are history and social conditions secondary; they are consulted not merely to realise an ethical programme but to determine what concrete possibilities present themselves for intervention. In this sense, not only is the historical and social situation read in terms of ethical demands, but the ethical programme is limited and perhaps partially determined by the situation. This is why much – though by no means all – political philosophy that falls under the category 'strategic' addresses itself to the concrete historical conditions under which the philosophizing takes place (1994: 7).

The idea here is that the normative and programmatic analyses of strategic political philosophy are self-reflexive: they recognise their embedded-ness within a particular context and the extent to which this context shapes and reshapes them. As the context shifts, so must the philosophy that would seek to analyse and, ultimately, change it. This is generally not true of formal political philosophy, which attempts to arrive at abstract and universal principles and prescriptions by disentangling itself from the vicissitudes of history and context.

Another important feature of strategic political philosophy, according to May, is that it usually 'involves a unitary analysis that aims towards a single goal' (1994: 10). Marxist philosophy, for example, locates the source of power within the substructure of economic relations with a mind to the eventual abolition of capitalism: 'Political and social change, if it is to be significant, must rest upon a transformation at the base [...]. All problems can be reduced to the basic one' (10). The same is true of certain strands of radical feminism which reduce all oppression to patriarchal dominance. Strategic feminist philosophy of this sort therefore relies on radical critique of gender relations with a mind to 'overthrowing' patriarchy. In all cases, the basic idea is that oppressive power emanates from a unitary source that must be combated and destroyed in order to achieve the goal of liberation.

The third and final type of political philosophy that May discusses is 'tactical political philosophy' (1994: 11). Like strategic philosophy, tactical philosophy subsists in the tension between the is-pole and the ought-pole, but it does not attempt to reduce political analysis to a central and foundational problematic. For the tactical philosopher, any attempt to locate power in a single centre radically circumscribes the sphere of possible intervention. Tactical political philosophy instead acknowledges the 'many different sites from which [power] arises and [...] the interplay among these various sites in the creation of the social world' (1994: 11). Power does not originate in or flow from these sites but rather builds up around them in varying degrees. One of the central theses of May's *The Political Philosophy of Poststructuralist Anarchism* is that 'poststructuralism, particularly as it is embodied in the works of Foucault, Deleuze, and Lyotard, has defined a tradition of the type of political philosophy... called "tactical" ' (1994: 12). The same is true, he thinks, of various 'classical anarchist' writers such as Proudhon, Bakunin and Kropotkin. Anarchism is a 'tactical philosophy' because it recognises the multifarious and diffuse nature of power and refuses to reduce all particular instances of oppression to a more basic form. In the next section, I shall explore anarchist philosophy in greater detail.

4.2 Anarchism as political philosophy

To many it may seem odd to regard anarchism as a genuine 'political philosophy' at all since, unlike some of the others mentioned previously, it has never been, nor ever aspired to be, a fixed, comprehensive, self-contained and internally consistent system of ideas, set of doctrines or body of theory. On the contrary, anarchism, from its earliest days, has been an evolving set of attitudes and ideas that can apply to a wide range of social, economic and political theories, practices, movements and traditions. As a result of its theoretical flexibility and open-endedness – or perhaps as a contributing factor to it, or perhaps both – anarchism has historically tended to emphasise revolutionary praxis over analysis of, and discourse about, revolutionary strategy (Graeber, 2004: 54). This explains why some Marxist-Leninists have accused anarchism of being an 'anti-intellectual', 'unscientific' and/or 'utopian' doctrine, and why some anarchists, in turn, have regarded political theory with impatience and suspicion, if not outright disdain.

Although anarchist theory has a unique tactical dimension, it also has a long and impressive history as a distinctive formal – and specifically ethical – philosophy. Moreover, both tactical and formal philosophy have played and continue to play a crucial role in anarchist interventions in working-class and labour movements. Too often the writings which were disseminated to, and hungrily consumed by, workers in these movements are dismissed as 'propaganda'. However, insofar as they articulate and define political, economic and social concepts; subject political, economic and social institutions to trenchant critique against clear and well-defined normative standards; offer logical justifications of their own positions; and advance positive alternative proposals; why should these writings *not* be regarded as philosophical texts and analysed accordingly? Obviously they should, and the fact that they have been so long ignored by political philosophers, historians and other scholars has everything to do with academic prejudice and nothing to do with the intellectual and philosophical merit of the writings themselves.

In scholarly literature, the term 'classical anarchism' is most often used in reference to the pre-1918 European anarchist movement (e.g., Crowder, 1991). Once in a while, however, 'classical anarchism' seems to be something like a catch-all for the work of three thinkers – Pierre-Joseph Proudhon, Mikhail Bakunin and Peter Kropotkin – whose ideas are allegedly close enough that we are justified in treating them all as a single, homogeneous unit. As it turns out, 'classical anarchism' in this sense is an academic myth. Proudhon, Bakunin and Kropotkin – indeed, most anyone who could be identified, or would have identified herself, as an anarchist prior to 1918 – disagreed on a wide array of issues: for example, whether and to what extent the use of violence is justified in revolutionary activity, what the role of labour unions is or should be, what the role of women in the movement should be, whether to advocate free love or to maintain 'conventional' sexual partnerships, how to answer the so-called 'Jewish question', whether and to what extent to collaborate with other revolutionary and left-wing parties, how and when the revolution will be initiated and how post-revolutionary society will be organised. In fact, anarchists probably disagreed more on balance than they agreed. Yet somehow, despite these often massive differences of opinion, they *mostly* managed to stick together without internal purges, executions, assassinations or jailings. How was this possible?

As L. Susan Brown (1993: 106) notes, 'Anarchist political philosophy is by no means a unified movement [...] Within the anarchist "family" there are mutualists, collectivists, communists, federalists, individualists, socialists, syndicalists, [and] feminists.' Different 'anarchisms' may provide different definitions of anarchy, different justifications for pursuing anarchy, different strategies for achieving anarchy and different models of social, economic and political organisation under anarchy (Brown, 1993: 106; cf. Rocker, 1938: 20–1). Notwithstanding such differences, all 'anarchisms' are properly so called in virtue of endorsing certain distinct ideas and practices. The question, of course, is what such ideas and practices might be.

One common misconception, which has been rehearsed repeatedly by the few Anglo-American philosophers who have bothered to broach the topic such as A. J. Simmons (1996) and R. P. Wolff (1970), is that anarchism can be defined solely in terms of opposition to states and governments. Simmons (1996: 19) writes, for example, that 'commitment to one central claim unites all forms of anarchist political philosophy: all existing states are illegitimate.' From this it allegedly follows that the 'minimal moral content' of anarchism is just that the subjects of illegitimate states lack general political obligations (22).

Wolff's and Simmons' definition of anarchism, and all others like it, is *extremely* idiosyncratic in view of the anarchist tradition we are discussing. The word 'anarchy', which comes from the Greek *anarkhos*, does not principally mean 'without a government' or 'without a state', but rather 'without authority'. As David Wieck (1979) notes, 'anarchism is more than anti-statism, even if government (the state) is, appropriately, the central focus of anarchist critique' (139). As 'the generic social and political idea that expresses negation of all [repressive] power' (1979: 139; cf. Kropotkin, 1970b: 150), anarchism is committed first and foremost to the universal rejection of coercive authority. To be sure, the various schools of anarchism may disagree among themselves concerning *how* coercive authority ought to be opposed. But they are generally agreed that coercive authority includes all centralised and hierarchical forms of government (e.g., monarchy, representative democracy and state socialism), economic class systems (such as capitalism, Bolshevism, feudalism and slavery), autocratic religions (whether fundamentalist Islam, Roman Catholicism or many others), patriarchy, heterosexism, white supremacy and imperialism (Rocker, 1938: 20; Proudhon, 1969; Morris, 1995: 35–41). All anarchisms are properly so called in virtue of endorsing a common moral position. At the deepest and most fundamental level anarchism as *philosophy* is an *ethics*; everything it affirms or denies, champions or condemns, must ultimately be understood in ethical or moral terms.

But what exactly is this moral commitment which all anarchists share in common? It has already been intimated. The ethical core of anarchism is the claim that all forms of coercive authority are morally condemnable. Notice that the form of this claim is evaluative (i.e., having to do with values) rather than normative (i.e., having to do with norms or principles of conduct). In other words, it is not a prescription or a recommendation but rather a value judgement, one that asserts that coercive authority is, in essence, 'bad'. When one consults the writings of the anarchists, moreover, one finds this assertion, this *condemnation*, repeated so often that it takes on the appearance of a motto. This strongly suggests that anarchism is founded first and foremost on a conception of the good – an *axiology* – rather than on a conception of the right. But in what does this conception of the good consist? The universal condemnation of coercive authority is a negative judgement – it specifies what is 'bad' but does not directly indicate what is to be regarded as 'good' or 'praiseworthy'.

The answer to this question depends entirely on what 'good' stands in opposition to the 'evil' of coercive authority. It also depends, quite crucially, on what is meant by 'coercive authority'. As we mentioned earlier, authority is a type of power relation – one that involves not just the *de facto* capacity to exercise power over others, but also a *de jure* license or warrant to exercise power over others. Defined in this way, authority cannot reasonably be regarded as evil in itself. Indeed, all the anarchist thinkers we have discussed recognise that there are many types of authority relations, not all of which are objectionable. As Richard Sylvan (1993: 221) notes,

> Consider, for example, the relation of a student to an authority in some field of knowledge, who can in turn back up expert judgments by appeal to a further range of assessable evidence [...]. [A]nyone with time and some skill can proceed past the authority to assess claims made.

Such authority relations, which Sylvan calls 'transparent' or 'open', stand in opposition to

> '[O]paque' (or 'closed') authorities, who simply stand on their position or station [...or] appeal to a conventional rule or procedure ('that is how things are done' or 'have always been done') without being able to step beyond some rule book... which has been enacted (for reasons not open to, or bearing, examination) by a further substantially opaque authority.
>
> (1993: 221)

Anarchists have typically objected to opaque authority relations because they lack precisely what authority in general claims to have – that is, adequate justification. In other words, opaque authority is arbitrary, which in turn implies that people have no reason to recognise its power over them. Submission to arbitrary authority is objectionable in itself because it 'divest[s] the personality of its most integral traits; it denies the very notion that the individual is competent to deal [...] with the management of his or her personal life' (Bakunin, 1974: 202). Put another way, arbitrary authority violates psychological and moral autonomy – the ability of the individual to think and act for herself in accordance with reason and conscience (Fromm, 1986: 10; Goldman, 1998: 435).

Without a theoretical or moral justification, opaque authority invariably backs up its power with coercion and violence. Anarchists oppose coercion for the same reason they oppose opaque authority more generally: because it violates the 'self-respect and independence' of the individual (Goldman, 1998: 72). As Bakunin (1970) says, authority that purports to be 'privileged, licensed, official, and legal, even if it arises from universal suffrage...' will inevitably be enforced through violence 'to the advantage of a dominant minority of exploiters' (35). Compelling obedience to, or recognition of, authority through the use or threat of coercion (violent or otherwise) constitutes a fundamental denial of individual liberty, and for this reason alone deserves condemnation. In opposing 'coercive authority,' therefore, anarchists oppose arbitrary authority coupled with the use or threat of coercive means to underwrite said authority. They do so, moreover, because coercive authority is by definition at odds with individual freedom.

Yet there is more to anarchism than this. After all, while anarchists obviously value freedom, the same is true of liberals and non-anarchist socialists. In fact, several of the most radical early liberals understood coercive authority in the same basic way as anarchists did, and opposed it for the same basic reasons. Of particular relevance here is the English political philosopher William Godwin, who argues in *An Enquiry Concerning the Principles of Political Justice* that freedom is logically incompatible with government. Indeed, Godwin valued freedom to such an extent that he advocated the abolition of the state. (It is not surprising, for this reason, that Godwin is often regarded as an important precursor to modern anarchism.)

We must recall, however, that the 'freedom' which Godwin and other classical liberals value is *negative* freedom ('freedom from'). To be sure, negative freedom is also valued by anarchists, and the liberal conception of negative freedom was extremely influential in the development of early anarchism, especially in post-Revolutionary France. Yet Proudhon, the first thinker to refer to his own political theory as 'anarchism', devotes most of his attention to the abolition of private property and the collective ownership of the means of production rather than the elimination of governments. When he does talk about eliminating governments, he does so only to motivate his positive proposal – namely, the establishment of a federal system of voluntary associations. The point, simply put, is that Proudhon was a socialist, not a liberal, and like all early socialists his primary ethical and political concern was not so much freedom as it was *justice*.

As we noted earlier, justice for the socialists is a function of equality, which is surely the *summum bonum* of socialism if anything is. Like other socialists, Proudhon understands equality not just as an abstract feature of human nature but as an ideal state of affairs that is both desirable and realisable. This state of affairs does not involve forcing human beings into a 'common grove' or making them into 'will-less automatons without independence or individuality'. It does not mean 'equal outcome' but 'equal opportunity'. Thus Alexander Berkman (2003: 164–5) writes the following:

> Do not make the mistake of identifying equality in liberty with the forced equality of the convict camp. True anarchist equality implies freedom, not quantity. It does not mean that every one must eat, drink, or wear the same things, do the same work, or live in the same manner. Far from it: the very reverse in fact [...] Individual needs and tastes differ, as appetites differ. It is equal opportunity to satisfy them that constitutes true equality. Far from levelling, such equality opens the door for the greatest possible variety of activity and development. For human character is diverse [...]. Free opportunity of expressing and acting out your individuality means development of natural dissimilarities and variations.
> (cf. Bakunin, 1994: 117–18; Guerin, 1998: 57–8)

It is worth recalling at this point that the word 'anarchy' refers not only to the absence of coercive authority but to the absence of a 'chief', 'head' or 'top' – in other words, to the absence of concentrated power exercised 'from the top down'. Anarchist equality, therefore, entails the equal distribution of power, which in turn implies the categorical rejection of centralisation and hierarchy. Such equality is necessary, moreover, in order to maximise individual freedom – not just 'freedom from' (negative liberty) but 'freedom to' (positive liberty).

Positive liberty, as Emma Goldman (1998: 439) explains, is necessary for a human being 'to grow to his full stature ... [to] learn to think and move, to give the very best of himself [... to] realise the true force of the social bonds that tie men together, and which are the true foundations of a normal social life'. This quotation underscores two indispensable features of the anarchist conception of freedom: first, that freedom involves the capacity of the individual to create herself, to resist what Foucault calls 'subjectivation' by cultivating new identities and forms of subjectivity; and second, that freedom is a capacity that emerges in, and is made possible by, social existence (as Proudhon (Quoted in Buber, 1958: 30) says, 'all associated and all free [...] the autonomy of the individual within the freedom of association').

The second feature belies a crucial difference between anarchism and liberalism. In a state of negative freedom, the rational, egoistic and atomistic agent of liberalism recognises her interests (understood not just as personal desires but as various ends determined by universal human nature) and takes means to achieve them. For the anarchists, however, 'the making of a human being is a collective process, a process in which both the community and the individual participate' (Bookchin, 1986: 79). Human subjectivity is produced in part by social forces, which can be either positive or negative, as well as by the individual force of self-creation (i.e., 'positive freedom').

The realisation of individual freedom, as Bakunin stresses, depends on recognising and 'cooperating in [the] realization of others' freedom' (quoted in Malatesta, 2001: 30). 'My freedom', he continues, 'is the freedom of all since I am not truly free in thought and in fact, except when my freedom and my rights are confirmed and approved in the freedom and rights of all men and women who are my equals' (30). As Malatesta (1965: 23) further notes,

> We are all egoists, we all seek our own satisfaction. But the anarchist finds his greatest satisfaction in struggling for the good of all, for the achievement of a society in which he [sic] can be a brother among brothers, and among healthy, intelligent, educated, and happy people. But he who is adaptable, who is satisfied to live among slaves and draw profit from the labour of slaves, is not, and cannot be, an anarchist.

In sum, freedom and equality are, for the anarchists, symbiotic concepts: individual freedom is positively constituted by and through social relations, which are in turn positively constituted by and through individual freedom.

The first feature of the anarchist conception of freedom is merely a reiteration of a point made earlier – namely, that freedom is a practice of self-creation, 'the freest possible expression of all the latent powers of the individual [...the] display of human energy' (Goldman, 1998: 67–8). At the same time, the 'desire to create and act freely [and] the craving for liberty and self-expression' are not innate characteristics but rather capacities that can be variously liberated or repressed. Freedom therefore has both a negative and a positive dimension. On the one hand, it must be understood as a precondition for self-creation, the 'open defiance of, and resistance to, all laws and restrictions, economic, social, and moral' which impede the cultivation and expression of individuality (Goldman, 1998: 67–8). On the other hand, freedom is coextensive with the process of self-creation itself, understood as the cultivation not only of individual subjectivity but also of social subjectivity or consciousness manifested concretely in healthy social environments (67). It is precisely this emphasis on freedom that distinguishes anarchism from other socialist theories, especially those that developed in the nineteenth century. For Engels and Lenin, no less than for Blanqui and Saint-Simon, the freedom of the individual is subordinate to the end of economic and social equality. This explains in part why anarchists are referred to – and refer to themselves – as 'libertarian socialists'.

Strictly speaking, then, freedom and equality are not distinct concepts for the anarchists. At the same time, it would be a mistake to suggest that anarchism simply fuses the liberal concept of freedom with the socialist concept of equality in a kind of synthesis. Rather, anarchist 'freedom-equality' is simply an expression of – a way of speaking about – human life itself. By life, moreover, we do not mean biological life but rather the immanent processes of change, development and becoming in terms of which Proudhon, Bakunin and Kropotkin *inter alia* (among other things) describe existence. In both its potential to change and its actual transformations, in both its singularity and universality, human life is a reflection of the 'unity in multiplicity' which Proudhon ascribes to the universe as a whole. Individual and social, social and ecological, ecological and global, global and cosmic – these are just so many levels of analysis which, if they can be said to differ at all, only differ in terms of scope. For the anarchists, *'Il y a seulement la vie, et la vie suffit'* ('there is only life, and it is enough').

It is this hybrid concept – which we might term 'vitality' – to which anarchist ethics ascribes the highest value. Domination and hierarchy, in turn, are condemnable to the extent, and only to the extent, that they oppose this concept. Perhaps at the level of pure ethics it is enough to describe this opposition in terms of limitation: domination and hierarchy inhibit, impede, obstruct and ultimately destroy life, and that is why domination and hierarchy are evil. For our purposes, however, a higher degree of specificity is necessary: we must explain not only *that* domination and hierarchy oppose life but also *how* they do. May (1994: 47) has argued, quite rightly in my view, that the principal mode of political domination is *representation*, the generic process of subsuming the particular under the general.

In the political realm, representation involves divesting individuals and groups of their *vitality* – their power to create, transform and change themselves. To be sure, domination often involves the literal destruction of vitality through violence and other forms of physical coercion. As a social-physical phenomenon, however, domination is not reducible to aggression of this sort. On the contrary, domination operates chiefly by 'speaking for others' or 'representing others to themselves' – that is, by manufacturing images of, or constructing identities for, individuals and groups.

These modes of subjectivation, as Foucault calls them, are in some instances foisted upon individuals or groups through direct or indirect processes of coercion. In other instances, modes of subjectivation are enforced and reinforced more subtly – for example, by becoming 'normalised' within a community. The result is that individuals and groups come to identify with the normalised representation, to conform to it, and so to regulate themselves in the absence of any direct coercion. Along these same lines, the anarchists were the first to acknowledge that representation is not a purely macropolitical phenomenon. Representation can and does occur at the micropolitical level – that is, at the level of everyday life – and needs to be avoided and resisted accordingly.

Deleuze (1977: 209) claimed at one point that Foucault was the first to teach us of 'the indignity of speaking for others'. Had Deleuze read Proudhon, Bakunin or Goldman, he might have come to a very different conclusion. For indeed, if anyone deserves credit for this 'discovery' it is the so-called 'classical anarchists'. It was they, after all, who first ascribed the highest moral value (and not merely dignity) to the ability of human beings and communities to 'speak for themselves', to act creatively upon themselves and to open up and pursue new possibilities for themselves – in short, to *live*. So, too, it was the anarchists who realised that political oppression is fundamentally constituted by wresting this ability from others, and, more importantly, that this 'wresting' involves 'giving people images [representations] of who they are and what they desire' (May, 1994: 48). It matters little whether that representation is legislated through an electoral process or imposed by a revolutionary vanguard, for the effect is the same. 'The life-giving order of freedom', Bakunin (1974) writes, 'must be made solely from the bottom upwards [...]. Only individuals, united through mutual aid and voluntary association, are entitled to decide who they are, what they shall be, how they shall live' (206–7). When that power is taken over by or ceded to hierarchical, coercive institutions of any sort, the result is oppression, domination and un-freedom: in a word, *death*.

Although I have established that anarchism is defined in part by a theory of value, this theory of value does not directly entail or endorse a principle of anti-authoritarianism, nor any other explicitly normative principle. On the contrary, it is clear that 'the critique of representation in the anarchist tradition runs deeper than just political representation,' extending into a far wider range of discourses, including morality. Kropotkin (1970a: 105), for example, argues that the value of individual and communal vitality precludes 'a right which moralists have always taken upon themselves to claim, that of mutilating the individual in the name of some ideal'. In practice, if not also in theory, the prescription of universal normative principles and moral mandates is just one more form of representation. As Kropotkin argues, the authority of such principles – the motivating force that they supposedly hold over us – depends crucially on totalised conceptions of a universal human nature or essence, on representations of 'the human being' as such. This is, again, the very substance of oppression.

In the place of normativity, the anarchists offer two alternatives: first, an anthropologico-genealogical description of the origins and functions of moral systems; and second, a pragmatic or procedural theory of action referred to as 'prefiguration' (Graeber, 2004: 62; Purkis and Bowen, 2005: 220). The first alternative, which is articulated most fully by Kropotkin, examines morality as such from an anthropological, sociological and evolutionary-psychological perspective. It goes on to explore the extent to which particular systems of morality, ranging from Kantianism to utilitarianism, have functioned in practice as mechanisms of domination and control (Morris, 2002). Kropotkin is therefore not interested in the question of whether, how and to what extent particular practices can be morally justified; rather, he is interested in the question of how systems of morality – particularly those systems which allegedly provide normative grounds for the condemnation of oppressive practices – come to be oppressive practices in their own right.

The second alternative refers to a practical principle observed more or less uniformly by anarchists over the past two centuries, namely, the 'prefigurative principle'. Borrowing from Benjamin Franks' work on the subject (2006: 97–100; 2009: 101–2), simply stated, the 'prefigurative principle' demands coherence between means and ends (Goldman, 2003: 261). That is, if the goal of political action is the promotion of some value and, by extension, opposition to whatever is at odds with that value, the means and methods employed in acting must reflect or *prefigure* the desired end. A helpful example is provided by Bakunin, who criticised certain Marxists for employing hierarchical, coercive methods in pursuit of egalitarian, libertarian ends: 'How could one want an equalitarian and free society to issue from authoritarian organization? It is impossible!' (Quoted by Bakunin in Kenafick, 1984: 7).

One can also point to the debate between Kropotkin, who disavowed the individual use of violent 'propaganda by deed', and the Russian revolutionary Sergei Nechayev, who advocated the use of terrorist tactics (Nechayev, 1989). As Paul Avrich notes, whereas Kropotkin insisted that means and ends are 'inseparable', which in turn implied that anarchists should not use the violent methods of the state in pursuit of the abolition of the state, Nechayev believed firmly that the end alone justifies the means (7–8; 29). More than one scholar has noted that Nechayev's uncompromising consequentialism shares more in common with Leninism than with the anarchism of the nineteenth and early twentieth centuries (Prawdin, 1961; Quail, 1978). That anarchism, as well as later anarchist movements within the New Left (Breines, 1982: 52–3) and in contemporary political struggles (Graeber, 2002, 2007), is distinguished very conspicuously by its strong commitment to the prefigurative principle – one that follows directly from the anarchist conception of power.

Anarchists hold that power relations, including those of an oppressive variety, can never be wholly abolished. This implies, among other things, that anarchy is defined by the ongoing process of contesting and reducing oppression rather than the utopian ideal of destroying oppressive structures and relations once and for all. In order to avoid reproducing oppressive power relations, moreover, the means and methods employed in this process ought to be consistent with their intended aims; the tactics used in pursuit of the value of freedom should themselves embody or reflect that value.

The prefigurative principle is not a normative prescription but a pragmatic recommendation (or, to use Kant's terminology, a 'hypothetical imperative'). The point of prefiguration is not to establish a foundation for normative judgement. The word 'ought' does not specify what is morally 'right' or 'wrong', but rather what is practical, prudent and consistent. To this extent, the prefigurative principle provides a general procedure for action that does not rely upon transcendent moral concepts or totalised representations of human nature. Within the broad ethical boundaries established by prefiguration and the general anarchist commitment to freedom and equality, there is enormous room for diversity of opinion. There is also a great, pressing and omnipresent demand for action at the expense of talk.

Taken together, these considerations begin to explain why anarchists have not distinguished themselves as especially 'sophisticated' philosophers even though it is clear that anarchism has an extremely sophisticated philosophical core. They also gesture at why anarchists have always maintained a fundamental unity-in-diversity as concerns political theory. In all events, it is clear that anarchism is an independent political philosophy whose unique theoretical and ethical approach distinguishes it from liberalism, Marxism and other political traditions. It is also clear that anarchist political philosophy has both a formal and a tactical dimension, combining a critique of existing conditions with concrete proposals for intervention.

4.3 Political philosophy as an anarchist practice

In its self-mythologising, anarchism is occasionally said to have evolved piecemeal among the peasants and labouring classes of Europe – again, as compared to Marxism, which was allegedly cooked up all at once in Marx's brain (!!). Errico Malatesta (1965: 198) is typical when he claims that anarchism 'follows ideas, not men, and rebels against the habit of embodying a principle in any one individual [...and] it does not seek to create theories through abstract analysis but to express the aspirations and experiences of the oppressed'. As is often the case there are tiny grains of truth to be found in the mythology. Proudhon, Voltairine de Cleyre, Goldman and Rudolf Rocker, for example, all came from poor families (Rocker was orphaned) and were mostly self-educated. In contrast, Bakunin, Kropotkin, Malatesta, Élisée Reclus and Gustav Landauer were all very well-educated; the first two were Russian aristocrats and the rest were squarely bourgeois. For the most part, therefore, anarchist theory was very much a product of literate, mostly middle-class minds. Its alleged 'simplicity', whether it is a merit or a fault, cannot be attributed to rural or working-class origins.

As a movement, however, European anarchism was from the start almost exclusively associated with the peasants and the working class. Furthermore, whereas Marxist socialism initially took hold in France,

England, Germany and the Low Countries, libertarian socialism (anarchism) initially found its strongest footholds in Spain, Italy, Southern and Eastern Europe and European Jewish communities. We need not concern ourselves with the underlying causes of these geographic and cultural disparities. Suffice it to say that anarchism's early popularity among workers explains why so many anarchist texts were published as newspapers, newsletters, pamphlets, brochures, transcripts of speeches and flyers rather than long-form books – because, for example, the former are cheaper and can more easily be read by working people between shifts or during breaks. In the late nineteenth and early twentieth centuries, therefore, the pamphlet became a standard genre for countless anarchist writers, including de Cleyre and Emma Goldman in the United States, Jean Grave and Sébastien Faure in France and Carlo Cafiero and Pietro Gori in Italy. Even denser works by Proudhon, Bakunin, Kropotkin and others were reprinted in excerpted or serialised pamphlet form to facilitate reading by busy workers.

Compared to a Marxist tome, which is typically long, dense and extremely technical, an anarchist pamphlet from the same period is brief, simple and fiercely but elegantly written. Not surprisingly, the anarchists' propensity towards *belle écriture* (beautiful writing) was often disparaged as frivolous by scientific socialists, a charge which contributed mightily to anarchism's reputation for theoretical shallowness. (Lukács, Antonio Gramsci and Rosa Luxemburg are remembered not as stylists so much as philosophers, whereas Gori, if he is remembered at all, is revered not for his brilliant essays but for his beautiful poems and songs.) In reality, this is only further evidence of anarchist pragmatism. For one thing, working people seldom had education enough to comprehend the intricacies of Marxist dialectics. For another thing, few of them had the time or inclination to teach themselves something as seemingly useless and remote from their everyday experiences as dialectical philosophy. Not only *could* anarchist philosophy be written in a simple and enjoyable-to-read manner; it was *obliged* to be written that way. After all, the point was not just to 'educate' but to inspire, uplift and even entertain as well.

We learn from Paul Avrich's *oeuvre* (see especially Avrich, 1970, 1989) that philosophy played a vital role in working-class anarchist culture. Because working families valued education, perhaps above all else, reading and studying philosophical texts was both a common and a highly valued activity. In New York, Chicago, Boston and other cities throughout the United States, anarchist groups and radical labour unions formed reading clubs in order to promote philosophical and cultural literacy throughout the entire community. Among the anarchist workers, it was taken for granted that being educated was part and parcel of being revolutionary. It was also understood, however, that because knowledge is not freely given to the powerless by the powerful, the powerless must seek knowledge themselves and share it with one another. This sentiment was the driving force behind the establishment of dozens of libertarian educational projects, from countless informal anarchist book clubs to the first Modern School in New York City in 1911.

A few points are worth noting here by way of summary. First, anarchism has always been committed to a kind of 'populism' as concerns political theorising. Simply put, if the people to whom a political theory applies are by and large unable to understand, appreciate or relate to that theory, there is something wrong either with the theory itself or, more likely, with the manner in which the theory is articulated. I would add this commitment to David Graeber's (2004: 1–3) list of reasons why anarchism has never been especially popular among academics. Generally speaking, academics seem to have a *de facto*, if not *de jure*, commitment to theoretical elitism. (Why this is so I will leave to sociologists to explain.) Because we are generally under no obligation to make ourselves clear to anyone except other scholars in our disciplines or sub-disciplines, we almost inevitably end up communicating our ideas in a less-than-populist manner. If it turns out that most of us actually prefer it this way, it is easy to understand why most of us are not anarchists. But this just underscores the absurdity of dismissing anarchism as 'philosophically and theoretically unsophisticated' because it refuses, and has always refused, to play the game according to our (academic) rules. On the contrary, it is precisely anarchism's unyielding populism that gives us reason to take it seriously as a *genuinely* revolutionary and working-class philosophy.

Second, anarchism has always been committed to the inseparability of theory and praxis. Marxist-Leninists talk about this a great deal too, but that is exactly the problem according to anarchists. 'Inseparability' here is not *just* a theoretical or conceptual talking point. A work like Bakunin's *God and the State*, for all its logical and philosophical flaws, was intended to inspire both thought *and* action. All good anarchist philosophy is like this – authored with a mind towards drawing rooms *and* barricades, classrooms *and* streets. You cannot change the world without understanding it, and you cannot understand the world without trying to change it. What good is it in writing a book called *A Theory of Justice*, say, if it does not provide any possibility for meaningful political intervention? On the other hand, what good is it in protesting against the government or the corporations if one is unable to explain *why* she is protesting or *what* she would like to see take their place? Anarchists have always understood this dialectic, which is why anarchist philosophy has always taken its particular and peculiar shape. If anarchist philosophy does not take up certain problems, it is because they are irrelevant as concerns real-world struggle, because they do not allow for meaningful political intervention.

Third, anarchist texts tend to be relatively brief and simple because, with a few important exceptions (e.g., Proudhon's oeuvre), anarchist philosophy is not comprehensive or systematic. Anarchism obviously has nothing comparable to *Capital* or *State and Revolution*. What is more, the anarchists occasionally borrowed from other political movements, including Marxism, and were usually quite fair in giving credit where it was due. From the 1860s, European socialists of all stripes accepted Marx's general critique of capitalism even if they rejected other aspects of Marxist theory. This was certainly true of the anarchists, who never developed a comprehensive economic philosophy of their own. (Interestingly, although anarchists argued along with Marx that capitalism exploits workers, adopted the labour theory of value and even made a habit of using Marxist language, they went a step further by claiming that exploitation was immoral and unjust. As scientific socialists, Marx and Engels rejected ethical language of this sort. But as Malatesta once said, working people care about what is right, not about what is scientific.)

Fourth, and crucially, let us not forget that the anarchist movement I have been discussing thus far had all but vanished by the end of the Second World War. (This is yet perhaps another reason for anarchism's being ignored in academia.) Anarchism has been struggling towards resurrection ever since, and while there have been a few false starts (e.g., in 1968 and 1999), we are only now beginning to witness a genuine rebirth. Why is that? To begin with, there are anarchist scholars everywhere now, whereas before there were only anarchists. They say the spirit of anarchism never dies, and while that is probably true, having the spirit of something is not the same thing as knowing that spirit or understanding it. Surely the *enragés* of 1968 and the anti-globalisation protesters of 1999 were anarchists in spirit. But were they the same kind of anarchists as those of 1900? In some broad sense, perhaps, but from a strictly historical and political vantage, the answer is 'no way'.

Amazingly, we have probably learned more about the classical anarchists in the past 4 years than we knew about them in the entire period running from 1968 to 1999. The reason for this, simply put, is that many of those former anti-globalisation protesters have since earned doctoral degrees and are doing important – in some cases ground-breaking – research on all conceivable aspects of anarchism. This was not the case 10 years ago. Now, new texts are being translated and interpreted every day and our knowledge of classical anarchism is growing and changing as a result, especially in the area of philosophy. Anarchism is no longer quite as obscure, its texts no longer hidden away in dusty archives. The more it is brought to light, the less it can be ignored by scholars who would rather have nothing to do with it and had been much happier without it. This is especially true in my own discipline of philosophy.

4.4 Conclusion

The recent resurgence of scholarly interest in classical anarchism has been accompanied by hopeful developments in anarchist activist circles. For example, the lifestyle and identity politics which had prevailed among American radicals since the heyday of the New Left are slowly giving way to class-based, labour-oriented politics. Perhaps the best illustration of this phenomenon is the colourful and conspicuous re-emergence of the Industrial Workers of the World (IWW), the Wobblies, who of late have been applying themselves full force to the organisation of workers in the service sector. It is also worth noting that many of the aforementioned scholars are also committed activists. As such, we can reasonably expect their academic research to shape, inform and influence their own political activities and those of other activists in several interesting ways. Indeed, this is already happening at annual and semi-annual conferences for anarchist scholars and activists around the world.

For the time being, however, it is clear that anarchist philosophy is mostly ghettoised within academic and activist subcultures. The question is not just how to bring anarchism (back) to working people, but how to make it theirs (again), as well as ours, the academics, the activists. Short of major political, social and cultural changes, my sense is that this will require certain kinds of people – people we have mostly lost and desperately need to find again: firebrand agitators and 'rabble rousers' of the Bughouse Square variety; soapbox orators and makers of sidewalk speeches; poor men's intellectuals who can ease complicated thoughts into smooth, supple prose; pamphleteers (bloggers?) with poets' hearts and tongues of gold. The anarchist philosophers of old were not only talented intellectuals but also gifted 'people persons' who had charisma, charm and leadership skills. There is no shortage of great ideas in contemporary anarchism. What we contemporary anarchists need, it seems, are great people to bring them to life.

Bibliography

P. Avrich (1970) *Anarchist Portraits* (Princeton, NJ: Princeton University Press).
——— (1989) *Anarchist Voices: An Oral History of Anarchism in America* (Princeton, NJ: Princeton University Press).
M. Bakunin (1970) *God and the State* (New York: Dover).
——— (1974) *Selected Writings* (New York: Grove Press).
——— (1994) *The Basic Bakunin* (Buffalo, NY: Prometheus Books).
A. Berkman (2003) *What Is Anarchism?* (Edinburgh: AK Press).
M. Bookchin (1986) *The Modern Crisis* (Philadelphia: New Society Publishers).
W. Breines (1982) *Community and Organisation in the New Left, 1962–1968* (New York: Praeger).
L. S. Brown (1993) *The Politics of Individualism* (New York: Black Rose Books).
M. Buber (1958) *Paths in Utopia* (Boston: Beacon Press).
G. Crowder (1991) *Classical Anarchism* (Oxford: Clarendon Press).
G. Deleuze (1977) 'Intellectuals and power' in D. Bouchard and S. Simon (eds) *Language, Counter-Memory, Practice* (Ithaca, NY: Cornell University Press), 205–17.
B. Franks (2006) *Rebel Alliances: The Means and Ends of Contemporary British Anarchisms* (Edinburgh: AK Press).
——— (2009) 'Vanguards and paternalism' in N. Jun and S. Wahl (eds) *New Perspectives on Anarchism* (Lanham, MD: Lexington Books), 99–120.
E. Fromm (1986) *Man for Himself* (London: Ark Paperbacks).
E. Goldman (1998) *Red Emma Speaks* (New York: Humanity Books).
——— (2003) *My Disillusionment in Russia* (Mineola, NY: Dover Publications).
D. Graeber (2002) 'The new anarchists', *New Left Review*, XIII: 61–73.
——— (2004) *Fragments of an Anarchist Anthropology* (Chicago, IL: Prickly Paradigm).
——— (2007) 'The twilight of vanguardism' in J. Macphee and E. Reuland (eds) *Realizing the Impossible: Art Against Authority* (Edinburgh: AK Press): 250–3.
D. Guerin (1998) *No Gods, No Masters* (Oakland, CA: AK Press).
N. J. Jun (2007) 'Deleuze, Derrida, and anarchism', *Anarchist Studies*, XV(ii): 132–56.
I. Kant (1965) *The Metaphysical Elements of Justice* (Indianapolis: Bobbs-Merrill).
K. Kenafick (1984) *Marxism, Freedom and the State* (London: Freedom Press).
P. Kropotkin (1970a) *Revolutionary Pamphlets* (New York: Dover).
——— (1970b) *Selected Writings on Anarchism and Revolution* (Cambridge, MA: MIT Press).
A. Leftwich (1984) *What Is Politics?* (London: Wiley-Blackwell).
G. Lukács (1971) *History and Class Consciousness* (Cambridge, MA: MIT Press).
E. Malatesta (1965) *Errico Malatesta: His Life and Ideas* (London: Freedom Press).
——— (1974) 'Towards anarchism' in M. Graham (ed.) *Man!: An Anthology of Anarchist Ideas, Essays, Poetry and Commentaries* (London: Cienfuegos Press).

—— (2001) *Anarchy* (London: Freedom Press).
T. May (1994) *The Political Philosophy of Poststructuralist Anarchism* (University Park, PA: The Pennsylvania State University Press).
B. Morris (1995) 'Anthropology and anarchism', *Anarchy: A Journal of Desire Armed*, XLV: 35–41.
—— (2002) 'Kropotkin's ethical naturalism', *Democracy and Nature*, VIII(iii): 423–37.
S. Nechayev (1989) *Catechism of the Revolutionist* (London: Violette Nozieres Press and Active Distribution).
R. Nozick (1974) *Anarchy, State, and Utopia* (New York: Basic Books).
M. Prawdin (1961) *The Unmentionable Nechayev* (London: Allen and Unwin).
P. J. Proudhon (1969) *What Is Property?* (London: William Reeves).
J. Purkis and J. Bowen (2005) 'Conclusion: How anarchism still matters' in J. Purkis and J. Bowen (eds) *Changing Anarchism* (Manchester: Manchester University Press), 273–8.
J. Quail (1978) *The Slow-Burning Fuse* (London: Paladin).
J. Rawls (1971) *A Theory of Justice* (Cambridge, MA: Harvard University Press).
R. Rocker (1938) *Anarchosyndicalism* (London: Secker and Warburg).
A. J. Simmons (1996) 'Philosophical anarchism' in J. Narveson and J. Sanders (eds) *For and Against the State* (Lanham, MD: Rowman and Littlefield).
R. Sylvan (1993) 'Anarchism' in R. Goodin and P. Petit (eds) *A Companion to Contemporary Political Philosophy* (Oxford: Basil Blackwell), 213–29.
D. Wieck (1979) 'Anarchist justice' in H. Ehrlich, C. Ehrlich, D. De Leon and G. Morris (eds) *Reinventing Anarchy* (London: Routledge and Kegan Paul), 215–43.
R. P. Wolff (1970) *In Defense of Anarchism* (New York: Harper and Row).

Part II
Anarchism, Property and Autonomy

5
Autonomy, Taxation and Ownership: An Anarchist Critique of Kant's Theory of Property

Kory DeClark

> The love of freedom is a universal trait.
> —Emma Goldman

5.1 Introduction: Kant and property

Property fundamentally affects liberty. When any two individuals occupy space in a finite area, the choices of one will, in principle, and usually in practice, limit the liberties of the other. For instance, if I am sitting in a public park, then you can sit anywhere you please so long as you do not want to sit in the very space I occupy, for I am already sitting there and you have no right to move me. But if, as it turns out, you *own* the park, then some would say you *do* have a right to sit in the space I currently occupy, for I have no right to be there. Property, by limiting the sphere of our available and legitimate actions, has this clear and elemental effect on liberty.

In his *Metaphysics of Morals*, Immanuel Kant attempts to derive a robust, a priori theory of property, and thereby the state, from fundamental moral truths. Any persuasive argument for the legitimacy of these institutions should be of interest to anarchists, for they traditionally reject both. Kant's argument – which was published in 1797, only 4 years after William Godwin's *Enquiry Concerning Political Justice*, and therefore predates all concerted work on modern anarchism – should be of special interest to anarchists for two reasons. First, the moral foundations on which Kant claims to justify his property system (which, it is worth noting, eerily resembles the contemporary institution of property) would later become axioms of anarchist moral theory. Most significantly, this includes the innate freedom each individual possesses, which includes, for Kant, a natural equality that prevents any person from binding others to an extent that she herself cannot be bound. Each human being is, therefore, her own master.

Second, in the covert manner customary of political philosophies, Kant's simple and intuitive argument appears to have, over the course of the last 200 years, helped to inform, or at the very least aligned with, the political dogma that legitimates property rights in the public mind. The point, then, of considering the Kantian argument – which if successful would do much to undermine the anarchist moral position – is to evaluate the logical and intuitively plausible route by which one might derive and justify an extensive property system from basic anarchist axioms, and to demonstrate its inadequacy. Moreover, by exploring the link between anarchism's political ideology and western moral philosophy, we are able to (i) investigate more formally the rapport between anarchist theory and certain strands of popular political and moral thought, (ii) begin to locate and evaluate any significant problems the latter face as they develop beyond their anarchist foundations and (iii) identify murky but powerful challenges moral philosophy poses for some anarchist viewpoints.

It is important to note before we begin that, like those of any political position, strands of anarchism vary considerably in some areas. The concerns I express in this chapter I intend to be relevant to most of them. Therefore, in order to remain maximally inclusive, by 'anarchism' I shall mean a theory that has as two of its defining features the strict observance of individual self-direction within the bounds of one's rights and duties, or liberty, and a rejection of hierarchical power structures based on domination, promoting in their place horizontal organisations based on voluntary participation (see Schmidt and van der Walt, 2009). Societies guided by these principles could admittedly take very distinct forms; nevertheless, each would be distinctly anarchist (perhaps with a few additional qualifications), and nothing I say in this chapter requires that we refine such a broad definition (Diagram 5.1).

5.2 Ownership and limits to property

Kant's ultimate guiding principle for right action – the *Universal Principle of Right* (UPR) – delimits the parameters of his theory of property: 'Any action is *right* if it can coexist with everyone's freedom in accordance with a universal law, or if on its maxim the freedom of choice of each can coexist with everyone's freedom in accordance with a universal

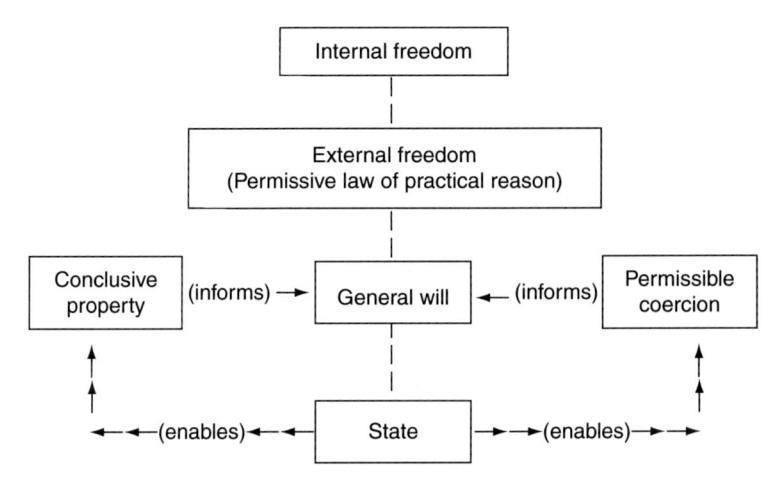

```
                    ┌──────────────────┐
                    │ Internal freedom │
                    └──────────────────┘
                             │
            ┌────────────────────────────────────┐
            │          External freedom          │
            │ (Permissive law of practical reason) │
            └────────────────────────────────────┘
                             │
┌────────────┐           ┌─────────────┐           ┌─────────────┐
│ Conclusive │ (informs)→│ General will│←(informs) │ Permissible │
│  property  │           │             │           │  coercion   │
└────────────┘           └─────────────┘           └─────────────┘
      ↑                        │                         ↑
      │                        │                         │
   ←(enables)←─┐           ┌───────┐           ┌─→(enables)→
               └───────────│ State │───────────┘
                           └───────┘
```

Diagram 5.1 Overview of the structure of Kant's argument for property.

law' (1996: 231)*. Kant's interest not simply in freedom, but in *everyone's* freedom, forms the anarchistic cornerstone of his position, anticipating (among many others) Errico Malatesta's injunction: 'Freedom for everybody and in everything, with the only limit of the equal freedom for others' (1977: 53).

The right to possess objects of one's choice is, for Kant, necessary for freedom. Possession takes two forms. When I have something in my hand, I have *physical* possession of it. But this does not make it mine, for, as far as it goes, once I set it down anybody else can pick it up and use it as they please without wronging me. However, if I am wronged by another's unauthorised use of it, even while I am away, then of it I have what Kant (1996: 245–6) calls *intelligible* possession.

Intelligible possession is ownership. You own object O just in case you are wronged by my unauthorised use of it, and I am unauthorised in using it – I wrong you if I use it – just in case you have a *right* to O. A *right* is a kind of freedom. It is a practical relation between individuals that modifies the liberties of some to ensure the right-holder's uninhibited ability to use her means to achieve her ends (230). So, when I own O I stand in a relation of rightful possession to you with respect to O, such that I have a claim on you to not interfere with my use of it without my permission (so long as my use does not violate *others'* rights). You wrong

---

* The page numbers in the Kant citations refer to the pagination from volume 6 of the original Prussia Academy edition of Kant, not to the Mary Gregor collection, though it is the latter where the quotations were obtained.

me when you violate this right by using O, and I own O just in case your use would violate my right.

In Kant's view, the existence of this sort of property relation depends on the reciprocal authorisation between members of a society to use coercion, in accordance with UPR, to enforce their rights against one another (233). The idea is that, were there no coercive force to guarantee the preservation of rightful relations between agents, one would have little reason to believe that others would respect one's rights, and any such society would quickly devolve back to a state of nature (or would be kept from moving out of it initially). Therefore, a state, as the only means of generating this collective authorisation, is a necessary (and desirable) condition for property.

It is important to note that Kant's argument can plausibly be extended from property to possession. Given that there is good reason to believe people would remain envious of one another's possessions even in the ideal circumstances specified by theories of distributive justice that have fairness as their central aim (see, e.g., Dworkin, 1981), nobody can know whether and what sort of coercive force would be necessary for the maintenance even of just distributions of *possessions* in a large, modern society that forbade private property. Thus, since all anarchist strands must support some version of property *use*, proponents of any given strand of anarchism ought to find Kant's claim threatening proportional to the degree their theory permits large, modern societies.

5.3 Property and freedom

Why and how would individuals initially move into a 'rightful condition', a civil society, or state, in which they could acquire property rights? Kant's explanation follows a rich philosophical history that approaches the question of property by way of (hypothetical) genealogy. We can start by breaking his argument into three basic stages (see Weinrib, 2003).

The first stage begins with Herbert Read's (1954) 'value of all values'; it is, for Kant, each individual's single innate right: *freedom*. Individuals have an equal, innate right of 'independence from being constrained by another's choice' in accordance with UPR (1996: 237). A key constituent of this notion is that each person has the right of 'being *his own master*' (238; Kant's emphasis). It is this sort of non-dependence that Kant values most highly within a property system and is what most firmly ties his view to the anarchist position at the foundational level. However, moving beyond this freedom to direct our own lives – what Kant calls our *internal* freedom – we quickly recognise that, as living beings, our survival necessitates that we both modify and consume *external* resources (space, land, food, oxygen, etc.). Consequently, any plausible property system, anarchist or otherwise, must justify our use of these 'objects' (or call for our extinction).

In response, Kant begins in the second stage to derive these *external* rights – rights to things – from our internal freedom. Individuals in a state of nature, he claims, have 'possession in common' of the earth, meaning that nobody has a unique claim to it. One can quickly point to the general problem this creates: If everyone equally possesses the land's resources, how can any individual utilise any portion of these resources for her needs while acting in accordance with UPR? Kant's strategy in answering this question will be significant later, so it will be helpful to reconstruct his *reductio ad absurdum* for acquisition here (1996: 247–50):

A1. Suppose that it is not within our rightful power to make use of an object of choice when that use cannot coexist with everyone's freedom in accordance with a universal law.
A2. Freedom would then *deprive itself* of choice, rendering otherwise usable objects *unusable*.
A3. But freedom's *telos* is to *promote* choice, since choice is an outer freedom. This would be a contradiction.

A4. Therefore, it must be within our rightful power to make use of an object of choice.

In other words, freedom cannot *restrict* human action, for this would betray freedom itself. Ultimately, I'll argue that this conclusion, while correct, does not justify the robust system of property rights that Kant eventually defends. However, the anarchist, who often eschews a priori argumentation, should note that it does seem to provide the *permission* or *provisional rights* persons need to use things in order to live freely. This is Kant's *permissive law of practical reason*.

While the relationship between internal freedom and external objects of choice generates each person's provisional rights to those objects, our principal interest here is Kant's attempt to graduate these rights from *provisional* to *conclusive*. The task is considerable, for even an agent's *provisional* possessions begin to limit the possible choices, and thus, clearly, the freedom of every other. Therefore, *to move beyond a mere provisional right and obtain a conclusive right to some object O, one must be able, while acting in accordance with UPR, to, by her unilateral will, obligate all others to refrain from using O* (255).

This move, when limited in scope to personal possessions, is surely necessary, though its moral justification is usually assumed rather than defended. For, would even the anarchist allow whoever so desired to trample destructively through the garden I have created and depend on for food? May my friends and I occupy the house that you and your people have (by yourselves, using resources you have gathered) built for your family? The question challenges anarchism's moral underpinnings: How do we derive rights for possessions without deriving them for *property* (taken to include the means of production)?

Kant's proposal is at once intuitive and palatable and again reflects anarchist thought. Because, in Kant's philosophy, the equal freedom of each individual is fundamental (237), in order for an individual to deprive others of something they have equal claim to – the land for my garden, or the wood for your house – those affected must *freely agree*, in at least some limited sense, to their own deprivation. You must, of your own volition, *give me* the right to my garden, just as I must give you the right to your house (though you may be so kind as to offer to share it). Imperative to the anarchist is only that this sort of agreement is not one of repressive obligation – of the rich manipulating the poor, or the strong the weak – but that each person acts as she desires, assuming *for herself* an obligation (Pateman, 1985; Graham, 1996).

Thus, for an individual to obtain intelligible possession of any object, *all* persons must together will that its possessor has that right. But how? Kant's answer, which commences his divergence from what I have called the anarchist core of his theory, is this: my *unilateral* will can bind others to respect my empirical possession of an object so long as my possession exists in a *civil condition* – a state – which embodies the *omnilateral* or *general will*. Only such a condition both unites the wills of all a priori and generally protects rightful relations between agents through the threat of coercion (Kant, 1996: 255–6, 259), thereby generating conclusive property. But notice that, if Kant's solution is adequate, *then it is itself a challenge to anarchist theory*, for it obliges us to accept conclusive property (and conceivably even possession) through the spectre of force.

5.4 The limitations of Kantian property rights

Kant's core theory, and plausibly any theory according to which individual freedom is of primary importance, I'll argue, cannot support an extensive form of property. It will help to consider a schema of the argument explicated in the previous sections:

B1. An action is right if it can coexist with everyone's freedom in accordance with a universal law. Whoever hinders me in so acting wrongs me (231).   Universal Principle of Right

B2.	Freedom – independence from constraint from another's choice – is the only innate right of every human being, which all possess equally (237).	Principle of Innate Freedom
B3.	By B2, in conjunction with practical considerations concerning the human condition, we deduce the *permissive law of practical reason*, which gives us *provisional* rights to external objects of choice (247).	By A1–A4, Section 5.3
B4.	However, possession is merely provisional so long as each individual wills only unilaterally that an object of choice be hers. However, such a unilateral will, when conjoined a priori with the will of all (the general will), generates *conclusively* rightful possession, by which all are bound only by those limitations that they themselves will (264, 316).	Postulate
B5.	A civil condition embodies the general will – it is the will of all (311).	Postulate
B6.	In a civil condition one's provisionally rightful possessions (which one has willed to be hers, and has taken physical possession of in accordance with UPR) become conclusively rightful possessions.	By B3–B5

The most conspicuous and interesting part of Kant's dialectic is his elimination of interpersonal equality and, as we will see, an important element of personal freedom over the course of the three basic stages (represented by B2–B4). Most troublesome, however, is the formula's dependence for its deduction on the *willing subsidisation* by their (hypothetical) agreement of those individuals *who stand to lose the most freedom* in the resulting rightful condition.

In Kant's state of nature each person possesses an innate right to her body and the space it occupies. This original position represents a fundamental internal equality, which for many of us has great intuitive appeal, and for some represents the only legitimate road to freedom (see, e.g., Bakunin, 1972: 76). But this original conceptual position says nothing of external objects, which are introduced only in the second stage of Kant's argument. In it our outer freedom, manifested as choice, permits our taking empirical possession of useful objects, by which we obtain a provisional right that equates merely to their *permissible use*. Like seats on a bus, each person has only a right to the seat she occupies, and only because and for as long as she occupies it; for, when she moves to another seat nothing prohibits someone else from taking the seat she left, just as nobody can (rightfully) prohibit her from taking any other unoccupied seat she chooses.

Notice, however, that from the moment external objects are introduced the equality of the first stage is vulnerable. The provisional acquisition of any object is based on an act, and because the physical and mental capacities of individuals differ according to their luck in the 'natural lottery', the ability of each to execute that act (or to defend each acquisition) will vary. This point is particularly poignant for the anarchist (save, perhaps, the most extreme strands in the individualist tradition) who must defend, to some degree, an ideal balance between freedom and equality (on this balance see Nozick, 1974: 160; Cohen, 1995: 19–38; Otsuka, 2003: Chapter 1). But no matter how this is done, inequalities created by provisional acquisition are at least largely controlled by natural limitations on human capacities. In the third and final stage, those parameters, which represent the only integrated fortification of our original equality, are removed. As we enter a Kantian civil condition, the limit to what one can acquire, and thus, practically speaking, the limit to the *power* that one can thereby obtain, *disappears* (Kant, 1996: 265; also see Weinrib, 2003: 797).

As we saw, however, in order for any individual to acquire property conclusively, her possession must be willed *omnilaterally*. According to Kant, this requires a civil condition. But the move from the state of nature to a civil condition (from B3–B4 in our formalisation) requires a conceptual dependency on the *original contract*, in which 'everyone (*omnes et singuli*) within a *people* gives up his external freedom in order to take it up again immediately as a member of a commonwealth' (Kant, 1996: 316; my emphasis). But as the world population grows in a finite area, and as the power that one can enjoy as the result of generations of acquisition escalates beyond anything resembling safe limits, we must question whether even a small minority of society's population *would* consent to such a contract, much less its collective whole. As Weinrib explains,

> My range of rightful possibilities is now confined to what might be left over from others' efforts at accumulation. The possibility of amassing land makes it conceivable that [...] all the land may be appropriated by others, leaving me literally with no place to exist except by leave of someone else.
>
> (2003: 815)

Weinrib's comments closely resemble those of T. H. Green, who separately observed that the landless majority in a capitalistic society 'might as well, in respect of the ethical purposes which the possession of property should serve, be denied rights of property altogether' (Q. Green in Waldron, 2008).

But what is most interesting about Kant is that, like the anarchist, he takes a hard-line position with respect to the sort of self-preservation that would cause one to *reject* civil society in these circumstances. Individuals, Kant holds, have a *duty of rightful honour* (DoRH) that is closely related to the innate right of freedom to which we were introduced in the first stage of Kant's argument. According to DoRH, one must '[assert] one's worth as a human being in relation to others' (Kant, 1996: 236). This means that persons must act according to their own interests; in fact, 'a condition in which the determination of this interest is given over to someone else is impossible from the standpoint of right' (Q. Kant in Weinrib, 2003: 811). For, as we saw, the innate right that all originally possess equally gives each individual the quality 'of being *his* [or her] *own master*' (Kant, 1996: 238). Kant's rhetoric in these passages aligns him, at least in this respect, with even the most individualist of those considered anarchists. Consider, for example, how Max Stirner's language echoes Kant's: 'I am my own,' Stirner writes, 'only when I am master of myself, instead of being mastered... by anything else' (1995: 153). Our question, then, is how Kant's position drifts from the anarchist's, given their agreement on these foundational points. In terms of his theory we might ask the question this way: What does DoRH engender for most if not a wholesale rejection of the sort of original contract Kant envisions? How can one respect one's own self-directedness while entering into Kantian civil society?

Kant's response appears to underlie the right he entrusts to the would-be state to tax its citizens in order to provide for the basic needs of the poor (Kant, 1996: 326), which marks a practical advance in his argument. According to Kant, redistribution allows individuals to maintain their freedom within the context of property, and thus to (hypothetically) consent to the original contract and thereby move towards a rightful condition while respecting DoRH (318; 326).

How might one respond to this? Natural rights deriders (Kropotkin and Malatesta, for example) would surely deny that Kant's rights-talk has any veracity to begin with: 'The anarchist thinker', Kropotkin says, 'does not resort to metaphysical conceptions (like "natural rights," the "duties of the state," and so on) to establish what are, in his opinion, the best conditions for realizing the greatest happiness of humanity'

(1970: 47); or, in Malatesta's words, 'The "natural laws", [and] "moral laws" [...] of the Kantians [...] are all metaphysical fantasies which get one nowhere' (1977: 74–5). But even those sceptical of the natural rights they attribute to Kant's view cannot so easily dispel his logic: Should all originally enjoy equal freedom, and should all then *voluntarily* contract according to their own preferences (save moral boundary-crossings), how can the anarchist reject the result, even when that result is a state?

I will not reproduce Kant's argument here (see Weinrib, 2003: 818–19), but let me note an important distinction that he must draw for its validity. The type of dependence that violates DoRH, on Kant's view, is a sort of direct relation between the poor and their fellow citizens that potentially leaves the impoverished at the mercy of those comparatively richer. Obliging the *state* to subsidise the basic needs of the poor, therefore, prevents a coercive condition in which the poor are forced into what would otherwise be considered an objectionable dependence on other individuals.

This raises a deep concern about the compatibility of property and freedom within Kant's system. Even as a potential beneficiary of the state's duty to prevent starvation (and the like), why think that a base-level, state-subsidised subsistence, in a world of plenty, would move even the least entrepreneurial of human beings to sign away the greater autonomy they hitherto enjoyed? To fully expand and defend this argument, we would have to examine a number of complicated issues that we cannot reasonably approach here – for instance, what constitutes a 'base-level' existence? why can redistribution provide only this level of compensation? and so on. The important point is that this concern finds a prominent target in Kant, who is often considered, within the historical canon of analytic philosophy, above all a champion of one's mastery over oneself. For what sort of mastery, in the system of property upheld in the *Metaphysics of Morals*, is available to the *majority* of persons under such a system – to the only moderately skilled, the impoverished, or simply those unfortunate enough to come into existence after the entirety of the earth's surface has been swallowed by their predecessors?

But let us concede, for argument, that it is at least *possible* that the state's obligation to provide for the poor *could* satisfy DoRH, which would thereby permit otherwise vulnerable persons to move towards a rightful condition. It is not impossible, after all, that some individuals would find sufficient comfort in the state's welfare. Nonetheless, this is not the more interesting question we ought to be pressing (though we shall come back to it later). In fact, it misses two more fundamental problems facing Kant's a priori system of rights. The first is the problem of arbitrariness: What a priori (or even empirical) reason do we have for meeting the demand to respect DoRH by allowing the state to redistribute wealth, rather than substantively modifying another part of the system (e.g., eliminating private property)? The second is the problem of justification: does the Kantian argument actually show that private property is justifiable?

Consider first the problem of arbitrariness. A major appeal of the Kantian system is that its deduction ignores messy empirical facts. Rights, and thus property, can be understood a priori just by thinking rationally about the relationships between concepts. This makes Kant's account impressively systematic, and its application appealingly universal. However, we find that our concerns about DoRH are met with uncharacteristic arbitrariness. Kant's solution – that the state shall redistribute wealth – seems *ad hoc*. Why *this* solution? It is certainly not because redistribution prevents other rights violations – the move is perplexing, some would claim, because it *so clearly* allows for violations of other rights (see Nozick, 1974: 169). Why propose, then, that potential citizens capitulate to the prospective institutionalised destitution of Kantian civil society, when other arrangements – for example, species of usufruct exhibited in tribal and other cultures, variations on the use-ownership 'possession' programme of Proudhon's mutualism or participatory economic models currently in development (see Albert, 2004: Part I) – would plausibly get closer to creating meaningful freedom within the state? It is curious that Kant would arbitrarily (conscientiously?) settle on the process presumably least offensive to potential property owners, even when that process could dramatically limit the scope of liberties for the population's majority.

But let us temporarily set this aside and address the problem of justification. The lynchpin of Kant's argument for property is the subargument in B3 (which we previously expanded in A1–A4). Kant's cryptic argument, once deciphered, is actually quite straightforward: It would contradict our very being to deprive ourselves of the use of usable things, so long as we can use those things in accordance with UPR. That seems right. But notice that this says nothing about *ownership*.

When I merely *use* something, say, a book from the library, I treat that thing differently than I would something I own. Not least important is that I plan to give it back (without having scribbled in the margins), for I know that other people may need to use it. I also understand that, because it is unfair (and inefficient) to take more books than I can productively use (the excess sitting idly in stacks on my desk when others might need them), the library may reasonably expect me to limit the number of books I borrow at one time. Contemporary ownership ignores these and related restraints. There are essentially no limits to what I can own, nor are there (significant) restrictions, based on a concern for others, on how I may use or treat those things. It seems reasonable, then, to demand a justification for the move from *use* to *ownership*, and from *possession* to *property*. One might imagine that such an argument would turn up in the subsequent steps, Kant having arguably just established the permissibility of *use*. But it never does. It is mysteriously absent from the text.

One might suggest, however, that I have missed the point. It might be said that the very purpose of the permissive law of practical reason is to allow persons the outer freedom they need to pursue their ends, and that this most fundamental freedom is the sort that necessitates restricting others from using objects of one's choice. That is, perhaps the *important* kind of human freedom *requires* property (see, e.g., Friedman, 1982). Is this plausible? First, even if it is, Kant still fails to defend such a claim. It takes additional work to demonstrate that persons need property to realise the sort of autonomy that Kant (may or may not) identify as our ultimate end. So we still require a compelling argument.

But there is a stronger response. And to consider it, let us suppose that Kant *had* provided some sort of argument. It remains that different systems of property rights deliver different sorts and strengths of rights. Some systems promote a very limited type of property that restricts any range of liberties, such as the amount of land one can acquire and the uses one can put it to (see Ryan, 1981). By contrast, a more robust, *laissez-faire* system – towards which we have been moving for the last half century (see, among many others, Klein, 2007) – sets essentially no limits, allowing owners to do anything they wish with what is theirs (so long as they do not violate the 'negative' rights of others). What system does the Kantian argument justify? Seemingly the *weakest* system compatible with autonomy! For, recall, the system itself remains ineffectual until each and every person included in the original contract – namely, everyone – (hypothetically) agrees to it while respecting DoRH. But, one might ask, did not we concede that the right of the state to tax and redistribute to the poor could satisfy DoRH? Yes. But the theoretical *sufficiency* of the system in this respect does not guarantee its *acceptance*.

Consider that the price of a good you desire might be sufficiently low at store S to warrant purchasing it. But if store V is selling the same good for much less, then, *mutatis mutandis*, you will purchase the good at V rather than at S. The Kantian case is similar. Redistribution may in some contexts be a sufficient provision to move towards a rightful condition, but it is not a necessary one. Variations on other systems – particularly need-based distributive patterns envisaged in strands of communist anarchism – could offer the same impetus but with greater total freedom, rendering these much more appealing to potential citizens. Thus, while public acceptance of the Kantian system would not be logically contradictory, it would certainly require myopic citizens. Unrestricted property systems, even redistributive ones, threaten to offer very little reassurance that citizens will not end up economically dependent in a way that would violate DoRH. So, by Kant's own lights, individuals may permissibly select a more promising system, even if lesser systems would be sufficient in their absence. And, in any case, if an individual could (hypothetically) feel that by accepting the Kantian system she may inevitably be a mere means for others without being at the same time an end for them, she *must* oppose the system, *even if her dependency will be on the state.*

This last notion is central to my final argument. According to Kant, only a dependency on the actions of other individuals is objectionable from the perspective of DoRH, and so the state's duty to provide for the poor does away with related concerns that persons might have about moving into a civil condition. But this claim appears patently false. When your life's trajectory is dramatically delimited by the social or economic position you occupy in a particular institutionalised framework, what difference does it make to you what form the body of individuals takes that you are made dependent upon? (One difference might be that state redistribution takes the form of an *entitlement*, while this is not necessarily the case under private redistribution. Though there is nothing formal preventing any society from understanding their private redistribution schemes as entitlements, the point deserves more attention than we can provide here.) In fact, the case against Kant is arguably stronger than one might first suppose, for his property system on some interpretations allows for an even *greater* loss of freedom than others of seemingly equal physical consequence. For a coarse example, consider the following two ways that the social genealogy might go for a finite piece of land (an island, say) newly inhabited by 100 individuals representing five equally large groups (group A, B, etc.).

Scenario One. The groups settle on different parts of the small island and survive by hunting and gathering. Food is usually plentiful, and the groups coexist quite well. In the third year, however, food is scant, and arguments develop over fishing ponds. These arguments lead to war between the groups. Eventually group A subjugates the other groups by force. The A's confine the other groups to a small portion of the island, providing them with survival essentials while requiring that they hunt and gather more food each day than the A's can consume and store, the excess of which the A's callously discard.

Scenario Two. The groups, during the first year, decide to break the island up into five equal sections, moving into a civil condition in which each group's provisional rights to their land is made conclusive. Each group elects an emissary to join a small, representative judiciary/police force. In the third year, the head of the A's shrewdly offers to trade a small fishing hole on his land for the B's large, though currently unproductive, orchard, for which the A's have discovered a better cultivation strategy. The B's (voluntarily) accept. Soon after, the fish in the fishing hole unexpectedly migrate while the A's fruit trees begin to flourish. Similar trades take place between the A's and the other groups, leaving all but the A's with insufficient resource-rich land. The A's leverage their position to make increasingly lucrative deals with the other groups, who accept (voluntarily?) to temporarily escape starvation. In less than one generation the A's acquire the entire island. They now *employ* the other groups and *rent* them a small portion of the island on which to live and work. The state, which now operates exclusively by dint of taxes paid by the A's (with capital generated solely by the *other* groups' labour), provides the labouring groups with what essentials they need for a meagre survival beyond what they can afford after spending their wages. The groups work long hours, hunting and gathering more food each day than the A's can consume and store. But the labouring groups have no right to this food, and the A's callously (but legitimately) discard the excess.

There are a few points to notice here. First, if we accept Kant's argument, then an unacceptable state of dependency exists only in Scenario One (S1), for the *de facto* dependency in S1 transfers in Scenario Two (S2) to the state. The question is this: From the perspective of the labouring groups, how does the route that the wealth they produce takes, while trickling back to them – after being reduced to an amount on which they can barely subsist – make any sort of fundamental difference to their freedom? What sort of freedom is available to the population in S2 that those in S1 lack? It seems that the oppressed in S2 are, if anything, *less* free.

To see this consider that S1 is a desperate case, while S2 is, once we control for simplifications, unremarkable. In the former, the A's perpetually violate individuals' rights. The form of slavery described in S1 is an extreme form of oppression, one that we have, especially on Kantian grounds, reason to abhor. But S2 is, *according to the same guidelines* (and from the *laissez-faire* perspective), quite different. S2 is an example, if anything, of a state running in good order, operating according to 'voluntary' contractual agreements (compare Nozick, 1974; Graham, 1996). It may be unfortunate for the majority of islanders that things wound up as they did, but there is nothing *wrong* (from a rights-perspective) with such a condition. This marks the fundamental distinction between the two cases. In S1, members of the oppressed groups presumably harbour an inalienable and righteous sense of having their rights continuously and shamelessly violated. We would *encourage* them to run away, or to fight back. However, in S2 this feeling would be as unlikely as its commensurate actions would be illegitimate. Revolutionary acts in S2 would wrong *the A's*, whose economic (and thus political) power is in this context presumably justified.

Interestingly, however, S1 and S2 are remarkably similar from the perspective of the 'unfortunates'. They 'enjoy' the same living standards and the same daily work. In each case they lack control of both the means and the product of their labour and would be violently coerced into compliance should they try to control either (in S1 by the (illegitimate) militia, in S2 by the (legitimate) police). Moreover, the long-term prospect for change in S2 is arguably *bleaker* than in S1, especially if members of the oppressed groups have learned to act 'rightly'. This is primarily because the A's hegemony in S2 generates in the oppressed what Murray Bookchin describes as 'an instilled mentality for ordering reality'. Such 'awe and apathy in the face of state power', he warns, 'are [the] products of social conditioning that render this very power possible' (2005: 164–5). History has shown that power perpetuates itself in just this way (see Chomsky, 2002: esp. 231–48, 260–6). So, while in S1 everyone at least *knows* that their oppressors are iniquitous, in S2 people eventually convince themselves that the current conditions are normal, deserved and to be expected. And on such an account they would sadly be right.

5.5 Conclusion

We have attempted, in this chapter, to see whether some central tenants of moral theory, shared by both Kant's philosophy of right and many strands of anarchism, can coherently lead, as Kant has presented it, to propertied societies protected by coercive elements of the state. Though his is not the only argument of this kind, the highly intuitive path that Kant presents makes his view worth examining seriously.

It is worth repeating here that, because Kant's conclusion must run against most authentic strands of anarchism, it has not been necessary to align our critique with any particular strand. Aside from gaining some insight into the problems that might exist in this (or any) argument for property, a primary benefit of critiquing a deduction as methodical as Kant's, for proponents of any strand, is that it carefully brings to light many of the problems an acceptable political theory must address. The concerns we raised for Kant's theory – and perhaps the charge of arbitrariness is most pertinent – have focused on the move from use to ownership. This is a particularly relevant focal point for proponents of anarchist theory, for each must offer her own consistent and unified argument that justifies property use while (in most cases) rejecting private property.

I have argued that a central weakness of Kant's argument, for his purposes, is located in his flavour of hypothetical consent, for this allows any individual to (hypothetically) reject political systems that may put her liberty at risk over time. To defend against this attack, one would presumably need to offer some justification for the view that private property is somehow necessary for human flourishing – a view I find implausible. Any viable anarchist moral theory must, in my view, centre its position on a respect for individuals and the agreements one has made with others. It is significant, then, that Kant's argument represents a form of contractualism. For, while the sort of hypothetical consent it invokes is less defensible than that of modern versions (most notably Scanlon, 1998; Rawls, 2003), the concerns we raised for Kant should remain relevant for these and other evolving moral theories that take their cue from him. Because anarchism finds it roots not only in socialism, but also in liberalism (Rocker, 2004: 9), for which contractualism is a major part, proponents of anarchism stand only to gain from familiarising themselves with the details of this approach, and taking from it what they can.

Bibliography

M. Albert (2004) *Parecon: Life After Capitalism* (London: Verso).
M. Bakunin (1972) *Bakunin on Anarchy: Selected Works by the Activist-Founder of World Anarchism*, ed. Sam Dolgoff (New York: Alfred A. Knopf).
M. Bookchin (2005) *The Ecology of Freedom* (Oakland, CA: AK Press).
N. Chomsky (2002) *Understanding Power*, eds. P. Mitchell and John Schoeffel (New York: The New Press).

G. A. Cohen (1995) *Self-Ownership, Freedom, and Equality* (Cambridge: Cambridge University Press).

R. Dworkin (1981) 'What is equality? Part 2: Equality of resources', *Philosophy and Public Affairs*, 10 (4): 283–345.

M. Friedman (1982) *Capitalism and Freedom* (Chicago, IL: University of Chicago Press).

R. Graham (1989) 'The role of contract in anarchist ideology' in D. Goodway (ed.) *For Anarchism: History, Theory, and Practice* (London: Routledge).

——— (1996) 'The anarchist contract' in the R. A. Forum http://raforum.info/article.php3?id_article=3447, date accessed: 17 February 2010.

I. Kant (1996) *The Cambridge Edition of the Works of Immanuel Kant: Practical Philosophy* (New York: Cambridge University Press). (Note: Pagination refers to Volume 6 of the Prussia Academy edition).

N. Klein (2007) *The Shock Doctrine* (New York: Metropolitan Books).

P. Kropotkin (1970) *Kropotkin's Revolutionary Pamphlets*, ed. R. Baldwin (Toronto: Dover Publications).

E. Malatesta (1977) *Errico Malatesta: His Life and Ideas*, ed. V. Richards (London: Freedom Press).

P. Marshall (2008) *Demanding the Impossible: A History of Anarchism* (London: Harper Perennial).

R. Nozick (1974) *Anarchy, State, and Utopia* (Oxford: Blackwell).

M. Otsuka (2003) *Libertarianism Without Inequality* (New York: Oxford University Press).

C. Pateman (1985) *The Problem of Political Obligation* (Oxford: Polity Press).

J. Rawls (2003) *A Theory of Justice* (Cambridge: Harvard University Press).

H. Read (1954) *Anarchy and Order* (London: Faber and Faber).

R. Rocker (2004) *Anarcho-Syndicalism: Theory and Practice* (Oakland: AK Press).

C. Ryan (1981) 'Yours, mine, and ours: Property rights and personal liberty' in J. Paul (ed.) *Reading Nozick* (New Jersey: Rowman and Littlefield).

T. M. Scanlon (1998) *What We Owe to Each Other* (Cambridge: Harvard University Press).

M. Schmidt and L. van der Walt (2009) *Black Flame: The Revolutionary Class Politics of Anarchism and Syndicalism* (Oakland: AK Press).

M. Stirner (1995) *The Ego and Its Own*, ed. David Leopold (Cambridge: Cambridge University Press).

J. Waldron (2008) 'Property' in E. Zalta (ed.) *The Stanford Encyclopedia of Philosophy* (Fall 2008 Edition), http://plato.stanford.edu/archives/fall2008/entries/property/, date accessed: 17 February 2010.

E. J. Weinrib (2003) 'Poverty and property in Kant's system of rights', *Notre Dame Law Review*, LXXIII(iii): 795–828.

6
The Ethical Foundations of Proudhon's Republican Anarchism

Alex Prichard

In this chapter I will set out a general introduction to the ethical foundations of Proudhon's anarchism. I will contextualise it within Proudhon's own intellectual development, the arguments his contemporaries and near contemporaries were making, and against the socio-historical background of late-nineteenth-century France. This aspect of his thought has not been widely discussed in the English language literature (Harbold, 1969; Hoffman, 1972), leading to little understanding of how the central animating concept of Proudhon's life's work – justice – fits into his economic theory. This is what I will do here. In this way I aim to illustrate why Proudhon believed that people's workplaces and economic futures were not things to be gambled with by distant individuals on frenetic markets or governed according to the (un)informed whim of politicians. He called for an approach to property that undermined the moral justification for private title and buttressed a theory of democratic worker control. By locating democracy at the heart of people's lives – at their place of work – Proudhon argued that civic participation would gain far fuller expression. Since it is in our places of work that we feel our rights and duties most keenly, the extension of the republican impulse into this domain of life was absolutely crucial to Proudhon and a moral imperative for the realisation of social justice. Active individuals and collectives, engaged in the daily business of democratic political economy; this was how Proudhon understood republicanism. To tame the market and structure the economy in more equitable ways, Proudhon called for the federation of trades, towns and regions, and he believed that through this twin process of the socialisation of title through democratic worker control and the federation of the plural social cleavages of society, capitalist anarchy would be brought under control, while moral and socio-political autonomy would be returned to the people.

Proudhon's theory of ethics was naturalistic. He believed ethics were fundamentally driven by our instincts and mollified by our conscience and our reason. That said, Proudhon was also deeply historical, arguing clearly that our instinct is always realised within specific historical and social contexts. While instinct is what unites us, it is the diversity of cultures which, in practice if not in principle, divides us. He argued against the rationalists, particularly Immanuel Kant, but retained their ethical defence of the individual. He took liberally from Auguste Comte, whose positivist sociology drew on the most up-to-date scientific findings to argue that our fixed biological natures and the material teleology within society guided history, but rejected Comte's total denunciation of free will. Proudhon sought to retain Comte's understanding of the biological origin of morality and the social contexts for its realisation; he also wanted to retain the idea that society was qualitatively distinct from the individual, but he refused the crude positivist 'Religion of Humanity' that Comte believed flowed inexorably from his own scientific findings.

In painting this picture of Proudhon's moral and political philosophy I will also draw extensively on Proudhon's published texts and the relevant secondary literature. My approach deviates somewhat from the standard treatment of Proudhon's republicanism. This is Steven Vincent's (1984) excellent *Pierre-Joseph Proudhon and the Rise of French Republican Socialism*. Through a close reading of some of Proudhon's best-known works and set against rich historical contextualisation, Vincent demonstrates that 'Proudhon had a consistent vision of society and its needs, a vision which is pre-eminently moral, and which revolves around his desire to install a federal arrangement of workers' associations and to instil a public regard for republican virtue' (1984: 3–4). Vincent's focus is political and social rather than ethical, so he draws on Rousseau and Montesquieu's thought for the antecedents of Proudhon's political philosophy. I focus on Proudhon's theory of justice and while I inevitably come to similar general conclusions to Vincent, I arrive at them from a quite different angle.

Perhaps the central distinction between my approach and Vincent's will be my focus on Proudhon's undisputed *magnum opus*, *De la Justice dans la Révolution et dans l'Eglise* (1988/1990 [2nd edn 1860]). By his own admission, Vincent does not engage with this text 'in any detail' (1984: 225), but this text, which in its current edition is over 2000 pages long and is divided between 12 *études* or studies, gives us a radically different perspective on Proudhon's republican anarchism. In it we find the basics of Proudhon's theory of human nature, his understanding of the origin of the moral sentiment, how this sentiment is shaped by social forces and how our conscience drives social change. I will show that Proudhon's radically anti-reductionist social theory was critical and emancipatory in part because it denied the absolutist and reductionist theories of his day.

In order to demonstrate the significance of his thought in his own time, I will show how Proudhon's ideas were influenced by and fundamentally critical of the epochal ideas of Kant and Comte. The former was one of the most influential moral philosophers of the period, the latter the founder of modern positivism. Taking this route will take me some distance from the exegesis offered by Vincent, though what I will show, by arriving at similar conclusions, is that Proudhon was no muddle-headed eccentric, but an original and far-sighted political and moral philosopher in his own right, and one whose ideas fuelled a tradition of political thought that radically re-configured the intellectual relationship between morality and right, liberty and authority and property and society.

The chapter is structured in the following way. In the first part of the chapter I will set out the context in which Proudhon developed his moral philosophy. What I will show is that there is some confusion in the secondary literature as to the meta-theoretical and meta-ethical foundations of Proudhon's theory. Was he a rationalist or a sociologist, a positivist, individualist or something else? Through a brief discussion of the basic ideas of Comte and Kant I will be able to show the points of convergence and divergence between their ideas and Proudhon's and, hopefully, clarify some of the confusion surrounding the interpretation of Proudhon's philosophy. I will then summarise Proudhon's theory of justice. In the second part of the chapter I will show how this theory of justice connects to Proudhon's theory of property and how both came to be seen as central to what I consider to be the essence of his republican anarchism. Proudhon was not simply an iconoclast. Like all anarchists he had a vision of how society could be more justly organised according to more enlightened principles of ethics and political economy. Unlike many to follow him, Proudhon's vision was sustained by thousands of pages of philosophical analysis and historical evidence.

6.1 Rationalism, positivism and immanence

All too often it has been claimed that Proudhon's thought was too confused to offer coherent answers to serious questions about ethics and politics. To get some idea of the confusion Proudhon's position has generated, consider the opinion of Henri de Lubac. He has argued that

[Proudhon's] method, however hostile to metaphysical abstraction, was the very reverse of any Empiricism. It was equally remote from Auguste Comte's Positivism and Marx's historic Materialism [sic]. Although Proudhon detested the word it was an 'Idealism', too, in its own way. Neither would it be impossible to link it up with Kant's Moralism.

(de Lubac, 1948: 143)

This is a confusing summary to say the least, but de Lubac does suggest that Proudhon was a neo-Kantian, and in many respects de Lubac is right. He is certainly correct, and most serious commentators follow him here that it is Kant as opposed to G. W. F. Hegel that exerts most influence on Proudhon's ideas, but whether Proudhon can be considered a Kantian is debatable. That said, in perhaps the best-known book on Proudhon's political thought, one that takes a decidedly rationalist and deductive approach to it, Alan Ritter claims that Proudhon is best read *as* a neo-Kantian and *in* neo-Kantian ways. Ritter's deductive 'analytic approach' (1969: 3) casts Proudhon's method as one that evaluates all moral precepts insofar as they are consistent with an absolute commitment to 'respect'. Ritter highlights a certain element of moral realism in Proudhon's thought which he then subsequently determines is inconsistent with what he identifies as Proudhon's tendency towards neo-Kantian deontology. To marry realism to deontology would, of course, be a fatal inconsistency in Proudhon's thought, and Ritter indeed concludes that '[j]udged by its own pretensions, Proudhon's theory of morals is a failure' (1969: 92–3).

But to draw such a conclusion Ritter had to be sure he had correctly identified Proudhon's 'pretentions' and it is arguable that he did not. In order to sustain this argument, Ritter must claim that Proudhon was most certainly *not* an empiricist, still less a Comtean sociological positivist (as de Lubac suggests), since to sustain this would imply that deductive coherence was by no means the limit of Proudhon's moral theory. So, Ritter (1969: 34) claims that

In his published writings, and even in his letters, sociological propositions are rare and incomplete. We are told repeatedly that 'the stimulus of society' affects men's behaviour and ideas, but learn little about the scope and limits of this stimulus, or why and how it occurs. The hints of a theory of social psychology in Proudhon's published work whet our curiosity without satisfying it.

This is, unfortunately, wildly inaccurate. Proudhon may not have been a positivist, but that does not mean he was not sociological in his approach. For example, in *The Sociology of Pierre-Joseph Proudhon 1809–1865*, Constance Hall has argued that for Proudhon justice was immanent *in man and in society*, and by analysing historical and social conceptions of justice over time, one could better account for *social* cohesion and *social* order (Hall, 1971: 90). Furthermore, Celestin Bouglé and George Gurvitch, two hugely influential early-twentieth-century French sociologists, published important works on Proudhon, and both saw him to be a disciple of Comte (Bouglé, 1911; Gurvitch, 1965: 31–46, cf. Berth, 1912; Ansart, 1997). The key ideas Proudhon seems to have taken from Comte were those of 'collective reason' and 'social statics' and a philosophy that saw history as the unfurling of human reason in changed material contexts – which was not too dissimilar from Kant's (Kant, 1991a).

That said, Proudhon chose to describe his own work as a *'science sociale'*, rather than 'positivism', in order to distance himself from Comte's technocratic 'Religion of Humanity' that was to be led by a sovereign cadre of 'Priest Scientists' (Noland, 1970; Haubtmann, 1980, Copley, 1989; Ansart, 1992). Not aligning himself with the predominant systems of thought at that time has confused later analysts such as de Lubac, but this does not mean he was completely idiosyncratic nor that his ideas took nothing from his contemporaries. In trying to decipher Proudhon's philosophy we need to answer some simple questions and contextualise his answers to get some idea of the intellectual coherence of his thought. So, let us start at the beginning and ask: what were his basic ontological, epistemological and ethical assumptions, and who were the main influences on his thought?

Despite their differences, the evidence suggests that Proudhon was deeply influenced by both Comte and Kant. Proudhon claimed to have been reading Tissot's translation of Kant's *Critique of Pure Reason* from as early as 1839 (Vincent, 1984: 62). However, it was not until Joseph Tissot published his translation of Kant's 1797 work *Principes Métaphysiques du Droit, suivis du Projet de Paix Perpétuelle*, which included translations of 'What is Enlightenment?', 'Perpetual Peace', 'Theory and Practice' and the 'Contest of the Faculties', in 1853 that Proudhon became familiar with Kant's political and moral philosophy. It is clear from his published writings and his unpublished notebooks that he was profoundly moved by Kant's critical method, his theory of right and his theory of the antinomies (Castleton, unpublished). In a letter to Joseph Tissot, who became a close friend, Proudhon stated that '[i]n reading

Kant's antinomies, I saw in them, not a proof of the weakness of our reason, nor an example of dialectical subtlety, but a veritable law of nature and of thought' (cited in de Lubac, 1948: 144). Much as Hegel had attempted, Proudhon argued that the antinomies were real as well as ideal. Indeed, in *The Principle of Federation*, it is the antinomy between liberty and authority which Proudhon traces historically from ancient times to our own, both as a conceptual trade-off given meaning by changed understandings of our place in the worlds and as a political one between social and political classes (Proudhon, 1979).

Pierre Haubtmann, Proudhon's most diligent biographer, tells us how Proudhon went to visit Tissot to talk about Kant's work in June 1856 – around the time he began work on his four-volume *tour de force*, *De la Justice dans la Révolution et dans l'Eglise*. The questions of practical reason that preoccupied Kant were also at the forefront of Proudhon's mind at this time, though for quite different reasons. Whereas Kant was the quintessential recluse, what marked Proudhon out during the late-1850s was the fact that people regularly came to see him or wrote to him for advice on moral and social problems. Indeed, such was his level of engagement with sections of the public that he even described himself as a 'consultant moralist'! In 1859, soon before the publication of the second edition of the work, Proudhon claimed, in typically Enlightenment language, that *De la Justice* would be 'a sort of encyclopedia in which the principle, the law, the method and the end is *right*' (Haubtmann, 1987: 30–57; Copley, 1989: 212).

In many respects, Proudhon's debt to Kant is typical of the period. As Sudhir Hazareesingh has shown, most late-nineteenth-century French republicans were neo-Kantians (Hazareesingh, 2001) and Hegel had not had much impact because he remained largely untranslated (Kelly, 1981). French liberals held fast to a methodological and civic individualism, rationalism and a teleological view of nature and of history. Most advocated the moral and republican value of universal federal republics in ways that were akin to Kant's theory of 'Perpetual Peace' (Barni, 1868; Proudhon, c. 1900; Bakunin, 1990). However, unlike Tissot, who Proudhon chastised for remaining too close to Kant (Navet, 1994: 55), Proudhon took his analysis and ideas in ways that were ultimately antithetical to the Kantian project. The main influence here was Comte, and what Proudhon took from him was his sociological method and his naturalist ethics.

Comte is perhaps less well-known to Anglo-American moral philosophy, to anarchist studies too no doubt, but his influence on nineteenth-century French thought was second only to Saint-Simon, Comte's tutor and mentor in his early years (Pickering, 1993). Comte's influence on Proudhon would have pre-dated Proudhon's first political writings, such was the Saint-Simonian intellectual ferment of the Restoration period (1814–1848), but we find very little by way of direct citation or reference. In the introduction to the Marcel Rivière edition of Proudhon's *De la Création de l'Ordre dans l'Humanité* (1849), the editors Bouglé and Cuvillier make it clear that Comte's *System of Positive Philosophy* is a key influence on the work but remains largely un-cited. Comte echoes throughout Proudhon's formulation of his 'relational ontology' and it is clear that he uses Comte's famous historical 'law of the three stages'. They also note that in the introduction to the second edition to the work, Proudhon himself sees the resemblances between the two works but claims he discovered the ideas on his own (Bouglé and Cuvillier, 1927: 17–18). This may be the case, but if either position is correct, it is clear that Proudhon was no Kantian rationalist and further research linking his thinking to Comte would undoubtedly be fruitful.

However, perhaps more interesting than a lack of referencing is an event that took place in late 1854. On their publication, Comte sent complimentary copies of the first two volumes of his *Système de Politique Positive* to Proudhon, with an odd invitation to join him in proselytising his positivist 'Religion of Humanity'. The invitation is hugely surprising, not least because Proudhon was one of the most famous social critics of his day and unquestionably diametrically opposed to Comte's technocratic and authoritarian politics. Proudhon obviously declined the invitation for many of the same anti-dogmatist reasons he gave in turning down a similar invitation from Marx and Engels in the early 1840s (Haubtmann, 1980: 183–96). However, as Haubtmann's readings of Proudhon's notebooks show, Proudhon read the volumes in considerable detail. Proudhon was inspired by Comte's theory of social forces, of the sociological and ideational principles of order, but he was also particularly struck by Comte's linking of sociology to biology and the teleological theory of history akin to Kant's.

To understand this influence, and to correctly locate Proudhon's thought in this epochal debate in the history of European thought, I will now briefly recap the main issues at stake. The core meta-theoretical problem of eighteenth- and nineteenth-century philosophy was epistemology. The most pressing question was, as Proudhon put it, in the absence of God and Divine Right to rule, how can we know what is *right* and 'on what should we base [...] the moral law and the political order'? (Proudhon, 1988/1990: 1144). Answers to this question, and there were many of them, were hugely ambitious and charged the intellectual ferment of the Enlightenment. Those who denied Voltaire's relativism often believed themselves to have found the Rosetta Stone that would once and for all divine the rational foundations of the future intellectual, moral and political order (Manuel, 1965).

Kant and the rationalists argued that there was a natural, if broken, correspondence between our ideas about the world and the world itself, but that while reality may not be directly knowable, it was rationally deducible. The problem was that since all perception was mediated then we could not directly know the 'thing in itself'; we could only deduce the nature of a thing from logic *or* induce its nature from observation. Newton had shown that the world 'out there' was governed by the material laws of nature, but if we as humans were to be morally and politically free, Kant argued that morality had to have an independent ontological status. We had to be able to find truth out for ourselves, because our rationality was a God-given quality and if we were to use it to our fullest extent, all barriers to it had to be shown to be overcome in principle. Kant believed that moral truths were deducible in the same way as mathematical truths were, and he also believed that the answers given by rational moral analysis would correspond to the world out there in much the same way as mathematics does (Körner, 1955; Scruton, 1982).

Kant's critical project sought to demonstrate that the structure of logic and reason are in transcendent harmony with the phenomenal world 'out there', and the dogmas of religion and the sophistry of politics had to be pierced. The purpose of the critical project was to discover these universal laws of cognition and of morality, smash the sophistries of the age and use the newly discovered moral law to determine the correct constitution of the transcendent political order. By so doing, morality, exactly like mathematics, would compel duty and obedience to the moral law. Kant believed that it was precisely the failure of past thinkers to correctly deduce this moral law, and the consequently spurious nature of the political laws built atop them which plunged Europe into revolutionary wars.

Crucially, however, if moral laws were to be binding, there could be no pollution of the ideational by the material realm, for the material led to determinism and only the ideational to freedom. Kant (1964: 58) argued the following:

> pure philosophy (that is, metaphysics) must come first, and without it there can be no moral philosophy at all. Indeed a philosophy which mixes up these pure principles with empirical ones does not deserve the name of philosophy (since philosophy is distinguished

from ordinary rational knowledge precisely because it sets forth in a separate science what the latter apprehends only as confused with other things). Still less does it deserve the name of moral philosophy since by this very confusion it undermines even the purity of morals themselves and acts against its own proper purpose.

This was a deliberate attempt to move away from the passionate romanticism of Rousseau, and Hume's subjectivism. In the 'Idea for a Universal History', Kant argues, *contra* Rousseau that the passions are 'pathological' where duty is concerned (Kant, 1991a: 45). Moral right, like mathematics, is rationally deducible from the structure of logic and from a critique of reason itself, not from our emotions. Once this structure has been correctly deduced, reason can show us how we ought to change society in order to make it correspond to the dictates of the discoveries of an enlightened mind. It is impossible to develop this in any more detail here, but it is clear that for Kant, the 'categorical imperative' (Kant, 1964: 89), translated into the terms of political right, forms a universal and transcendental foundation for moral duty. Moral duty, divined by the adept, forms the foundation of all positive laws. Whether you understand the law, agree with it or not, it is your absolute duty to obey the sovereign (Nicholson, 1976).

For Comte, this philosophy of reason and of morality was simply untenable. Law could not be made by kings and politicians; what do they know about the world? As far as Comte was concerned, only the scientists were qualified to legislate for humanity, and Comte made it his life's work to demonstrate why. Differences did not end here. Comte's empiricist epistemology was also the polar opposite of Kant's rationalism. For Comte, 'truth' was

> [a] conception that shall harmonise with the total sum of impressions received from *without*. The less distinct these impressions are, the greater is the effort of the mind to substitute its own combinations, which are very subtle and far-fetched. When there is a strong desire for a decision, and yet no external facts sufficient to justify it, it is sometimes founded on purely internal reasons, due simply to a strong relation of the Heart upon the Intellect.
> (Comte, 1968a: 575)

This distinction between the rationalists and the positivists should be clear: what Kant took for transcendental reason, Comte thought, was instinct – and a pretty inaccurate one at that. Moral and mathematical axioms do not spring up in our minds fully formed; they must be learnt and taught and they are based on painstaking observations. By Comte's analysis, human cognitive functions are not dualistic but a 'complex result'; rather than transcendentally ideal, they are an 'irreducible' property of human 'social evolution' (Comte, 1968a: 543). Thus, he argues, 'the Brain should never be considered apart from the rest of the organism' (543). The special functions of intellect are what he calls 'composite results, due to the combined action of the elementary intellectual functions'. Finally, he argues that 'from the Biological point of view, this dependence of the Intellect on Sensation is perfectly analogous to that of the bodily Functions upon the Environment which controls the whole vital Existence' (Comte, 1968c: 15). There is little here that echoes Kant's epistemology.

From this perspective, everything we think we 'know' has been imparted to us from the outside, by habit and biological and environmental necessity. Our free will is not set aside from the material processes that govern history, but an intrinsic part of it. *Pace* Kant, Comte argued that we are ruled more by our passions and our bodily functions than by our intellect, by society more so than by our own ideas. Society was real and had causal influence on our ideas, whether we liked it or not. Philosophical idealism, Comte argued, is 'as injurious to morality as it is erroneous in philosophy' (Comte, 1968b: 29).

Comte's positivism was also deeply moral as well as historical and normative. Comte argued that history had evolved through three stages: the religious stage, the metaphysical or philosophical stage and the positivist stage. In the religious stage, man anthropomorphises nature, believes the whims of the weather are morally significant and ultimately believes Gods to have fixed our moral natures. In the metaphysical or philosophical stage, which Comte saw as originating with the scientific discoveries of the Arabs regarding the movement of the stars and the forces of nature, of mathematics and so forth, man takes his own intellect to be indicative of a transcendent order. It is only with the advent of positivism that man (women had quite different but equally fixed natures and roles) can fully realise his total dependence on the material and social realm and this realisation is synonymous with moral *progress*.

In the positive stage of history, the moral law must be deduced from the facts as they are experienced, while social law was to be formulated on the basis of what society needs. The social good can be empirically ascertained by the scientists and society governed to that end. This gives no room for free will since not only is history driven by an internal *material* teleology, but its endpoint can only be deduced from the facts by the scientists, those historically preeminent and providentially necessary 'Men of Genius'. As Comte stated it: '[the] nature of things [...] absolutely prohibits freedom of choice by showing, from several distinct points of view, the class of scientists to be the only one suited to carry out the theoretical work of social reorganisation' (Comte, 1998a: 97). These would be a cadre of 'Priest Scientists', as Comte called them, who would preach the Positivist 'Religion of Humanity' which would contain all the moral, civic, political and economic rules for a smoothly functioning society, and of course, Comte would be its self-anointed 'High Priest'. As Frank Manuel has argued, '[t]he impression is inescapable that in the positivist religion there is a total loss of personality as man is merged in the perfect transcendent unity of Humanity' (Manuel, 1965: 281). Raymond Aron argued that Comte 'made an exact diagram of his dreams, or of the dreams each of us may invent in those moments when he takes himself for God' (Aron, 1968: 90).

One does not need to be an anarchist to find this fundamentally disturbing. Liberals like John Stuart Mill, originally a close friend and correspondent of Comte's sharing much in terms of their utilitarianism, described Comte's liberal technocracy as one of the worst despotisms ever devised (Mill, 1993, cf. Scharff, 1995). But we can see that there is a clear division here, both ethical and political and both rest on basic ontological and epistemological assumptions. The rationalist individualism at the heart of liberalism and the communistic materialism at the heart of positivism were diametrically opposed. Proudhon attempted to chart a course between the two.

First of all, the claim that ethics might have biological and historical, as well as social and intellectual, roots had a profound effect on Proudhon's ideas on the subject. He repeats Comte's position when he argues that

> KANT forced himself to construct morality, like geometry and logic, on an *a* priori conception, outside all empiricism, and he failed. His fundamental principle, the absolute commandment, or the *categorical imperative* of Justice, is a fact of experience about which his metaphysics are powerless to give an interpretation.
> (Proudhon, 1988/1990: 309)

Proudhon concurs with Comte that if reason is phenomenal and influenced by social forces it must be open to sociological, psychological and biological analysis. However, he argued that justice was no more reducible to 'a relation declared by pure reason as *necessary* to the social order' than is it, *pace* Comte, 'a *commandment* instructed by a superior authority to an inferior being' (Proudhon, 1988/1990: 1376; emphasis added). Proudhon argued that 'justice is immanent to the human soul; it is in itself a foundation, and it constitutes its highest power (*puissance*) and its supreme dignity' (136). This tells us clearly what justice is not, but in order to find out what justice is, we must unpack this final quote a little bit more.

Proudhon's clearest and most concise answer to the question regarding the nature and origin of justice lies in the tenth *étude* of *De la Justice*, in his study entitled 'Love and Marriage'. Given his widely known sexism, it is perhaps unsurprising that few have ventured there for enlightenment on his theory of morality. Still, what he has to say is quite striking. He opened his discussion like this:

> We have seen that, *à propos* of free will, all [bodily] functions suppose an organ: where [then] is the organ of justice? We speak of the conscience; but conscience is a word, the name of a faculty in which we affirm that Justice is its content. (1988/1990: 2057)

His argument is that basic observations and sensations suggest that humans intuit the right thing when we *feel* it as good and the reverse as bad, much in the same way as things generally smell bad when they are off, and better when they are edible (1373). Proudhon therefore theorised that the moral organ was in fact the whole body (2057). We rationalise and think and this is the mark of our individual moral autonomy. Yet we also feel and react unthinkingly; we recoil from pain and feel hurt. But what hurts us emotionally and disgusts us morally will be socially structured in important ways.

Like Comte, Proudhon embeds this individual, biological moral faculty in a theory of 'social forces'. For Comte, social facts are aggregates that are irreducible to their parts and qualitatively dissimilar. Proudhon concurred that what Comte called 'social facts' or 'collective ideas' are superior to the sum of their parts and 'very different, also often the inverse of my own conclusions'. But, he argued, 'this conversion [from individual to social fact...] does not imply the condemnation of the individual; it presupposes it' (1261). Without free and willing agents, social forces would be either completely random or historically exactly the same. The fact of the matter is that society is neither. Its characteristics are relatively enduring but also changeable.

Moreover, if the body is the source of justice then it ought to be protected and respected, and the personalities and bodies of others no less so. The free, open nature of society demands it. In clearly Kantian ways, Proudhon argued that 'the end of man is in himself' (347). Proudhon develops his own take on the state of nature theory to illustrate his position.

> Although he was originally in a completely savage state, man constantly creates society through the spontaneous development of his nature. It is only in the abstract that he may be regarded as in a state of isolation, governed by no law other than egoism [...] Man is an integral part of collective existence and as such he is aware both of his own dignity and that of others. Thus he carries within himself the principle of a moral code that goes beyond his individuality. He does not receive this principle from elsewhere; it is intimate to him, immanent. It constitutes his essence, the essence of society itself. It is the characteristic mould of the human soul, daily refined and perfected through social relations.
>
> (1988/1990: 117)

Proudhon has here charted something of a via media between Comte's hard empiricism and Kant's rationalism. We are free-thinking agents, but not infinitely so. We may be socialised, but we are always individuals first. Proudhon makes clear, here and elsewhere, that morality is structured first within human consciousness and is changed and reflected back at us in the societies we create. Social forces, forces we may not identify with but help sustain by our daily participation in them, constrain and enable our own rationalised sense of right and wrong, while the institutions we build and that embody these ideas constrain and enable us in material ways. Progress and change are possible, but not infinitely so, because not only do our underlying natures change more slowly, but political institutions are also particularly enduring. Morality is thus particular and social, unavoidably contextual, but most importantly *immanent*. Later in the work, Proudhon argues that to talk in terms of immanence makes one 'a true anarchist' (637). But what does this term mean? How does Proudhon understand this term?

In French, 'immanence' means to be contained in or intrinsic to something; it can also, in its more theological sense, relate to a sense of omnipresence. Proudhon would likely have been using the term in a manner similar to that used by the secular (if mystic) Saint-Simonian pantheists of his period. That is to say that by this framing, justice is an emergent property. It emerges from the clash of the ego and the community; it manifests as social norms that cannot be reduced to individuals since many rarely subscribe to them. Immanent justice is an irreducible synthesis between instinct and reason, the individual and society. Justice exists out there as well as within our conscience – it is omnipresent as well as always in a process of becoming.

Because both collectives and individuals are the preconditions of justice, they must *both* be protected. In his writing on war, Proudhon shows how conflict is at the heart of morality; conflict not only between peoples and their different conceptions of right, but also within us, between our innate conscience and our inherited social ideas (Prichard, 2007). War is the ultimate manifestation of conflict and Proudhon is quite clear that force, justified by social conventions regarding right, is what sustains political orders – not ideas alone. When our ideas about what is right changes, expect conflict. Conceptions of social justice constitute the structure or context within which these new ideas must compete, and the dynamic process of social stasis and change continues anew. Comte wanted this process to come to an end; Kant thought it unlikely that it would because men were too stupid or lazy. Proudhon praised our ability to challenge authority as one of the marks of our individuality and our humanity.

Despite all this conflict, order is the normal state of social relations and central to this, as Ritter (1969) recognised, is the principle of 'respect'. However, this principle, I would argue, ought to be read in a philosophically realist way, that is to say both socially *and* individually, both rationally *and* sociologically, since respect presupposes a 'relational social ontology' or social context, as well as a conscious and conscientious rational individual. Respect demands mutual recognition, and individual dignity must be sustained through *reciprocal* processes of empathy. By identifying one's own moral dignity with that of another and respecting the reciprocal nature of that exchange, society is formed. Thus, Proudhon argued the following:

> right is the faculty of each to require the respect of human dignity in his person; duty is the obligation of each to respect this dignity in the other. At base, right and duty are identical terms, in as much as they are always the expression of demandable or due respect.
> (Proudhon, 1988/1990: 299–300)

At this point in our discussions we can now see where Proudhon fits in terms of the intellectual currents of his day. I have argued that Proudhon had a sociological ontology (defined in a Comtean way) and that epistemologically he considered himself an 'ideo-realist'. I cannot be more precise here than to argue that this position took cognitive and rational faculties seriously, but was not blind to the sociological influences on our cognition (for more on this see Ansart, 1967: Chapter 5). Morally or ethically, Proudhon was a 'partisan of immanence', which implied that justice was always in a process of becoming (Proudhon, 1988/1990: 637).

Because of the sociological and relational ontology of Proudhon's ethical theory we can see how he would be a natural ally of republicanism, as Vincent argued. This is because for Proudhon human virtues were *mutually* agreed. 'Mutualism', Proudhon's term to describe his thinking here, captures this relation succinctly. Proudhon also saw moral activity as transformative and always in conflict with both our innate sense of right and social mores. There simply was no transcendental foundation for morality and conflict was at its heart. For Proudhon justice is thus immanent to man *and* society and reducible to neither. Moral history can show us where and how ideas have changed or become embedded, and over time, and with education and investigation into the wonders of the world around us, Proudhon also believed that our moral ideas would become ever more enlightened.

6.2 Justice, property and republican anarchism

In this second part of the chapter I want to develop the above discussion by illustrating how Proudhon's theory of justice linked to his theory of property. By linking property and justice in this way I hope to illustrate the ethical foundations of Proudhon's republicanism in more detail. What I will show is that Proudhon used his naturalistic ethics to undermine liberal absolutist and communist theories of property and also to provide ethical weight to his anarchist republicanism.

In the first part of *What Is Property?*, Proudhon argued that natural law theories of property ultimately need state sanction to uphold what ought to be natural – which makes them anything but. If they were truly natural they would surely be self-regulating systems akin to those found in the animal kingdom. The typical fall-back position for natural law theorists was our supposedly malign nature, which sanctified force to uphold a law which is in our best interests in spite of ourselves (Kant believed this sort of law also had historically palliative side effects). Secondly, Proudhon argued that while everyone who wrote about property realised that it was originally held in common, most ultimately seek to justify unequal distribution on the basis of rational principles: utility, duty, right and so on. What was originally held in common thus needs a transcendent or *external* principle to defend something internal but ultimately *un*natural in human society.

To illustrate this, Proudhon resurrected the Lockean labour theory of property. However, Proudhon argues that far from creating property as Locke had presumed, labour actually destroys the private*ness* of property. He made this argument based on his assumption that since no productive process is undertaken in isolation or in asocial contexts (tools and materials always come from somewhere), an asocial right to exclusive use of the product was illogical and thus immoral. Thus, Proudhon argued that any exclusive right to the product of labour must again be enforced according to principles that are *external* to the productive process itself. Proudhon's sociological ontology and his 'ideo-realist' epistemology are there for all to see and his theory of justice as immanent to man and society (as opposed to transcendently deducible alone) was clearly there in embryo too (Proudhon, 1994).

Proudhon's arguments had not much changed by the time he came to write his final work on property in the early 1860s. However, here, rather than attacking liberal property theory from a rational and analytical perspective, he took a historical path to the same conclusions. As he put it:

> The recognition of the institution of property is the most extraordinary act, if not most mysterious, of the collective Reason [...] there is nothing simpler, or clearer than the fact of material appropriation: a corner of ground is unoccupied; a man comes and there establishes himself, exactly like an eagle makes its nest, the fox its burrow, the bird on the branch, the butterfly on the flower, the bee in the hollow of tree or of a rock. This is no more than, I repeat, a simple fact, requested by the need, achieved by instinct, then affirmed by selfishness and defended by force. This is the origin of property. Then comes the limited liability Company, the Law, General reason, and universal Assent; all divine and human authorities, which recognises, consecrates this usurpation [...] Why? Here Jurisprudence is disturbed, lowers its head, begging not to be questioned.
> (Proudhon, 1997: 41)

Here Proudhon argues that a natural impulse to possession, common to man and animals, is transformed in society, over time, to proprietorship – the right to use and abuse. We know from *What Is Property?* that jurisprudential theory was far from coy about the origins of private property, but what it presumed to be a natural trans-historical justification was actually a historically specific resurrection of Roman law (Pockock, 1985). With the emergence of more complex societies, there emerged more complex theories and practices of property and of association. In fact, with

> [t]his understood, we will notice that the general laws of history are the same as those of the social organization. To write the history of a people's relations with property is to say how it survived the crises of its political formation, how it produced its powers, its bodies, balanced its forces, regulated its interests, equipped its citizens; how it lived, how it died. Property is the most fundamental principle with which one can explain the revolutions of history [...] no nation has surpassed this institution; but it positively governs history [...] and it forces nations to recognise it, punishing them if they betray it.
> (Proudhon, 1997: 120)

Human society's relationship with property has evolved and understanding the evolution of this history is to tell the story of the evolution of political community as such. Transcendent principles of property demonstrate more about how a class thinks of itself and its obligations than it does about any transcendent order. Take the liberal and Jacobin socialist arguments. In relation to the first, Proudhon argued that 'if each proprietor is sovereign lord within the sphere of his property, absolute king throughout his own domain, how could a government of proprietors be anything but chaos and confusion?' (Proudhon, 1994: 211). Imposing one's 'will as law' (210), the essence of bourgeois theories of property in the self, would result in 'anarchy' in the worst sense of the term, and yet this is 'the ideal of the economists who attempt strenuously to put an end to all governmental institutions and to rest society upon the foundations of property and free labour alone' (Proudhon, 1989: 20).

The Jacobin socialist option of state or collective control of production and property was equally problematic for Proudhon. The idea of a principle of distributive justice, such as the Saint-Simonian dictum, *'From each according to his ability. To each according to his needs'*, originally a principle of meritocracy but during the Second Republic a political creed, was 'unproductive and harassing, applicable only to quite special conditions [...] equally opposed to the advantageous use of labour, and to the liberty of the workman' (Proudhon, 1989: 84–5). The idea that some ultimately arbitrary centre could divine the principle of a just distribution held two further problems for Proudhon. First, the experience of the 1848 Luxembourg Commission in Paris, where state support of the economy produced indigence and economic collapse, showed the state socialists had failed when offered the opportunity to put the doctrine into practice.

Secondly, this hoarding centre was always liable to corruption as spectacularly demonstrated by Napoleon III's coup d'état 3 years later. Proudhon summarised by arguing that '[private] property is the exploitation of the weak by the strong; communism is the exploitation of the strong by the weak,' which also imposes 'a pious and stupid uniformity [...] on the free, active reasoning unsubdued personality of man' (Proudhon, 1994: 197, 196). With the advent of the Second Empire in 1851 and the rise of a new liberal and *dirigiste* technocracy, with individuals penned up in the new industrial factories and paying taxes to the state, Proudhon came to characterise this period as 'industrial feudalism' (Proudhon, c. 1990: 36).

Proudhon decided that the solution was to 'REPUBLICANISE [...] PROPERTY' (Q. Proudhon in Vincent, 1984: 143), by politicising the economy rather than seeking political representation in the formal political sphere. The question he asks repeatedly throughout his works is 'which principles' ought to underpin society? Proudhon advocated a commutative theory of justice. Aristotle had famously distinguished between legal, distributive and commutative justice. The first defines the relations of the parts to the whole; the second defines the relation of the whole to its parts or, for ease of expression, the relationship of the state to the rest of society; and the third governs reciprocal obligations and presupposes neither centre nor sovereign (for a full discussion of this see Simon, 1987). Proudhon believed that the principles of social order presupposed by the liberal elite fell into the former classification – concerned as they were to formalise their liberties. The second was related to the Jacobin socialists and the liberal technocracy, who, when in power, sought to stipulate in no uncertain terms the obligations of the parts to the whole. Proudhon's anarchism was commutative in that it sought to lay down a social and horizontal principle of justice. Paraphrasing Pascal, Proudhon argued that in his revolutionary society, the 'centre is everywhere, its circumference nowhere' (Proudhon, 1989: 282).

In order to remove the necessity of state force to sustain unjust social relations and to found property relations on a principle of commutative justice, Proudhon argued that labour and property relations had to be understood for what they were, not for what the liberals and Jacobin socialists would like them to be (on Jacobin socialism see, for example, Lobère, 1961). This is where Proudhon's moral and social philosophy (outlined in the previous section) was put to political and socio-economic use. The first thing to reject was the absolutism of liberal conceptions of property. As he argued in *Theorie de la Propriété*,

> As a disciple of Kant and Comte I reject the absolute as much as I do the supernatural; I recognise only intelligible, positive laws, like astronomy, the body, zoology, law, political economy [...] Republican in principle, in the mean time a partisan of constitutional guarantees, I fight with all my force against this absolutism which the French people sacrificed in the body of Louis XVI and yet wish to make me adore in property.
>
> (Proudhon, 1997: 107)

As a student (if an autodidactic one) of 'positive laws', Proudhon opposed the absolutist conception of property with his own '*science sociale*'. As I have shown, Proudhon argued that at base, we have animal instincts towards what is right and wrong that have been shaped on the margins by history and context, but which retain a basic humanity that is relatively enduring, both historically and culturally. However, unlike Rousseau who believed man to have an innate goodness, that only needed a change in institutions to usher it forth, or the more persistent alternative that posited an evil human nature in order to justify coercive laws, Proudhon believed man was both 'an angel and a brute', given to both sublime inspiration and venal brutality. But underlying this surface variation is a deeper continuity.

In *What Is Property?* Proudhon (1994: 174–80) argued that humans display three degrees of sociability. Our social instinct or 'first degree of sociability' is the biological context in which ethics emerges. We share most of the basic human moral impulses with animals, such as caring for infants, forming groups and friendships with reciprocal social relations. This first degree of sociability is supplemented, Proudhon (1994: 180) argues in his first major work, by our 'memory and penetration of judgement'. We are thus able to reflect on how our society is structured, and if we do so honestly, Proudhon argues, we would see that because none can supply all their desires unilaterally, society demands sharing, cooperation and industry. With all products originally held in common, reciprocity and social equality have structured our innate sense of justice. This explains why human and animal societies tend towards equality and are outraged by inequality. Justice, in this context, is a feeling for equality and a sense of indignation at injustices, and despite

Kant's hopes, 'instinct [on this issue] is not modified by knowledge of its nature' (Proudhon, 1994: 180). Proudhon argues that while our diversity of talents is marginal to our underlying human equality, and the inequality of talents is precisely why we need society, this inequality among humans (and not among animals) leads us to specialisation, which inevitably leads to esteem for one another and for exquisite talent. This in turn generates a sense of *equity* which qualifies the underlying equality, and it is this principle, Proudhon argues, which separates us from animals. 'Equity', Proudhon (1994: 183) argues,

> is sociability raised to its ideal through reason and justice; its most usual manifestation is urbanity or politeness, which among certain nations sums up in a single word almost all the social duties [...] As justice is the product of social instinct and reflection combined, so equity is a product of justice and taste combined, that is of our faculties of judging and of idealising.

Equity, the third or highest degree of sociability, is the core of Proudhon's ethical ontology in his earliest work. It is naturalistic, sociological and biological. It is also critical. Proudhon argues that natural human community is arbitrarily undermined by private property and the consolidation of the means of social control in the state. Both the state and private property are anti-social because, by consuming without producing, they are *parasitical* upon it. By upsetting the natural equality of society through appropriation and expropriation, society is continually *imbalanced* and thus prone to shocks and crisis. Proudhon argued that by uncovering the laws of our natures and of society, which he of course claimed to have done, we would also be able to find more equitable foundations for political economy (Proudhon, 1998: 189–95).

Central to this was a labour theory of value and a republican anarchist theory of political order. Richard Vernon has argued that they are one and the same thing. Proudhon's ideas suggest the view that civil citizenship 'as a political value, was merely an arrest of the spirit of liberation, whose ends were not political at all' (Vernon, 1986: 66). They were in fact economic. Proudhon argued that our economic relations mirrored our social ones, with the *oikos* the natural and immediate locus of human society, expanding outwards in ever-*decreasing* bonds of social attachment. Second to the family is the workplace. Both are more ethically defensible because they are experienced daily.

It is not in the fraternity of revolutionary citizens but in the reciprocity among producers that unity is to be sought. Nor is it in the sharing of uniformity of status as citizens that unity is found but, precisely to the contrary, in the diversity of skill and situation that, in making individuals complementary to one another, also makes them cooperative.

(Cited in Vernon, 1986: 74)

For Proudhon, participation in the industrial process makes one an 'associate' and a 'citizen' (Proudhon, 1989: 216), more so than in the rarefied air of a nation-state. At work, conjoined with the broader production process and the needs of society, one finds the fullest expression of civic responsibility and duty, both towards one's associates and the needs of society. It is here that rights and duties are most keenly *felt* and met, simply because we spend the vast majority of our lives working as opposed to voting.

Thus we need not hesitate, for we have no choice. In cases in which production requires great division of labour, and considerable collective force, it is necessary to form an ASSOCIATION among the workers in this industry; because without that, they would remain related as subordinates and superiors, and there would ensue two industrial castes of masters and wage workers, which is repugnant to a free and democratic society.

(1998: 216)

These trade associations, historically and economically specific 'natural groups' as he also called them, are principally created to deny 'the rule of the capitalists, money lenders and governments, which the first revolution left undisturbed' (98–9). This would return the 'collective force' to the labourers and make capital the 'undivided property' of the plural associations of society as opposed to society as a whole, or wealthy individuals within it. In this respect, Proudhon sought to substitute the rule of the association for the rule of government, and political economy for formal politics and formal systems of law – not in the future, but now, through purposive collective action.

The political economy ought also to be functionally, regionally and politically federated, Proudhon argued. There is no use substituting the egoism of the individual proprietor or the state for the egoism of the association or commune. They must be organised according to the principle of social reciprocity like all communal social relations. In *The*

Principle of Federation, Proudhon recognised that federation is a liberal idea 'par excellence' (1979: 73). However, the liberals, like Rousseau, 'had put contract to use in legitimising the *state*; [and... Rousseau] had enclosed men irrevocably within so-called sovereign territorial units and thus foreclosed on the promise of liberation' (Vernon, 1986: 67). The real, as opposed to the ideal ontology of politics, was that set by a naturalist or realist political economy. Central to this ontology were what Proudhon called 'natural groups', or any group which 'willy-nilly impose upon themselves some conditions of solidarity [...] which soon constitutes itself into a city or a political organism, affirms itself in its unity, its independence, its life or its own movement (*autokinesis*), and its autonomy' (cited in Vincent, 1984: 218). These groups have moral worth derived from the individuals of which they are comprised and from their affirmation of political capacity and moral autonomy. For democracy to be truly representative it must recognise and reflect the will of these natural groups. But crucially, democracy must also be economic and direct, both within the economic groups and between them (Proudhon, 1982: 282). As Proudhon (1979: 67) argued,

> [h]owever impeccable in its logic the federal constitution may be, and whatever practical guarantees it may supply, it will not survive if economic factors tend persistently to dissolve it. In other words, political right requires to be buttressed by economic right.

For Proudhon 'Agro-industrial federation' should organise the economy outside the control of the state while securing the protection of the citizen from 'capitalist and financial exploitation' (70). Contrary to those socialist approaches current at his time, Proudhon believed that the state was to have no direct involvement in business; it was to be an 'initiator' without any executive role in the economy (45). The state we end up with here is a pale imitation of the *dirigiste* state Proudhon had to combat daily and certainly not the state he had in mind at the beginning of his critical project. As society changes, so will the institutions we build atop it. The challenge is to adequately theorise this change.

Like for Kant, though in a radically different way, federation seemed to institutionalise the requisite diffusion, separation and balance of responsibilities and duties required of republican citizenship. Federalism did not represent a transcendent order, but a loose principle of social organisation. Based on the Swiss model of his time, it also provided Proudhon with the most obvious institutional means through which to protect and integrate the natural cleavages of society without necessarily subordinating one to any other. As Vernon argues, Proudhon's blueprint for 'agro-industrial federation' should be judged by 'the opportunities for participation it affords' (Vernon, 1986: 94). Who would disagree? Proudhon sought a citizenship without a supreme *polis*, where the *oikos* was democratised and claims to right and wrong would be judged according to the progressive development of science and reason, and according to need and equity. In Proudhon's vision, citizens no longer left their belongings behind in the world of things to participate in the rarefied air of the state, but should see the economy as the true basis of republican virtue. In fact it is here that citizenship means the most as it is here that sociability and responsibility are most keenly felt. Proudhon advocated a gradualist (r)evolution which involved 'getting the association into operation' (Vincent, 1984: 146). As Proudhon argued, violent 'revolutionary action [...] would simply be an appeal to force and to arbitrariness [...] I would rather burn Property little by little than give it renewed strength by making a Saint Bartholomew's Day of property owners' (cited in Vincent, 1984: 93).

6.3 Conclusion

We are in the midst of an economic crisis. Because they lack the economic means to protect themselves and the political means to affect real social change in their favour, the poor will, as usual, bear the brunt of it. Proudhon's theory of justice, property and republican citizenship is designed to provide an ethical defence of the empowerment of the working class derived from a theory of morality that takes human sociability and complex reciprocity as primary (cf. Glassman, 2000). It is designed as a vision of social order that can inspire and motivate while it also provides arguments to understand the social order and how it might be more equitably ordered. It is also fundamentally designed to bring the state and capital to heel by returning social power to society's constituent units and its productive workers.

The assumption is that without the ability to trade shares in people's livelihoods like so many trinkets, and mortgage people's futures by bailing out banks using the rights assumed through political expropriation, society would not only be more just, but also be more stable and more productive. This can be achieved through the socialisation of title through worker cooperatives and trade and communal federations. Proudhon did not seek a rupture with contemporary society, nor did he seek to build an alternative elsewhere and 'drop out' of global society. His was a social theory that saw our destinies as common and our need to work together as given. It refused grandiose blueprints and absolutist principles; he refused communism and liberalism and yet took what was most valuable in both and integrated them. Proudhon's was the first theory of anarchism and thousands have since followed and adjusted his ideas. But at the time (and since) many have failed to see the value and historical significance of his writings. As Alexander Herzen, one of the most prominent Russian revolutionaries of the nineteenth century, observed at the time:

> The French seek experimental solutions in him, and, finding no plans for the [Fourierist] phalanstery nor for [...Cabet's] Icarian community, shrug their shoulders and lay the book aside [...] Proudhon is the first of a new set of thinkers. His work marks a transition period, not only in the history of socialism, but also in the history of French logic.
>
> (Cited in Jackson, 1957: 115)

What we have also lost is the narrative of how this intellectual rupture that Herzen highlights developed and then changed again over the following years. Such is our ignorance of Proudhon's ideas on property and moral philosophy, on war and order, and most other matters, that we have little sense of how foundational he was to the anarchist canon. Moreover, those who followed did not feel the need to engage with his ideas in detail and so we have lost any sense of intellectual *progress* and cannot see *regress* and *reinvention* when it appears. I do not wish to imply that Proudhon had all the answers – there are gaps and omissions in Proudhon's thought and the analysis I have given here is unavoidably partial and selective – but my hope is that this introduction to the ethical foundations of Proudhon's republican anarchism is suggestive enough that those within the anarchist tradition engage with it once again and that those currently outside that tradition use it to empower their own struggles, or use it as a foil for their own arguments in pursuit of social justice and equality.

Acknowledgements

I would like to thank Edward Castleton, Benjamin Franks, Ana Juncos, Ruth Kinna, Matt Wilson and an anonymous reviewer for comments, corrections and suggestions for improvement. All translations are my own and indicated by the source text. All remaining errors are also my own. This chapter was completed during the final months of an

ESRC Postdoctoral Fellowship, grant code: PTA-026-27-2404, for which I would like to acknowledge thanks.

Bibliography

M. Albert (2003) *Parecon: Life After Capitalism* (London: Verso).
M. Albert and R. Hahnel (1991) *The Political Economy of Participatory Economics* (Princeton: Princeton University Press).
P. Ansart (1967) *Sociologie de Proudhon* (Paris: Presses Universitaires de France).
―――― (1992) 'La Présence du Proudhonisme dans les Sociologies Contemporaines', *Mil Neuf Cent: Revue d'Histoire Intellectuelle*, X: 94–110.
―――― (1997) 'Proudhon À Travers Le Temps', *L'Homme et Société*, 123–24, pp. 17–24.
R. Aron (1968) *Main Currents in Sociological Thought 1: Montesquieu, Comte, Marx, Tocqueville: The Sociologists and the Revolution of 1848* (New York: Doubleday).
R. Axelrod and W. D. Hamilton (1981) 'The evolution of cooperation'. *Science*, CCXI, 1390–1396.
Bakunin, M. (1990) *Statism and Anarchy* (Cambridge: Cambridge University Press).
J. Barni (1868) *La Morale dans la Democratie* (Paris, France: Germer Balliere).
É. Berth (1912) 'Proudhon En Sorbonne', *L'Indipéndence* 27 pp. 122–40.
C. Bouglé (1911) *La Sociologie de Proudhon* (Paris: Armand Colin).
C. Bouglé and A. Cuviller (1927) 'Introduction' in P.-J. Proudhon, *De la Création de l'Ordre dans l'Humanité, ou Principes d'organisation politique* (*Oeuvres Complètes de P.-J. Proudhon*) (Paris: Marcel Rivière).
E. Castleton (unpublished) 'Notes on Kant for composition of *La Guerre et la Paix*', Bibliothèque d'Étude et de Conservation, Besançon (MS. Z 550 and MS. 2859).
S. Chambost (2004) *Proudhon et la Norm: Pensé juridique d'un anarchiste* (Rennes: Presses Universitaires de Rennes).
A. Comte (1968a, b, c, d) *System of Positive Polity* (4 vols.) (New York: Burt Franklin).
―――― (1998a) 'Philosophical considerations on the sciences and scientists' in H. S. Jones (ed.) *Comte: Early Political Writings* (Cambridge: Cambridge University Press).
―――― (1998b) 'Plan of the scientific work necessary for the reorganisation of society' in H. S. Jones (ed.) *Comte: Early Political Writings* (Cambridge: Cambridge University Press).
A. Copley (1989) 'Pierre-Joseph Proudhon: A reassessment of his role as a moralist', *French History*, III: 194–221.
H. de Lubac (1948) *Un-Marxian Socialist: A Study of Proudhon* (London: Sheed and Ward).
S. Edwards and E. Fraser (1970) *Selected Writings of Pierre-Joseph Proudhon* (London: Macmillan).
M. Glassman (2000) 'Mutual aid theory and human development: Sociability as primary', *Journal for the Theory of Social Behaviour*, XXX: 391–412.
G. Gurvitch (1965) *Proudhon: Sa vie, son oeuvre avec un exposé de sa philosophie* (Paris: Presses Universitaires de France).

C. M. Hall (1971) *The Sociology of Pierre-Joseph Proudhon 1809–1865* (New York: Philosophical Library).
W. H. Harbold (1969) 'Justice in the thought of Pierre-Joseph Proudhon', *Western Political Quarterly*, XXII: 723–41.
P. Haubtmann (1980) *La Philosophie Sociale de P.-J. Proudhon* (Grenoble: Presses Universitaires de Grenoble).
—— (1987) *Pierre-Joseph Proudhon, sa vie et sa pensée, 1849–1865* (Paris: Relié).
M. D. Hauser (2007) *Moral Minds: How Nature Designed Our Universal Sense of Right and Wrong* (London: Little and Brown).
S. Hazareesingh (2001) *Intellectual Founders of the Republic: Five Studies in Nineteenth-Century French Political Thought* (Oxford: Oxford University Press).
R. L. Hoffman (1972) *Revolutionary Justice: The Social and Political Theory of P.-J. Proudhon* (London: University of Illinois Press).
T. O. Hueglin (1985) 'Yet the age of anarchism?' *Publius*, XV: 101–12.
J. H. Jackson (1957) *Marx, Proudhon and European Socialism* (London: English Universities Press).
I. Kant (1853) *Principes Métaphysiques du Droit, suivis du Project de Paix Perpétuelle* (Paris: Librairie Philosophique de Ladrange).
—— (1964) *Groundwork of the Metaphysic of Morals* (New York: Harper and Row).
—— (1991a) 'Idea for a universal history with a cosmopolitan purpose' in H. Reiss (ed.) *Kant: Political Writings*, 2nd ed. (Cambridge: Cambridge University Press).
—— (1991b) 'Perpetual peace: A philosophical sketch' in H. Reiss (ed.) *Kant: Political Writings*, 2nd ed. (Cambridge: Cambridge University Press).
M. Kelly (1981) 'Hegel in France to 1940: A bibliographical essay', *Journal of European Studies*, XI: 29–52.
S. Körner (1955) *Kant* (Harmondsworth: Penguin).
L. Lobère (1961) *Louis Blanc: His Life and His Contribution to the Rise of French Jacobin-Socialism* (Evanston, IL:Northwestern University Press).
F. Manuel (1965) *The Prophets of Paris: Turgot, Condorcet, Saint-Simon, Fourier, Comte* (New York: Harper and Row).
J. S. Mill (1993) 'On liberty' in G. Williams (ed.) *John Stuart Mill: Utilitarianism, On Liberty, Considerations on Representative Government, Remarks on Bentham's Philosophy* (London: J. M. Dent).
G. Navet (1994) 'Les lettres à Joseph Tissot' in G. Navet (ed.) *Proudhon: Sa Correspondance et ses Correspondants: Actes du Colloque de la Société Proudhon, Paris, 6 Novembre 1993* (Paris: Société P.-J. Proudhon, E.H.E.S.S.).
P. Nicholson (1976) 'Kant on the duty never to resist the sovereign', *Ethics*, LXXXVI: 214–30.
A. Noland (1970) 'Proudhon's sociology of war', *The American Journal of Economics and Sociology*, XXIX: 289–304.
M. Pickering (1993) *Auguste Comte: An Intellectual Biography*, Vol. I (Cambridge: Cambridge University Press).
D. Pizzaro (2000) 'Nothing more than feelings? The role of emotions in moral judgement', *Journal for Social Behaviour*, XXX: 355–75.
J. G. A. Pocock (1985) 'The mobility of property and the rise of eighteenth century sociology' in J. G. A. Pocock (ed.) *Virtue Commerce and History: Essays in Political Thought and History, Chiefly in the Eighteenth Century* (Cambridge: Cambridge University Press).

A. Prichard (2007) 'Justice, order and anarchy: The international political theory of Pierre-Joseph Proudhon (1809–1865)', *Millennium: Journal of International Studies*, XXXV: 623–45.

P.-J. Proudhon (c. 1900 [no date supplied]) *Du Principe Fédératif et de la Nécessité de reconstituer le parti de la révolution. (inc) Si Les Traités de 1815 ont Cessé d'Exister* (Paris: Ernest Flammarion).

—— (1979 [1863]) *The Principle of Federation and the Need to Reconstitute the Party of the Revolution*, trans. Richard Vernon (Toronto, University of Toronto Press).

—— (1982 [1865]) *De la Capacité Politique des Classes Oeuvrières* (*Oeuvres Complètes de P.-J. Proudhon*) (Paris: Slatkine).

—— (1988/1990) *De la Justice dans la Révolution et dans l'Église: Études de philosophie pratique* [1860] (Paris: Fayard).

—— (1989 [1851]) *General Idea of the Revolution in the Nineteenth Century*, trans. J. B. Robinson (London: Pluto Press).

—— (1994) *What Is Property? or, an Inquiry into the Principle of Right and of Government* [1840], trans. Donald Kelly and Bonnie Smith (Cambridge: Cambridge University Press).

—— (1997) *Théorie de la Propriété* [1862], Electronic copy of Éditions l'Harmattan edition, published electronically by the University of Quebec in 2002, http://dx.doi.org/doi:10.1522/cla.prp.the, date accessed: 19 July 2009.

—— (1998) *La Guerre et La Paix, recherches sur la principe et la constitution du droit des gens* [1861] (Paris: Editions Tops).

A. Ritter (1969) *The Political Thought of Pierre-Joseph Proudhon* (Princeton: Princeton University Press).

R. C. Scharff (1995) *Comte After Positivism* (Cambridge: Cambridge University Press).

R. Scruton (1982) *Kant* (Oxford: Oxford University Press).

Y. Simon (1987) 'A note on Proudhon's federalism' in D. J. Elazar (ed.) *Federalism as Grand Design: Political Philosophers and the Federal Principle* (Lanham: University Press of America).

B. Turner (1986) *Citizenship and Capitalism: The Debate over Reformism* (London: Allen and Unwin).

R. Vernon (1979) 'Introduction' in P.-J. Proudhon, *The Principle of Federation or the Need to Reconstitute the Part of the Revolution* (Toronto: University of Toronto Press).

—— (1986) *Citizenship and Order: Studies in French Political Thought* (Toronto: University of Toronto Press).

K. S. Vincent (1984) *Pierre-Joseph Proudhon and the Rise of French Republican Socialism* (Oxford: Oxford University Press).

J. Waldron (1988) *The Right to Private Property* (Oxford: Clarendon Press).

7
Freedom Pressed: Anarchism, Liberty and Conflict

Matthew Wilson

7.1 Introduction

In the following work I want to ask some troubling questions about the concept of freedom in anarchist thought: what sort of freedom might we expect, once we are *free* from the state? How will anarchists maintain order, without denying certain freedoms? My first claim will be simply that these questions, crucial though they are to the anarchist project, remain largely unanswered. But I want to focus primarily on a perhaps greater challenge – a challenge that most anarchists do not appear to have considered.

I hope to demonstrate that this highly complex world, where communities embody plural and often conflicting values, presents a significant problem for anarchists and their hopes for a world 'without domination'. To make my argument, I begin by exploring this problem in relation to liberal thought; while there are clear and important differences between liberalism and anarchism, I argue that there is much anarchists can learn by looking at the difficulties that liberalism has in defending freedom and difference. Importantly, I argue these problems are far from being simple by-products of the liberal defence of the state, but are, rather, inherent difficulties that any libertarian theory faces.

There is not the space to outline in this piece how anarchists may meet the challenges I place before them here, beyond a few brief comments in the Conclusion; in any case, I would not venture to suggest that I have all the answers. It is my primary concern now, therefore, to highlight what I consider to be a considerable – though not necessarily insurmountable – problem for a philosophy that argues strongly for a world without hierarchical structures of social control.

7.1.1 A working definition of anarchism

Before we begin, I need to clarify a number of terms. Firstly, there is the need to define what I mean by anarchism, and who I refer to when I talk about anarchists. It has been noted often that anarchism is a broad church; for this reason, it is considered poor practice, especially in academic works, to refer simply to *anarchism*. However, I would suggest that my argument is best understood as an open challenge to any variant of anarchist thought.

While in the second part of this chapter, I refer more to contemporary, often activist-oriented anarchism, I do so because I am personally most interested in engaging with these areas of radical thought; the problems I discuss, however, are not problems that only this particular school of anarchism is vulnerable to. Of course, different *responses* to this challenge are to be expected, and some anarchists may view the problems I discuss as being more or less difficult to respond to, depending on how they consider issues such as power, ethics and so on.

One author who has touched on a number of the issues I raise is the postanarchist Saul Newman (Newman, 2001: especially Chapters 4 and 8). Newman's approach differs from mine in some significant ways: he adopts an openly poststructuralist approach, and uses a number of poststructural theorists to critically explore what he considers to be anarchism's metaphysical underpinnings. The following work neither *embraces* nor *rejects* poststructural critiques of humanism (or the postanarchist critiques of classical anarchism), but it does follow two important assumptions. The first assumption is that power is not simply the preserve of the state. Power exists in stateless societies, and this has consequences. It may be shared more equally, be put to more just ends, and so on; but it is there. We need not, for this argument, deny that the state, or a particular class, for example, has the power (or we could say, the possibility) to inflict and enforce its desires on the majority of people who are not in such a position. What is relevant is that, if and when the state disappears, the problem of power will remain. In this chapter I hope to demonstrate that in a very practical way.

The second assumption is that we must accept that moral disagreements are extremely unlikely to disappear entirely, as a result of rational deliberation, natural dialectics, or whatever else it may be argued will ultimately bring about a universally accepted standard of ethics. Even for those who believe we will, eventually, come to some final moral agreement, the fact surely remains that value conflicts are with us now, and will remain with us for the foreseeable future. If anarchism is to be of any use to us *now*, then, it must accept and deal with this reality.

7.1.2 A working definition of liberalism

I also use the term 'liberal' in a broad sense: I refer primarily to John Rawls, and to the ideas of neutrality and consensus that are commonly associated with mainstream contemporary liberal theory. As I use this discussion merely as a way of exploring the idea of value conflict, once again a broad approach is not only sufficient but also perhaps more helpful.

Of course, the state is always present, implicitly if not explicitly, in discussions about value conflict within liberal theory; the simple question that must be asked immediately then is whether there is anything to be learned from these debates. The equally simple answer is, yes. These discussions are ultimately about what happens when different ways of life clash. The state, it may be argued, exaggerates these problems, and almost certainly creates a number of them, or rather, produces the situations in which they are more likely to occur; but there should be no doubt that some social conflicts exist beyond the state.

7.1.3 Defining 'Values'

Finally, I use the terms 'morality', 'ethics', 'values' and 'the good life' as being more or less synonymous with one another; they are all used to convey the essential characteristic of deeply help beliefs that inform our actions.

7.2 Anarchism and freedom: An overview

Freedom is a key value for anarchists – just how key is one question I pose below – and yet, when we cast a critical eye on the ways in which freedom is understood within anarchism, we find abstractions, contradictions, but, more often than not, an unsettling quiet. Alan Ritter (1980: 9–10) opens his book *Anarchism*, by noting that 'Anarchists are commonly regarded as extreme libertarians on the ground that they seek freedom above all else,' but goes on to note that in fact anarchists rely 'on public censure to control behaviour', and asks how anarchists can be considered libertarians when they support such censure: 'Although [anarchists] have long deemed this question crucial', he continues, 'no acceptable answer has yet been found.'

At times, anarchists do indeed appear to be extreme libertarians, placing the value of freedom above all else. This view comes not only from caricatures offered by people who know very little about anarchism, but also from anarchists themselves. Bakunin, for example, famously declared anarchists to be 'fanatical lovers of liberty' (1957: 17).

116 *Anarchism, Liberty and Conflict*

This commitment to freedom, however, is often moderated by commitments to additional values, most commonly, equality. Herbert Read suggests that 'we must prefer the values of freedom and equality above all other values' (Read, 1947: 2). And as Ritter explains, 'Viewing anarchists as single-minded devotees of freedom is...erroneous': rather, their relationship to it 'is mediated and indirect' (Ritter, 1980: 39). Ritter offers a strong argument that suggests that anarchists – in his case, Godwin, Proudhon, Bakunin and Kropotkin – moderate their libertarian tendencies in numerous ways, and that while they condemn the state and other ideologies for restricting freedom, and argue that, conversely, it is anarchism which best ensures personal liberty, they are not committed to freedom above all else. More importantly, for our present argument, anarchists do not understand this commitment to freedom as a rejection of social order.

Indeed, anarchists are keen to stress that the representation of anarchy as chaos is incorrect; anarchism is about maintaining order, while rejecting the conventional arguments that suggest such order is only possible within a state. My first claim is simply that anarchists have failed to adequately demonstrate that their claims are worthy of support. To take the most obvious concern, crime: given the anarchists' rejection of police forces and prisons, we would expect to find clear and well-rehearsed answers to this problem. Yet more thorough discussions about crime in anarchist societies are in fact rare, and those that exist offer little comfort; the conventional argument is that most crime is economically or culturally driven, and in a more egalitarian and less aggressive society, the incentives that cause people to steal will no longer prevail (see, e.g., Cullen, 1993). Occasionally, however, anarchists are a little more honest. As Class War bluntly put it, anarchists do not have enough answers to the question: What do we do when the cops fuck off? (Class War, 1986: 3). Regrettably, this chapter must be one more that leaves the question of crime under-explored and unresolved.

7.2.1 What sort of freedom?

So what *do* anarchists think about freedom? Ritter argues that anarchists in fact support what he calls *communal individuality*, which, although he does not use the term, is suggestive of some form of positive freedom; freedom is one value among others, not the sole or highest value. Ritter in fact talks of freedom as a triadic concept, in which there is a 'relation of *subjects* who are free from *restraints* to reach *objectives*' (10–11). This does not offer a significantly different angle from that of positive freedom (at least not at the level I wish to discuss it here). To take this positive approach, we do not need to negate freedom's value, but rather conceive of it in a particular way.

David Graeber and Andrej Grubacic, however, contend that 'anarchism as a whole has tended to advance what liberals like to call "negative freedoms"' (Graeber and Grubacic, 2004: 5). In a similar vein, Giorel Curran states, 'To anarchists the values of liberty and autonomy are everything, and they staunchly resist all attempts to trample them' (Curran, 2006: 20). Yet Randall Amster declares 'the anarchist is mainly interested in positive liberty' (Amster, 2006: 99), and the collective Notes from Nowhere (2003: 1009) also appear to advance a more positive position: '[B]asic rights provide the security that is at the root of a positive understanding of freedom as a freedom to do or to be.'

So what sort of freedom do anarchists support? Do they simply support different forms, with some favouring negative and others positive freedom? A sympathetic response would be that this is indeed the case, and rightly so; after all, it would be somewhat paradoxical if anarchists were to demand conformity to one particular vision of freedom. I want to take a more critical approach and suggest that in fact, freedom remains a confused – and even abused – concept within anarchist discourses, and that what we might take for nuanced and differentiated positions, in fact, demonstrate a considerable degree of contradiction and a serious lack of clarity.

7.3 A problem shared: Learning from liberalism

As I mentioned briefly above, anarchists have usually understood the question of maintaining order, or, to put it another way, reducing conflict, with reference to some notion of the *anti-social*: the problems of, for example, aggressive, destructive or deceptive behaviour. However poorly this issue has been addressed, it remains the case that it has been this aspect of social order that has received the most attention from anarchists. As Kropotkin argued, once people 'free themselves from existing fetters [they] will behave and act always in a direction *useful* to society' (1970: 102, my emphasis): in other words, according to Kropotkin at least, there are ways of acting that are *un*useful, and ways of acting that are useful, to society. Some of the former category we call crime, or, increasingly, anti-social behaviour.

Now, liberal theorists have understood this basic *problem* of social order in much the same way; how do we prevent individuals from committing acts such as theft and murder, and so on? Whereas anarchists see the state as *producing* (at least a significant part of) this problem, liberals see the problem as naturally occurring and propose the state as its *solution*. Both, however, understand these clearly defined anti-social acts as being the focal point when the issue of social order, or disorder, is considered.

Furthermore, both liberalism and anarchism support the ideal of individual freedom and so both are concerned with state interference with this freedom. However, liberals consider the state necessary to maintain the sort of social order just discussed. They do not embrace it for its own sake, but rather as a problematic necessity. They therefore insist that the limits of state power be restricted to the maintenance of this basic social order, and no more. The state is not intended to interfere with our personal lives, or our personal values. To ensure this, liberals have developed the concept of *neutrality*: the state must be neutral between competing conceptions of the good life. It must not favour one morality over another (Klosko, 2000: 4; see also Waldron, 1989; Brenkert, 1991; Rawls, 2001; Kymlicka, 2002).

But in recent years, many critics of liberalism have argued convincingly that the idea of value neutrality is fundamentally flawed; not because they consider it morally questionable necessarily, but because they consider it an impossible ideal. These critics suggest that we need to look more closely at the inevitable problem of *value conflicts* (see Young, 1990; Carens, 2000).

The *separation* of public and private lives, where values are viewed as a private affair while our public lives are regulated by the state – but only within its remit of maintaining order – is ultimately impossible. The state cannot but regulate our private as well as our public lives, and it cannot remain neutral regarding visions of the good life. This is true for two reasons. Firstly, defining which acts are social and which are anti-social can never be a value-free decision. Secondly, in controlling a society's basic infrastructure – its cultural and educational resources, health and transport services and so on – the state is placed unavoidably in a position of having to choose between different courses of action in relation to its administration. However, because our values are not merely a private affair, and are in fact often linked in complex and multiple ways to the wider world, physically and discursively, the choices the state makes often have a direct impact, however unintentional, on our moral lives. What this means, ultimately, is that it is not simply narrowly defined anti-social acts, such as murder, that are prohibited and/or regulated by the state, but a whole range of acts and even beliefs that are more or less suppressed by its dominant values.

At this stage I want to pre-empt the response that anarchists are well aware of this critique, and that this is one very good reason why they are opposed to the state. I am not convinced that anarchists *have* in fact for the most part understood this problem in the way I intend to pursue it here: however, whether I am right or wrong on this point is not important for my argument. What concerns us here, and what I will demonstrate below, is that the issue of value conflict is a serious problem *even without the state*, and I would suggest that this certainly *is* an issue that has not been sufficiently addressed by anarchists.

To make my argument, I want to first explore the issue of conflict, and the liberal response of neutrality, a little more closely, before going on to discuss the anarchist understanding of diversity, which, I argue, mirrors in important ways these liberal ideas of neutrality. Although it should be clear when we turn to the discussion of anarchism that the state is no longer the sole cause of the problem, it is worth highlighting the fact that, in the preceding discussion, there is also no reason to consider the state as being relevant: the problems discussed remain problems, even when we take the state out of the picture.

7.3.1 Conflicting freedoms, conflicting values

As we have seen, contemporary liberal theory has articulated a strong commitment to individual autonomy that mirrors much anarchist discourse. Liberalism is premised on the idea of a broad-based concept of freedom that allows for a diversity of thought and action within it; this freedom provides a (morally) neutral setting in which diverse conceptions of the good life can flourish. John Rawls, for example, saw that any attempt to bring about a comprehensive moral unity within a given society would lead to unacceptable levels of state interference:

> [A] diversity of doctrines – the fact of pluralism – is not a mere historical condition that will soon pass away [...] diversity of views will persist and may increase. A public and workable agreement on a single general and comprehensive conception [of the good life] could only be maintained by the oppressive use of state power.
> (Rawls, 2001: 425)

But he also argued that the state was capable of acting as a sort of impartial security guard, which would step in to defend a set of 'basic rights and liberties' (442) when they were threatened. For this to happen, Rawls argued, a society would need to achieve what he called an 'overlapping consensus' (421–48, 473–96), in order that it could then provide a 'political conception of justice that can articulate and order in a principled way the political ideals and values of a democratic regime' (421). This consensus must be 'endorsed by each of the main religious, philosophical and moral doctrines likely to endure in that society from one generation to the next' (473). (As we shall see below, many contemporary anarchists have also argued that it is only by reaching consensus that a community can avoid resorting to some form of coercion.)

The problem with this approach is that the notion of basic liberties is an extremely contentious one: is it really the case that a community of diverse moral values will be able to agree on what these basic liberties are? Rawls appears to think so; and, interestingly, so do many anarchists. But freedoms, and all sorts of other values, often *conflict* with one another. And this is not merely a matter of theoretical conflict – it is to say that freedoms and values are often mutually incompatible on a practical level; one *necessarily* cancels out the other, at least to some significant degree. We can not then refer to some objective notion of freedom in order to decide between conflicting interests, because it is often precisely differing conceptions of freedom that are conflicting. As John Gray (2000: 70) notes,

> [Rawls] claims that giving priority to liberty does not require making choices among rival freedoms or making controversial judgements about the worth of these freedoms. [... Yet] claims about the greatest liberty cannot be value free. [...] Rawls writes as if any reasonable person can know what the greatest liberty is. The truth is that it is indeterminate to the last degree.

Rawls' ideal of freedom – a freedom that can contain diverse voices without significant conflict – is not value neutral; what Rawls considers as basic liberties may be considered trivial, or even oppressive, by someone else. However well-intentioned, a list of basic liberties is in considerable part also a list of one's own values; it cannot but reflect what we consider to be morally acceptable. This myth of the neutrality of freedom, then, allows a strong conception of the good life to be presented as a set of basic liberties, as a thin, liberal, 'meta-ethic', a safe space that does no more than protect the diversity of values within it.

7.4 Value conflict, without the state

When this problem is explored in relation to liberal thought, the emphasis is very often on what actions the state should or should not take.

However, it is hopefully clear that this is the case only because the state is the mechanism by which liberals hope to resolve conflict. The conflicts themselves exist independent of the state. And when such conflicts arise they do not need the state to come down in favour of one side of the dispute: without state interference, the conflict may simply continue (with whatever repercussions that entails), be resolved in favour of one or the other side, or be eventually settled amicably. Very often, in contemporary societies, the result is a mixture between the first two options; one side becomes and remains dominant and is generally unthreatened and untroubled by its opposition, while the other side remains in a condition of (more or less tolerable) oppression. Iris Marion Young has argued that a profound and systematic denial of freedom – what she calls structural oppression – can take place when such conflicts occur. Importantly for this argument, she notes that 'disadvantage and injustice' arise in such situations, 'not because a tyrannical power coerces them, but because of the everyday practices of a well-intentioned liberal society'. The oppression that results, then, is 'structural, rather than the result of a few people's choices and policies. Its causes are embedded in unquestioned norms, habits and symbols [...]. [I]n short, the normal processes of everyday life' (Young, 1990: 41). Bhikhu Parekh offers a similar argument:

> Every culture is also a system of regulation. It approves or disapproves of certain forms of behaviour and ways of life, prescribes rules and norms governing human relations and activities, and enforces these by means of reward and punishment. While it facilitates choices as Raz and Kymlicka argue, it also disciplines them as Foucault argues. It both opens up and closes options, both stabilizes and circumscribes the moral and social world, creates the conditions of choice but also demands conformity. [...] While valuing the indispensable place of culture in human life, we should also be mindful of its regulative and coercive role and the way it institutionalises, exercises and distributes power. Its system of meaning and norms are not and cannot be neutral between conflicting interests and aspirations.
> (Parekh, 2000: 156–7)

What really interests us here is the way cultures – which is also to say philosophies, political positions (even anti-political ones) and systems of morality, even libertarian ones – are argued to be *incapable* of neutrality. As Gray demonstrates, freedoms conflict and we must decide between them, explicitly or implicitly, and, as Young and Parekh argue, certain norms become dominant and thus seriously limit the freedoms of people wishing to live in different ways. So freedoms – and perhaps we should also say the beliefs and actions that are made possible by those freedoms – conflict, and when they do, one will very often have to submit to the other. To be neutral in these situations is simply to give no assistance to either claim; which will generally mean, to let the stronger side win. (By *stronger* I do not only mean physically stronger. There are countless other ways one side of a debate will be in a position to overrule the others' wishes. One of those ways, worth noting here, is by virtue of being able to claim 'neutrality' for their position, while accusing the other side of being authoritarian.) When these conflicts occur, then being neutral does *not* (always) give equal space for both parties to co-exist; it can simply allow space for one to suppress or deny or beat or disperse the other without any third-party interference.

Liberals argue that what Rawls called the 'fact of pluralism' meant that only a liberal politics could protect us from the 'oppressive use of state power'; as we shall see, anarchists also argue that diversity is inevitable – and should be positively embraced – and that it is anarchism which offers people the autonomy needed for this diversity to flourish. We have seen, however, that the liberal idea of neutrality does not defend this plurality as effectively as liberals had hoped; rather, it allows a state, and also, importantly, a culture, to present its own interpretations of liberty as being value-free, thus creating the possibility for it to deny certain other liberties and values while declaring itself to be neutral, or to be defending diversity, or freedom.

The question now becomes, what evidence is there that anarchist conceptions of freedom and diversity are immune to a similar challenge, especially when we remember the critiques of Young and Parekh, who argue that it is not simply state regulation, but also cultures, habits, norms and everyday practices that are capable of 'deciding' between conflicting freedoms and values? Young refers to the structural oppression caused, not by a tyrannical regime, but by a 'well-intentioned liberal society'; how much better will a well-intentioned anarchist society fare?

7.5 Freedom for all except fascists, homophobes, racists, vivisectors, dairy farmers, misogynists, capitalists, etc.

Anarchists have long been involved in anti-fascist work, and considerable energy has been put into fighting the British National Party (BNP) in Britain. The Notts Stop the BNP campaign, made up of 'trade unionists, socialists, anarchists and anti-fascists', has actively campaigned to stop the BNP holding their Red White and Blue (RWB) Festival. As part of the campaign

> the company who supply portable toilets to the BNP Red White and Blue event were [sic] targetted [sic] by militant antifascists. All companies who support the RWB can expect to be targetted also. If you make money by helping the BNP, we will cost you money!
>
> (Derbyshire Antifascists, 2008)

Another tactic used in this particular campaign was the gluing of the locks of the farmer on whose land the RWB Festival was taking place. The rhetoric leaves no doubt that the BNP is considered a legitimate target for such attacks, and that it must be 'stopped', 'silenced', 'defeated' and so on. Antifa, a militant anti-fascist group that 'comes from the anarchist tradition', is well known for its uncompromising position against fascists. Its 'members' have been involved in fighting (literally) with fascists, and, as with the above campaigns, they make clear their intentions to prevent the BNP and other far-right groups from campaigning.

What are we to make of this? Surely these actions are denying the freedom of certain individuals, with the (implicit) justification being that what they believe – and do – is wrong. But does this mean their freedom is not still being denied? Ronald Dworkin has argued that, in fact, freedom does only relate to those things we have a right to do, and that therefore there is, in this case, no denial of freedom (Dworkin, 2000). This seems both philosophically and morally dubious and leaves open many troubling questions, the most obvious being, who decides what we have a right to do?

Gray demonstrates this problem in relation to Rawlsian – and therefore much liberal – thought.

> If [...] we accept that curbs on racist speech are not mere contourings of freedom of expression but instead restraints on it, we are compelled to confront the awkward fact that basic liberties make conflicting demands. They do so not just [...] in a few hard cases, but [...] quite frequently.
>
> One basic liberty clashes with another, or with the same basic liberty, or with important social values that are not basic liberties. The distinction between basic liberties and other values is not categorical. It is breached whenever one liberty clashes with another. In

order to resolve conflicts between basic liberties we must assess which liberty is most important. To do that we must consider their impact on society.

(Gray, 2000: 78)

It would be easy enough to restate a position of freedom that explicitly excluded fascist discourses, but it is not simply fascism that poses these problems for anarchists. As Antifa notes, 'While our major target is fascism, we must be aware that bigotry in all forms (racism, sexism, homophobia, etc) needs to be fought, whether it comes from the mouths of fascists or from elsewhere' ('Founding statement').

It is interesting that the list of *isms* in the quote above ends with *etc*. Unintentionally, it raises the crucial point: what other beliefs, discourses and practices are denied access to the anarchist community? If Antifa and other anarchists can use coercion and other – at times violent – means, often limiting individuals' freedom, and this is justified because those whose freedom is being denied are racists or sexists, what might we expect from anarchists in relation to other *isms* about which they disapprove? (To put it another way, at what point does it become meaningless, or woefully Orwellian, to talk of freedom at all?)

The term *speciesism* was coined by Richard Ryder to deliberately draw parallels between the way non-human animals are commonly understood as being morally inferior to humans and other isms, such as racism and sexism. The argument for animal rights is becoming more and more popular within the anarchist movement, and anarchist support for freedom is now frequently being understood to embrace non-human life; not just animals, but also the natural environment, are, according to increasingly prevalent discourses within the movement, to be accorded their own liberty (Torres, 2007). And many anarchist animal rights activists have conducted similar campaigns against 'animal abusers' as those cited above by anti-fascist campaigners. Once again, the freedom of those involved in the mistreatment and killing of animals – and the destruction of the natural environment – is implicitly over-ridden by the rhetoric and practices of many animal rights anarchists.

Yet unlike fascism, the very idea of speciesism, and with it the notion of freedom for non-human animals, is denied by many anarchists who continue to see no ethical problem in the taking of non-human life (Purchase, 1994). If animal rights activists now justify coercing corporations involved in animal abuse, there is no obvious reason why they should 'allow' *other anarchists* to adopt their own systems of non-human domination. What would meat-eating anarchists make of their doors being glued shut by animal rights activists? Would they consider this a denial of *their* freedom? Or would vegan anarchists be expected to respect the freedom of their omnivorous neighbours – and neglect that of the animals they currently feel justified in defending?

Presently there appear to be few signs of tension regarding this issue. The popularity of discourses opposing 'blueprints' or prescriptive positions of any kind allows anarchists the (admittedly important) space within which they can live, work and fight alongside people with whom they disagree on certain issues without having to consider how these relationships might work in a truly – or even more – anarchic society; yet as we have seen, anarchists already take strong and principled positions against certain actions which they believe to be fundamentally wrong. What distinguishes some actions from others? What allows some differences to be tolerated, and others to be actively opposed? Diversity has long been championed by anarchists, and it is increasingly placed at the heart of contemporary discourses (Maeckelbergh, 2009), but what does diversity mean exactly? Is it limitless, or are there boundaries outside of which diversity becomes division? Despite its regular evocation, diversity is, I will argue below, a term that, like freedom, is all too often used with all too little reflection.

7.5.1 Elements of freedom: Diversity

Its ability to embrace a 'diversity of tactics' was, according to many, one of the principal strengths of the alter-globalisation movement, with the slogan 'one no, many yeses' being widely used to give voice to this (Kingsnorth, 2004). Although this movement was by no means exclusively anarchist, anarchism was at 'the heart of the movement' (Graeber, 2002: 62; see also Epstein, 2001), and so the discourses that arose from it are a good indicator as to what many contemporary anarchists are thinking. Movement actors and contemporary anarchists emphasised diversity. Yet, as Chris Hurl (2005: 1) notes, 'While the anti-globalization movement is often celebrated for its apparent diversity, it often remains unclear how this diversity manifests itself in practice. The ambiguous boundaries of the movement serve to obscure its specific social relationships.'

One activist who embodies this tension is José Bové, an activist who became something of a celebrity within the movement for his direct action against McDonald's (Goaman, 2004: 173). McDonald's has become a classic target for anti-capitalist campaigners, but much of the rhetoric against it comes from an animal rights perspective. Bové, however, is a dairy farmer. Recognising the conflicts that freedom raises, a writer from the anarchist collective CrimethInc. (2000: 104) states that 'we must create a world in which everything that is possible is also desirable... there will be no reason for guilt, no possibility of hypocrisy or conflict between desires [...] a world empty of meat and dairy products.' What would happen to this diversity – and José Bové – if this author succeeded in realising her anarchist vision? Would Bové become a legitimate target for having his locks glued?

For the most part, these troubling questions are not even being asked, let alone answered. In fact, the rhetoric of diversity follows much the same pattern as that of the discourses of freedom: a great many strongly held views that diversity is to be championed, with little or no reflection as to what this in fact means, and, importantly, rarely any suggestion that notions of diversity are invariably limited in some way. Within the discourse of diversity, this naïveté is perhaps even more surprising than it is with regard to freedom, because the limits to diversity are often quite apparent – and so the topic of (at times heated) debates.

> The Dissent! Network also jumped through hoops to remain inclusive, albeit with mixed results. At almost every gathering there was a discussion of who should be allowed to participate in the Dissent! Network. Could Christians, who might be proselytising an authoritarian religion? How about members of organised political parties? What exactly were the limits and nature of the PGA hallmarks, and who did they include and exclude?
> (Trocchi et al., 2005: 66)

While these reflections may appear to demonstrate an awareness of the problems, in fact we often find that many in the movement are able to assure themselves that, having considered these difficult dilemmas, they have opted for the inclusive approach, and thus resolved any issues diversity may pose. Welcoming those beyond the line up of usual suspects, which means allowing Christians and Green Party members, for example, into the network has allowed a continued feeling of a movement committed to diversity. Graeber and Grubacic declare that anarchism has often 'celebrated [its] commitment [to negative] freedom as evidence of [its] pluralism, ideological tolerance, or creativity' (Graeber and Grubacic, 2004: 5). The obvious and necessary question, however, rarely seems to be asked: how far does this 'ideological tolerance' actually go?

In large-scale mobilisations and protests, which have been used to argue for the feasibility of anarchist ideals, this diversity was itself regulated.

> Activists sought to ensure the coexistence of multiple strategic and tactical standpoints through the segmentation of the space-time of the event, for example, different 'blocs' were exhibited in Prague, different zones or territories of protest in Québec City and different days of action in Genoa. And yet this segmentation has often not been upheld. The segmentation of space is contingent upon the power of groups to maintain boundaries.
>
> (Hurl, 2005: 2)

What does it mean when a movement committed to a policy of 'no borders' instigates 'boundaries' of its own volition? How do boundaries differ from borders? What does the need for segmentation suggest? Is it an effective way of ensuring diversity, or should it remind us of the fragility of these coalitions, and of the problematic nature of the diversity they supposedly embody?

> When faced with property destruction, many activists were quick to dissociate themselves, with some going so far as to form a human chain protecting Nike Town. On several occasions 'nonviolent' activists physically confronted activists engaging in property destruction. They publicly condemned these actions and called for the arrest of those involved. [...] The organizational form adopted by the Direct Action Network was unable to deal with groups that did not adhere to their guidelines. There was no mechanism in place to deal with difference.
>
> (Hurl, 2005: 2)

In fact, resistance to talking about 'the movement' as one coherent set of ideas and principles arises exactly from the recognition that there are diverse and often antagonistic elements within the broader whole; yet what this actually means for the notion of diversity remains elusive.

7.6 Self-enforcing decisions

The problems raised above are at times exacerbated when certain values held by dominant or majority groups have a wide-reaching impact, so that it becomes difficult to avoid the physical reality created by those values. The more car drivers there are in a community, for example, the more the physical and social environment change accordingly (Ward, 1991; Wolf, 1996). However, following Carole Pateman, the anarchist writer Robert Graham suggests that when a minority disagrees with the majority, the minority ought to be allowed to disobey: although communities may make decisions based on majority rule, contra the consensus process, favoured by many contemporary anarchists (Maeckelbergh, 2009), 'What the majority can not do is force the minority to obey its decisions' (Graham, 2004: 22). But this ignores the reality that, unless the minority leaves the community entirely, the minority will, with regard to many decisions, be seriously impacted by those decisions. A society that allows hard drug use does not force me to consume those drugs, but if I remain in that society, I have to live with the consequences of that policy. Put another way: how would I *disobey* such a policy? Simply not taking drugs is not to disobey, and, importantly, it would certainly not help me address my concerns about serious drug use in my community. And if I block any decision to allow such drug use, as I would be able to do if my community followed consensus, then those people who wanted to use drugs would be similarly affected.

One solution, which has been proposed by many contemporary activist anarchists, is that of relocation (Seeds for Change, 2007; Gordon, 2008: 69; Maeckelbergh, 2009: 226). There is not the space here to discuss this in any detail, but I would suggest that such an idea is sufficiently problematic to make the simple claim that this is not a viable solution. Can we really expect a minority of potentially thousands of people to simply pack up and leave a community that they have potentially lived in for years, generations even? Where would they move to? What would happen to their land, their buildings and their loved ones who stayed behind? These and many other questions make the idea of relocation an entirely inadequate response.

As inadequate as it is, however, it at least stems from an acknowledgement that, if communities can not agree on certain courses of action, conflicts will at times become unavoidable. This is precisely why contemporary activists place such an emphasis on consensus. As with Rawls, anarchists understand that without such a consensus, the imposition of certain values over others becomes a very real possibility. Sadly, consensus is only a viable solution if a real consensus can actually be reached; the argument made by myself here, and many others elsewhere, is that, very often, it cannot. Consensus is an outcome, rather than a solution. Though to be fair, activists emphasise that consensus is very much about the *process* – it is not, in other words, supposed to be simply about reaching a consensual outcome. While this is a valuable insight, I would maintain that it is nonetheless consensus *as outcome* which activists refer to when the need for coercion is denied.

What is perhaps most important to realise, however, is that what is all too often possible is the establishment of a *perception* of success: the belief that consensus has been achieved when in fact it has not, or when it has been reached in such a way that raises concerns about its ultimate value. There are obvious ways that this might occur, and practitioners of consensus are usually keenly aware of them: the manipulation of individuals, the withholding of certain information, and so on. But there are other, less obvious ways in which the process can be corrupted.

For Rawls, the consensus process was backed up by a set of basic liberties which could not be questioned. This was a pragmatic response, intended to make the overarching aim of consensus viable. While anarchists might now reject this idea when presented in such an explicit manner, we have already seen how certain beliefs and actions are readily denied. It seems reasonable to assume that many of the values held now by anarchists, such as a commitment to anti-fascism, would be carried into an anarchist community, thus becoming the guidelines for an anarchist set of basic liberties.

7.7 Conclusions: Embracing values

In this chapter, I have raised a number of concerns regarding the discourses of freedom articulated by anarchists. I have argued that, while these discourses are widespread, and profoundly and strongly held, there appears to have been little critical reflection regarding the problematic nature of freedom, as a moral, political and analytical concept. I have argued that this presents a serious problem for anarchism, because the difficulties posed by freedom are in fact considerable; I have outlined some of the criticism levelled at liberalism to demonstrate these problems and to show that they are not simply theoretical issues, and that they do not simply affect liberals. I have gone on to suggest that the response of liberal critics is to suggest that other values – or notions of the good life – are always brought into the equation – consciously or otherwise – when problems of rival freedoms arise. Finally, I want now to suggest briefly that anarchists (and possibly others of different political persuasions) must themselves be more conscious of the values they support and take a more honest approach to the inevitable limits of freedom.

However much we may try to maintain a culture of freedom, decisions will have to be made when freedoms and values conflict. We can ignore the dilemma this presents us with – as I have argued is often the case – or we can confront it. Either way, our values will come into play to help us decide which freedom to defend, and which to deny or restrict. What is surely needed then is much greater honesty and clarity about the values we want to see promoted, and those we take umbrage with. There is not the space here to discuss what those values might be, but in any case I am not convinced that we should look to one particular moral rubric for advice. While I think recent positions by Franks (this volume) and Todd May (1994) are no doubt useful for thinking about these difficult questions, what appears to be more important than *how* we justify our acts is that we *do* justify them, and that we do so not solely with reference to freedom. We need to be prepared to argue for our values, but this first means we need to acknowledge them openly; they are often hidden not only from others, but also from ourselves. And we may well find that we disagree with some of our own judgements when they are revealed to us more clearly. This will be a difficult process for people committed to allowing other people their freedom, but if we do it collectively and with honesty, it will not fail to be a more just response to the unavoidable dilemmas that life will continue to throw our way.

This, I would suggest, is in large part what activists mean when they argue that consensus is as much about process as it is about results. The question is, once we recognise that consensus may not always be reached, does using the consensus process have the same impact? Or does it run the risk of becoming a formality, a fraud even, in the way that many would suggest supposedly democratic institutions currently are? The answers to these questions, and indeed to many of the questions I have raised, are unclear; what does seem clear is that if we ignore them, we then most certainly run the risk of making many of the same mistakes as the liberal theorists do.

Bibliography

R. Amster (1998) 'Anarchism as moral theory: Praxis, property and the postmodern', *Anarchist Studies*, VI(ii): 97–112.

Antifa (2009) 'Founding statement', http://antifa.org.uk/foundstat.htm, date accessed: 20 January 2009.

M. Bakunin (1957) *Marxism, Freedom and the State* (London: Freedom Press).

G. Brenkert (1991) *Political Freedom* (London: Routledge).

J. H. Carens (2000) *Culture, Citizenship and Community* (Oxford: Oxford University Press).

Class War (1986) 'What do we do when the cops fuck off?', *The Heavy Stuff* II.
CrimethInc. (2000) *Days of War, Night of Love* (Sundyberg: Demon Box Collective).
S. Cullen (1993) 'Anarchy and the mad axe man', *The Raven*, VI(ii).
G. Curran (2006) *21st Century Dissent: Anarchism, Anti-Globalisation and Environmentalism* (Basingstoke: Palgrave).
Derbyshire Antifascists (2008) http://www.indymedia.org.uk/en/regions/nottinghamshire/2008/08/405243.html, date accessed: 20 August 2008.
R. Dworkin (2000) *Sovereign Virtue* (Cambridge: Harvard University Press).
B. Epstein (2001) 'Anarchism and the anti-globalization movement', *Monthly Review*, LIII(iv): no page reference. http://www.monthlyreview.org/0901epstein.htm, date accessed: 22 March 2008.
K. Goaman (2004) 'The anarchist travelling circus: Reflections on contemporary anarchism, anti-capitalism and the international scene' in J. Purkis and J. Bowen (eds) *Changing Anarchism* (Manchester: Manchester University Press).
U. Gordon (2008) *Anarchy Alive: Anti-Authoritarian Politics from Practice to Theory* (London: Pluto Press).
D. Graeber (2002) 'The new anarchists', *New Left Review*, XIII: 61–73.
D. Graeber and A. Grubacic (2004) 'Anarchism, or the revolutionary movement of the twenty-first century', ZNet, http://www.zmag.org/znet/viewArticle/9258, date accessed: 20 January 2009.
R. Graham (2004) 'Reinventing hierarchy: The political theory of social ecology', *Anarchist Studies*, XII(i): 16–35.
J. Gray (2000) *Two Faces of Liberalism* (New York: The New Press).
C. Hurl (2005) 'Anti-globalization and "Diversity of Tactics" ', *Upping the Anti*, I, http://uppingtheanti.org/node/1334, date accessed: 29 August 2008.
P. Kingsnorth (2004) *One No, Many Yeses* (London: The Free Press).
G. Klosko (2000) *Democratic Procedures and Liberal Consensus* (Oxford: Oxford University Press).
P. Kropotkin (1970) *Kropotkin's Revolutionary Pamphlets* (New York: Dover Publications).
W. Kymlicka (2002) 'Liberal individualism and liberal neutrality' in G. W. Smith (ed.) *Liberalism: Critical Concepts in Political Theory*, Volume III (London: Routledge).
M. Maeckelbergh (2009) *The Will of the Many: How the Alterglobalisation Movement Is Changing the Face of Democracy* (London: Pluto Press).
T. May (1994) *The Political Philosophy of Poststructuralist Anarchism* (University Park, PA: Pennsylvania State University Press).
S. Newman (2001) *From Bakunin to Lacan: Anti-Authoritarianism and the Disclocation of Power* (Oxford: Lexington).
Notes from Nowhere (eds) (2003) *We Are Everywhere* (London: Verso).
B. Parekh (2000) *Rethinking Multiculturalism: Cultural Diversity and Political Theory* (London: Macmillan Press).
C. Pateman (1979) *The Problem of Political Obligation* (Chichester: John Wiley and Sons).
G. Purchase (1994) *Anarchism and Environmental Survival* (Tucson: See Sharp Press).
J. Rawls (2001) *Collected Papers* (London: Harvard University Press).
H. Read (1947) *The Philosophy of Anarchism* (Freedom Press: London).

A. Ritter (1980) *Anarchism* (Cambridge: Cambridge University Press).
Seeds for Change (2007) 'Doing it without leaders' in Trapese Collective (ed.) *Do It Yourself* (London: Pluto).
K. Soper (1993) 'Postmodernism, subjectivity and the question of value' in J. Squires (ed.) *Principled Positions* (London: Lawrence and Wishart).
B. Torres (2007) *Making a Killing: The Political Economy of Animal Rights* (Edinburgh: AK Press).
A. Trocchi, G. Rewolf and P. Almaire (2005) 'Reinventing dissent! An unabridged story of resistance' in D. Harvie, K. Milburn, B. Trott and D. Watts Ben: Trocchi et al. (eds) *Shut Them Down: The G8, Gleneagles 2005 and the Movement of Movements* (Leeds: Dissent and Autonomedia).
J. Waldron (1989) 'Legislation and moral neutrality' in R. Goodin and A. Reeve (eds) *Liberal Neutrality* (London: Routledge).
N. Walter (1979) 'About anarchism' in H. Ehrlich, C. Ehrlich, et al. (eds) *Reinventing Anarchy* (London: Routledge and Kegan Paul).
C. Ward (1991) *Freedom to Go: After the Motor Age* (London: Freedom Press).
―― (2008) *Anarchy in Action* (London: Freedom Press).
W. Wolf (1996) *Car Mania: A Critical History of Transport* (Chicago: Pluto Press).
I. M. Young (1990) *Inclusion and Democracy* (New York: Oxford University Press).

Part III
Alternative Anarchist Ethics

8
Anarchism and the Virtues

Benjamin Franks

8.1 Introduction

This chapter has a number of aims: the first is to briefly sketch out standard philosophical approaches to anarchism ('philosophical anarchism') drawn from the arguments of Robert Paul Wolff (1976) and more recent critical synopses by Dudley Knowles (2007) and Jonathan Wolff (2006). This outline of philosophical anarchism concentrates on identifying the main ethical principles and the classification of the moral agent. The second feature of this chapter is that it explains and illustrates a distinctive alternative anarchist ethic ('practical anarchism'), which is consistent with the main features of contemporary activism and scholarship on anarchism, but which also draws on the historical canon, such as Emma Goldman, Peter Kropotkin and Errico Malatesta.

This practical anarchism differs from, and avoids the weaknesses of, philosophical anarchism and the usual consequentialist or deontological interpretations of anarchism. This practical anarchism grounded in the texts of the wider historical and contemporary radical movements is shown to be consistent with virtue ethics. To this end, the chapter compares practical anarchism with the account of the virtues found in Alasdair MacIntyre's influential text *After Virtue* (2006) to illustrate a high degree of consistency and correspondence between the two.

Finally to make the case that practical anarchism succeeds as a virtue theory it needs to respond to, and overcome, a number of challenges. These challenges are that virtue theory requires (i) law (*nomos*) and (ii) a teleology, which, some noted theorists argue, are incompatible with anarchism. The chapter shows that while these criticisms of the virtue account of anarchism have strong evidential support these presumed weaknesses can be overcome. The first is refuted by demonstrating that anarchism can support – and indeed requires – stable behaviour norms, though they are not fixed. The second criticism is contested, by showing that grand narratives of liberation are necessarily produced by participating in, and generating, virtuous practices. However, these *telē* are not reducible to a single version *telos*. Consequently, it is possible to provide a coherent and defensible alternative to standard philosophical accounts of anarchism based on a quasi-Kantian liberalism.

8.2 Standard philosophical approaches to anarchism

Many recent texts on anarchism start by highlighting the problems of interpreting the term (Kinna, 2005: 4–5; Clark, 2007: 1–2; McLaughlin, 2007: 25). Many texts distinguish particular versions of anarchism by identifying key principles, and then assessing their consistency, practicality or their underlying epistemological assumptions. The next section will demonstrate that an approach based on identifying anarchism through isolating universal necessary and sufficient conditions is too limiting and inflexible. The standard philosophical account of anarchism is explored in greater detail by other chapters in this volume (such as those by Paul McLaughlin and Samuel Clark), so this is just a sketch – along with one or two variants from Alan Carter (1989, 2000), and Hillel Steiner and Peter Vallentyne (2001) – in order to set up a contrast to a different, *practical* anarchism.

8.2.1 Philosophical individualist anarchism

Individualist anarchism is based on the rational sovereign subject, as identified in neo- or quasi-Kantian liberal political philosophy. It considers the fundamental feature of anarchism to be a rejection of coercion. As David Keyt explains, 'The rejection of political authority, which gives anarchism its name, is not the first principle of the theory but a corollary of its views about coercion and force' (Keyt, 2005: 204). It is quasi-Kantian, as Onora O'Neill points out, because Kant's notion of rational autonomy is towards acting only according to universal principles, while quasi-Kantianism has no limitations other than respecting the freedoms of others (2002: 35–40, 73–95). The essential characteristic of anarchism, according to Keyt, is the defence of negative liberty.

This is a definition of anarchism, shared by such grandees of British political philosophy as Jonathan Wolff (2006: 31) and Knowles (2007: 249), who also interpret it as proposing an absolute prohibition on coercion and permitting only voluntary association. Anarchism rejects government because state practices necessarily require coercive interference in the form of forced obedience to regulations to which the individual has not consented (Lovett, 2004: 86; Knowles, 2007: 23–4, 29, 43; Knowles, 2009). In the place of state practices anarchist individualists regard consensual market relationships as the ideal model for social interactions. The major exponents of these forms of anarchism have been Robert Paul Wolff (1976) and Robert Nozick (1988).

Robert Paul Wolff outlines a rejection of all political institutions that are not the result of actual consent: 'If all men have a continuing obligation to achieve the highest degree of autonomy possible, then there would be no state whose subjects have a moral obligation to obey its commands' (Wolff, 1976: 19). Only in the case of freely agreed to laws, passed unanimously, would respect for autonomy be preserved. Imposing a legal obligation onto a sovereign subject without their consent would be illegitimate (Wolff, 1976: 23–4, 26). As communities grow in size, unanimous decision-making through direct democracy becomes increasingly inefficient (Wolff, 1976: 69). As a result, Wolff concludes that standard liberal, democratic structures provide no practical basis for a legitimate state (Wolff, 1976: 69).

Instead, Wolff, like Nozick (1988: 50–3), posits ideal social relationships based on consensual contracts. Despite Wolff (1976: 77) identifying some problems with classical liberal economic relationships, in particular the exploitation and economic 'enslavement' of individuals with relatively little economic power, he nonetheless regards this financial dependency to be the result of the ability of monopolistic or oligarchical institutions, whether private or state-centred, to manipulate the economy. In smaller communities with federated structures, such manipulative economic power would, argues Wolff (1976: 81), be avoided, and thus 'voluntary economic co-ordination' would protect individual sovereignty.

Individualist anarchism, for the purpose of this chapter, is synonymous with right-libertarianism. This identity does ignore a significant difference between them, namely, as to whether contract enforcement and protection of borders should be left to a legitimate, spontaneous minimal/ultra-minimal state as right-libertarians believe (Nozick, 1988: 51–3), or whether these functions too should be privatised, as anarcho-capitalists prefer. However, the main features of individualist anarchism and right-libertarianism are the same: a commitment to the quasi-Kantian sovereign subject with its rejection of an overarching teleology, and a concomitant commitment to social relationships based on free contracts. This quasi-Kantian account will be shown to be inconsistent with much anarchist thought and practice, as there are forms of coercion which are consistent with an anti-hierarchical liberatory theory. In addition, I will argue that philosophical anarchism has an inadequate account of moral agency.

8.2.2 Philosophical social anarchism

In the recent philosophical literature Hillel Steiner and Peter Vallentyne's (2001; Vallentyne and Steiner, 2001; Vallentyne et al., 2005) 'left-libertarianism' has become a rival to dominant right-libertarian interpretations of anarchism. It should be noted that Vallentyne and Steiner use the term 'left-libertarian' differently to theorists such as Maurice Brinton (2005), and, more recently, Ruth Kinna (2005: 24–5). These latter writers identify the term with those who overtly employ Marxist economic analysis and agency, but reject the traditional Leninist role of the state as a set of apparatuses capable of transforming society in an anti-hierarchical direction. By contrast, both Vallentyne and Steiner's version of left-libertarianism and Nozickian right-libertarianism are tied to the principle of complete self-ownership. The difference is that while the Nozickian version extends rights over the person to include sovereignty over the products of labour and to possession of natural or previously commonly held resources (1988: 150–82), left-libertarianism rejects such extension of dominion over natural resources and artefacts (Vallentyne, 2001: 5–8). Left-libertarians consider the right-libertarian case for initial acquisition, and consequently justice through transfer, as being epistemologically suspect and morally unacceptable on the basis of egalitarian outcomes. As a result, left-libertarians seek collective control of unearned resources (Vallentyne, 2001: 1–2, 10–13). In their account, all that distinguishes left-libertarianism from traditional philosophical accounts of anarchism is approval for state (or quasi-state) institutions to initiate egalitarian outcomes or mitigate oppressive power relations.

Closely aligned to left-libertarianism is Alan Carter's (1989, 2000) analytical anarchism, which overtly borrows from the tradition of 'analytical Marxism' by G. A. Cohen (1979) and Jon Elster (1985). Analytical anarchism is also based on the model of liberal agents acting out of rational self-interest, albeit ones who face substantive material or economic restraints, but unlike individualist anarchism and right-libertarianism, Carter considers particular types of non-egalitarian outcome to be problematic, though they are subservient to political inequalities (Carter, 2000: 231).

Carter stands in contrast to other philosophers who discuss anarchism, such as Richard Dagger (2000), Knowles (2007), Christopher Wellman (2001: 753) and Wolff (1976), who concentrate only on questions of political power, and in particular the question of the legitimacy of political authority. Thus, they tend to either largely ignore economic power-relations, or minimally accept Lockean rights of transfer, and consequently tend to support right-libertarian interpretations of anarchism. However, Carter's analytical anarchism, like Knowles, Wolff and the right- and left-libertarians, concentrates on only two sets of operators or agents: the state and the individual. This apparently restrictive cast of moral agencies (or characters), which is a substantial feature of analytical approaches, is highlighted as one of the areas of difference for a virtue account of anarchism and analytical anarchism.

So, in contrast with philosophical anarchism, this chapter presents an account of anarchism which is critical of both quasi-Kantian and utilitarian genres of ethical theory. This alternative version (referred to as 'practical anarchism') will be shown to be consistent with MacIntyre's *After Virtue*. In referring to the virtue form of anarchism as 'practical anarchism', it is not to suggest that alternative philosophical accounts, such as individualist anarchism, are necessarily 'impractical', just as referring to a 'philosophical anarchism' is not proposing that alternatives are not ethically, epistemologically or ontologically grounded. The distinguishing signifier is used both to indicate that this version is based on the actual methods of contemporary activists and to highlight that virtues are based within social practices. This practical anarchism is also in accordance with some (but not all) core features of more contemporary (post)anarchist theorists from the likes of Todd May's (1994) *The Political Philosophy of Poststructuralist Anarchism* and more recent theorists in this field like Jason Adams (2003), Lewis Call (2003) and Saul Newman (2001).

8.3 Alternative approach: Practical anarchism

The anarchism defined here shares many of the characteristics of philosophical anarchism, especially the social versions, such as that offered by Carter. It differs in two major respects: first, it does not define anarchism in terms of necessary and sufficient conditions, but instead follows Michael Freeden's (1996) methodology. Freeden argues that as well as 'evaluating [...] validity, and [...] offering ethical prescriptions' (1996: 6), as is the standard for analytic political philosophy, it is also necessary to study and identify the inter-relationships of core and peripheral concepts, and to locate these concepts spatially and temporally, exploring the manner in which concepts shift historically from core to periphery (and vice versa) and subtly alter their interrelationships and their meanings. This is a move that is not as alien to political or moral philosophy as Freeden presumes, for as MacIntyre argues, virtue ethical approaches support the use of historical resources to understand and apply evaluative concepts, as opposed to the relatively recent ahistorical methods of analytic philosophy (MacIntyre, 2006: 4, 11).

In the main egalitarian forms of anarchism, which have long traditions, there are a number of core features which have remained stable. These features are consistent with aspects of Carter's definition, namely, that anarchism's main concern is to challenge social relationships and practices that enhance or sustain political inequalities, and in particular the concentrations of power that characterise state institutions. In addition these main forms of social anarchism are committed to challenging concentrations of economic power (whether embodied in private or state institutions) and also to achieve this through methods that embody (or prefigure) these goals. As a result, in order to resist economic or political hierarchies, it might be legitimate, contrary to Keyt's definition, for anarchists to use certain types of coercive force. This does not permit indiscriminate violence, despite this being the popular stereotype of anarchism (Knowles, 2002: 249), for the use of compulsion is only justified if it is used by the less-powerful against the more-powerful and the newly constructed relationship is less hierarchical than the original position and allows for further challenges to domination. Where such an intervention against the powerful, such as the Leninist revolutionary party's assault on Tsarism, merely (re)produces another substantive authoritarian structure, then, as illustrated by Brinton (2005: 293–378), a founder of the libertarian socialist group Solidarity, such methods are rejected by consistent anarchists.

Research into the anarchist-influenced revolutionary syndicalist and overtly anarcho-syndicalist unions of the early twentieth century demonstrates that in non-academic circles, the socialist tradition of anarchism has historically had more proponents than the libertarian right (see van der Linden and Thorpe, 1990). These groups explicitly reject concentrations of economic power as damaging to human well-being, and consequently are critical of capitalism. As Kropotkin explains, anarchism promotes for humankind the fullest possible development of all his [sic] faculties, intellectual, artistic and moral, without being hampered by overwork for the monopolists, or by the servility and inertia of mind of the great number. He would thus be able to reach full individualization, which is not possible either under the present system of individualism, or under any system of state socialism.

(Kropotkin, 1910)

Similarly, and more contemporarily, large-scale anti-capitalist movements have developed, which John Carter and David Morland identify as having as 'anarchist shift in both its ideas and its politics' (2004: 8). Even critics of Carter and Morland such as Mark Neocleous (2005: 48–50) acknowledge that anarchist principles are a significant features of these 'anti-globalisation' movements.

To avoid the replacement of economic hierarchies by political ones, anarchists reject formal state structures, and seek tactics that do not replicate existing, or produce new, detrimental power relations. This corresponds with the position advanced by contemporary (post)anarchists, like Adams, Call, May and Newman. They differ from the analytical approaches in that they view oppressive (and constructive) power as having no irreducible origin. Instead, like MacIntyre, they view the social world as being constructed out of intersecting social practices. With the absence of a single source of authority, whether the state (Alan Carter) or the economy's technological base (Cohen), there is no single site or form of resistance which takes universal priority. The anti-reductive account of power is not unique to contemporary (post)anarchists but can also be found in the works of Malatesta (1984: 155) and Jean Grave (Guérin, 1970: 81).

With no single source of oppressive power, there is no ultimate conflict, or final resolution. Thus, without fixed determinate ends, anarchists tend to advocate methods that are consistent with their goals, a process referred to as 'prefiguration', as the tactics used are supposed to encapsulate the values desired in their preferred goals (Purkis and Bowen, 2004: 220; Gordon, 2006: 172, 203). As will be discussed below, this prefigurative characteristic of creating and maintaining fulfilling social practices that are co-operative, non-hierarchical and generate or perpetuate similar activity is one of the characteristics which makes practical anarchism particularly congruent with virtue ethics.

A further feature of practical anarchism that distinguishes it from the deontological approaches concerns its analysis of agency. The agents of change are not the universal, abstract individuals of deontological anarchism, removed from their social context and asserting their universal, negative rights, but shifting collectives of the oppressed, who (attempt to) evade, challenge or transform oppressive social structures. What links the subjugated agencies to produce their own forms of resistance to hierarchical powers is not only certain similarities in the oppressive forces they seek to transform and thus comparable targets and methods, but often a shared narrative. This is not to say that an identical teleology exists across the range of anarchisms; indeed a careful reading would identify changes in the framing purpose of anarchism across its histories and social contexts. However, what joins most of the contexts in which anarchism developed are shared narratives promoting the autonomous actions of the oppressed to (albeit temporarily or incompletely) challenge, alleviate or avoid hierarchies and create more enriching social practices.

8.4 MacIntyre and the virtues

In order to illustrate that this distinctive account of anarchism is consistent with MacIntyre's virtue ethics, it is first necessary to describe MacIntyre's ethical theory. This includes examining the features of MacIntyre's critique of existing moral theories, as these illustrate the differences between philosophical anarchism and the virtue version (practical anarchism). Through defining and defending anarchism as a virtue certain flaws found in both anti-hierarchical and virtue ethics are identified, in particular adherence to a type of essentialism – a fixed determinant account of the human subject – that this contemporary practical anarchic virtue theory avoids.

MacIntyre provides one of the pivotal texts for re-establishing virtue ethics, and in particular, Aristotelian version, within Anglo-American philosophy (the term 'Anglo-American' primarily refers to the geographical location of philosophical institutions rather than a synonym for the analytical tradition). For instance, Rosalind Hursthouse (2002: 3) cites MacIntyre's works alongside those of Elizabeth Anscombe, Philippa Foot, Iris Murdoch, Bernard Williams, John McDowell, Martha Nussbaum and Michael Slote, as 'put[ting] virtue ethics on the map'. MacIntyre's social version of the virtues is also most consistent with political theory in that it concentrates on the *polis* (the wider arena of power relations), rather than on individual emotional states. While the *polis* can be hierarchically organised (as indeed many are) including Aristotle's ideal state, they need not be. It is in the realm of social activity that the virtues are realised and thus this is consistent with the practical version of anarchism. Virtue ethics that concentrates on subjective states of being would have more in common with the individualist anarchism of Leo Tolstoy and Henry Thoreau.

After Virtue makes the case for a social version of virtues ethics. It starts with the controversial hypothesis that the abandonment of Aristotelian traditions in philosophy and their replacement with an avowedly anti-teleological, 'liberal Enlightenment tradition' – a category wide enough to include utilitarianism, Kantianism, analytical moral philosophy, Emotivism, Existentialism and orthodox Marxism – led to a crisis in ethics. This predicament is evinced, claims MacIntyre (2006: 1–2, 10), by the incoherent use of the language of ethics and the increasingly irresolvable nature of contemporary debates (2006: 6–7). These symptoms are a result of the devastation wrought to social, political and ethical thinking by the Enlightenment.

Enlightenment scepticism about ultimate grounds (the absence of a fundamental teleology of ethics) produced two different responses in moral thinking. The first was the growth of ethics that totally rejected teleological accounts of ethics, such as Kantianism, which views all goal-driven approaches as diminishing sovereignty and being precursors to tyranny (MacIntyre, 2006: 142–3). The second form of Enlightenment scepticism was an often-incoherent replacement of grander teleologies with a banal humanism, based on goals such as 'general happiness' (MacIntyre, 2006: 62–4).

In the place of rationalistic Enlightenment moral thinking, MacIntyre advances a theory of virtues based on Aristotelian ethics. A virtue, for MacIntyre (2006: 191), 'is an acquired human quality the possession and exercise of which tends to enable us to achieve those goods which are internal to practices and the lack of which effectively prevents us from achieving any such goods'. A theory of the virtues thus has three main components:

1. Virtues are teleological; they are aimed at creating a better person ('man-as-he-could-be-if-he-realised-his-essential-nature') out of the raw material of man-as-he-happens-to-be (MacIntyre, 2006: 52).
2. As virtues are social traits, they are predicated on the existence of basic, absolute rules (*nomos*) that allow a society to form and grow; such commandments include an absolute prohibition on murder (MacIntyre, 2006: 152).
3. That virtues are as diverse as they are immanent to different social practices (although similar virtues or mixtures of virtues can be

involved in different contexts) (MacIntyre, 2006: 187–8). Traditions embody the development of these social practices (MacIntyre, 2006: 222–3).

While, as Christopher Toner (2006: 596, 601) and Hursthouse (2002: 25–6) note, some interpreters of virtue ethics view Aristotle as primarily an egoistic philosopher for whom the aim of life is 'self-improvement' and individual flourishing, MacIntyre (2006: 222), by contrast, stresses the social nature of the virtues. Virtues require a wider socio-historical context in which the acts gain their meaning. Social practices, in which these immanent values are realised, interconnect to create the wider social world. As a result, the more people engage in virtuous activities, the more their society transforms into a flourishing community (MacIntyre, 2006: 155–6); similarly, the exercise of vices will lead to societal decomposition (MacIntyre, 2006: 194–5).

While most critics of anarchism would (wrongly) assume that it is the second principle based on the requirement for *nomos* that would be most problematic for anarchism, it is the first that is most challenging. For in fact, as will be shown later, the second criterion does not necessarily imply commitment to a state-based legislature. The first criterion is a problem, as MacIntyre's resurrection of Aristotelian ethics has often implied not only an overarching narrative to all human action, but one potentially based on a biologically essentialist view of the human subject (2006: 148). This is problematic, as a fixed concept of what it is to be human is epistemologically suspect, as there seems to be no appropriate methodology for discovering what constitutes humanity's universal quintessence. Nor is there any agreement among those who commit to essentialism on what constitutes humankind's fundamental nature. Further, if there is a fixed definite human nature, then this would restrict the possibility of radical change.

8.5 Anarchism as a virtue ethic

The main philosophical accounts portray anarchism as a liberal, deontological theory. Even Keyt (2005: 204, 213), who addresses anarchism with respect to the rival Aristotelian ethical theory, still regards anarchism as primarily based on a rejection of coercion. However, in wider social and political theoretical circles anarchism has been viewed as primarily a consequentialist movement. This is because the justifications for the brief outbreak of terrorist activity in the late nineteenth century, often credited to the anarchists, were couched in ends-based terminology (see for instance Nechayev (1989)). It should be noted that Alan Carter, citing historians such as George Woodcock and James Joll, questions whether these attacks were carried out by anarchists (1999: 225). However, consequentialist anarchisms fall foul of the prefigurative principle, and an account of anarchism based on virtue ethics is therefore more consistent with the broad stretch of anarchist writings and tactics.

8.5.1 Prefiguration

The repudiation of strict consequentialism has been the key ethical difference between anarchism and other political philosophies emanating from the socialist tradition, such as orthodox Marxism. Anarchism has been especially critical of Leninism, as Lenin (1975: 31) often evaluated strategy using ends-based criteria in, for instance, his defence of parliamentary tactics. Leninism is regarded by both liberals, such as Isaiah Berlin and Karl Popper, and libertarian socialists, such as the bioethicist David Lamb, as inherently authoritarian (for Popper (1981) and Berlin (1984) on quasi-Kantian grounds, while for Lamb (1997) on Hegelian ones).

From the earliest splits in the socialist movement between the followers of Bakunin and those of Marx, this ethical distinction has been primarily viewed as one of the relationship between means and ends, rather than differences over the ends themselves. James Guillaume, a follower of Bakunin, offered a challenge to the orthodox Marxists that neatly sums up the difference between anarchism and the Marxist tradition: 'How could one want an equalitarian and free society to issue from authoritarian organisation? It is impossible' (Quoted in Bakunin, 1984: 7). The means used, considered Guillaume, must embody the values of the desired goals. This view is repeated more recently by a range of contemporary anarchist writers and activists, such as the Anarchist Federation (1992: 20); Gordon (2006: 103–18, 233–6); IM in *Black Flag* (2001: 20); and Purkis and Bowen (2004: 220).

The Leninist group the International Socialist Organisation also accept this distinction, claiming that anarchist tactics are deficient precisely because of the commitment to prefiguration: 'The error anarchism falls into is believing that the means to achieve a classless, stateless society themselves must prefigure the end result' (D'Amato, 2007). The prefigurative principle, that the methods used should embody the goals, rejects not just Leninist consequentialism but liberal deontology. Deontology distinguishes between means and ends, but with primacy going to the former (Kant, 2008: 70–1).

In place of standard deontological ethics, anarchist prefiguration parallels MacIntyre's account of the virtues. Virtues, for MacIntyre, serve the teleological function of assisting individuals to flourish (*eudaimonia*) and this requires (and sustains) the right sorts of social arrangements (2006: 148–9). Thus, as MacIntyre stresses, different virtues take priority in different contexts rather than uniform obedience to a single Kantian set of predetermined, universal regulations (2006: 46–7). This is in concord with the rejection, by anarchists, of singular, universal forms of political strategy.

Anarchist prefigurative methods are identifiable as they are the types of practices that would collectively build up to create their anti-hierarchical version of the flourishing society. However, the employment of such methods is not justified consequentially. Anarchists, for instance, employ anti-hierarchical forms of social interaction (for instance, in their formal methods of organisation) not because they will bring about their ends more quickly than centralised authoritarian political structures, but because they produce the very forms of social relationship, albeit in miniature, that they hope to achieve in the longer term. This corresponds directly with MacIntyre's interpretation of the virtues:

> It is of the character of a virtue that in order that it be effective in producing the internal goods which are rewards of the virtues it should be exercised without regard to consequences. For it turns out to be the case – and this is in part at least one more empirical factual claim – although the virtues are just those qualities which tend to lead to the achievement of a certain class of goods, nonetheless unless we practise them irrespective of whether in any particular set of contingent circumstances they will produce those goods or not, we cannot possess them at all.
>
> (MacIntyre, 2006: 198)

The virtues are immanently realised in context-specific practices, and thus require different types of behaviour depending on circumstances. This is also true of anarchist prefigurative tactics. The anarchist curtailment of hierarchy, which underpins their account of justice, benevolence and courage, is realised differently in different social settings through different actions. For instance, at times of substantial police surveillance, meetings may be less public and transparent than under less controlled or repressive circumstances, thereby prioritising protective camaraderie. In more open societies, anarchist behaviours stress inclusivity and accessibility.

Against the portrayal of MacIntyre's virtue account as being consistent with anarchism is the objection that his virtue ethics is tradition-dependent and therefore conservative. This conservatism, it is argued, is incompatible with anarchism's radical (even revolutionary) ambitions. The objection is right in so far as virtuous activity is dependent on the practices that individuals and groups are initiated into and brought up in, and traditions are constituted out of particular types of historically linked practices. These traditions provide the basis for rationality and the ideals applied to understanding and evaluating individual procedures (MacIntyre, 2001: 4; 2006: 185–6). However, anarchism can still be congruent with MacIntyre's virtue ethics. First because as MacIntyre makes clear, traditions are not fixed, but evolve as a result of conflicts and arguments, within and between practices, and even lead to radical alterations within traditions (MacIntyre, 2001: 12–13; see also Horton and Mendus, 1994: 12–13). The second reason is that traditions themselves might embody anti-hierarchical principles. Historians such as Eric Hobsbawm (1971), Peter Linebaugh (2006) and E. P. Thompson (1991) have traced the development of radical social identities formed by long-standing collective activity based on values incompatible (and in conflict) with liberal-capitalist policies.

More recent anti-hierarchical social relations also evolve in response to the changes they bring to the societies in which they occur: for instance, in the development of 'clowning', a tactic in which some activists dress up as jesting entertainers and then follow security officials during their surveillance operations, and with exaggerated mimicry satirise the state operatives' behaviours. This tactic developed as a result of the intensification of policing focussed on anarchists as a result of earlier prefigurative tactics. The clown's buffoonery defuses some of the intimidation associated with large-scale monitoring and control, hinders oppressive strategies and thus encourages creative anti-hierarchical protest (Commodore Koogie, 2005: 127–33; Corporal Clutter, 2005: 255; Kolonel Klepto and Major Up Evil, 2005: 243–54). This is in agreement with MacIntyre's general account of the virtues. He identifies that the practice of the virtues alters according to context, and virtuous behaviours alter the social domain (MacIntyre, 2006: 190–1). Such different and changing types of prefigurative tactic also require different types of agent (or character) coming to the fore and undergoing transformation as a result of their actions.

Prefiguration is not uniquely anarchist. More conservative political movements, such as the pro-hunting lobby, or even racist political organisations, might endorse prefigurative tactics. Reactionary prefigurative political behaviours might include the active intimidation of immigrants as part of a wider political campaign to marginalise or drive out minority groups. So a commitment to prefiguration could be regarded as a necessary but not sufficient condition for anarchism, but might be more usefully regarded as a more core and stable feature of anarchism than for alternative ideologies. While other movements might utilise prefigurative behaviours, they rarely do so consistently or overtly. A further difference between anarchist and non-anarchist prefiguration is in the goals attempted to be prefigured and the types of agents bringing them about.

8.5.2 Agency and reason

Like the virtues and associated social practices, prefigurative tactics are diverse and alter according to social context. As MacIntyre describes, all human actions take place within social settings, such as an institutional arrangement, which have a distinctive history. The setting or arena is the result of previous interactions, and the involvement of individuals shapes these activities and produces the agents' identities. The identities and practices, which are co-productive, are often stable, but they can – and do – change over time (MacIntyre, 2006: 207).

The different arenas in which social practices take place also intersect (Macintyre, 2006: 206–7). Thus the social domain is made up of an interconnecting network. This distinguishes virtue theory from, say, the analytical Marxists who view one form of power, in Cohen's (1978: 162) case the material productive forces (technology), to determine all social formations. Cohen's Marxism has but one source of determining oppressive power: the material productive forces. Cohen's analysis either suggests that nothing can overcome this determining power (and thereby promotes acquiescence and passivity) or prioritises specific arenas of resistance (those engaged in overcoming or disrupting such developments) and particular types of agency (the proletariat).

A similar situation arises with analytical anarchism. This replaces Cohen's techno-primacy with state-primacy, in which the social world is the product of one determining power, namely, the apparatus of the state (Carter, 1989, 2000). This, too, either results in stasis, as nothing can overcome the determining forces, or creates just one type of agent (or character) capable of contesting this oppression: those in privileged positions to disrupt the state. Orthodox (and analytical) Marxism and analytical anarchism are incompatible with MacIntyre's virtue theory because of their fixed and unitary account of agents and settings.

Some postanarchists, such as Call (2002: 21) and Newman (2001), similarly criticise classical anarchism for its reductivist approach of seeing all oppressions emanating from a singular source. Yet this portrayal of earlier anarchists is highly questionable. Many early anarchists, like Grave (Quote in Miller, 1984: 131) and Malatesta (1984: 154), rejected the view that there was one strategic, central form of oppression and thus rejected the view that there was one central locus of resistance. As a result, they did not consider that one agent had a universally privileged position to overcome oppression on behalf of everyone else.

Acting on behalf of others (often without consent) is a form of paternalism, which is a form of hierarchy that anarchists have continually rejected. Much libertarian socialist criticism of orthodox Marxism has been addressed in terms of the latter's paternalistic approach to the economically oppressed. Lenin has been criticised for seeing all oppressions as economic and thus either the proletariat take priority in resolving all other social oppressions, which are merely epiphenomena – or that all oppressions can be analysed and strategically managed by the revolutionary party (see for instance May, 1994: 21; Brinton, 2004: 41–50). Instead, anarchism requires that the oppressed themselves take primacy in resisting and transforming subjugating forces. In some contexts, one type of identity might well take priority. In a racist environment, those who are subjected to discrimination would take precedence in transforming the prejudicial social arena, but this agent becomes secondary in contexts where oppression is primarily gender-based or economically based.

These differing oppressed identities take primacy as the moral agents of change. Because of the divergent forms of control and the particular types of moral subject, diverse prefigurative methods are required. No single form of response will be uniformly suitable across the domain of anti-hierarchical activity; nor does any single type of person, or character, form the sole model for moral action. This corresponds with the account of intersecting, albeit distinctive, settings which is a necessary feature of MacIntyre's Aristotelian virtue ethics. Both MacIntyre and the (post)anarchists hold that there is no universal account of the social world; each narrative is a product of (and produced by) the intersection of settings. Thus there are different types of rationality and different types of agent in each setting (May, 1994: 117–18; MacIntyre, 2001: 8; Newman, 2001: 78–80). Absolute relativism is avoided because of similarities between apparently different contexts and because different settings intersect, allowing for agreement and meaningful criticism (Horton and Mendus, 1994: 12; MacIntyre, 2001: 351–3).

MacIntyre's critique of moral thinking since the Enlightenment concerning moral agency is also in agreement with contemporary (practical) anarchism, with respect to a rejection of a single agency of change. Enlightenment morality is criticised by MacIntyre because in the form of either utilitarianism or (quasi-)Kantian deontology, it posits a single universal model of moral agency: in utilitarianism, the rationally calculating pleasure-centred individual and in liberalism, whether in its Rawlsian or Nozickian forms, the rational sovereign subject (MacIntyre, 2006: 62). Analytic Marxism (and analytical anarchism) is open to the same censure on account of its limited selection of moral agents: liberal, possessive individuals and state bureaucracies (MacIntyre, 2006: 33–4).

MacIntyre advances a number of powerful criticisms against analysing ethical dilemmas and promoting moral positions using the liberal model. The first set of criticisms is epistemological, in that they undermine Kant's claims to irrefutable moral principles derived from universal reason. MacIntyre contends that the identification of the universal, rational liberal subject as the sole model for moral agency is inadequately defended, and in the absence of any ethical teleological account for this model, an epistemological defence is all that could be offered. Second, because quasi-Kantian rationalism rejects a teleological account, its ethical pronouncements are either incoherent or detrimental to human welfare. These two criticisms run together in MacIntyre's assault on Kant's ethics.

There is a presumption in (quasi-)Kantian liberalism merely that the sovereign subject is one who uses universal reason. Yet as MacIntyre demonstrates in *Whose Justice? Which Rationality?*, there is no single universal rationality, but that reason is a product of various histories (2001: 9). Consequently, Kant's account of a pure, universal and rational ethic fails. MacIntyre shows that even Kant's fundamental maxim, 'treat people not solely as a means to an end, but an end in-themselves,' is non-universal as there are also rational alternatives to treating individuals as sovereign entities. MacIntyre's example is that an alternative maxim, 'treat only me as an end and everyone else as a means,' could also be universalised. It is conceivable that we could have a world of egoists, a plausible, if not particularly pleasant, possible world (MacIntyre, 2006: 46).

The 'rational' basis for Kant's universal rational doctrines is more apparent than real. The claims to universal rights based on individual sovereignty are inconsistent as no such universals have been discovered, nor could be discovered as our conceptual apparatus, including the terminology of rational analysis, is always partial and context-dependent (MacIntyre, 2006: 264–5). Indeed, when Kantians attempt to apply their universal theoretical framework they come up with different, albeit often deeply conservative, moral conclusions (MacIntyre, 2006: 48–9). Such inconsistency in Kant's rational system, plus its inability to resolve pressing social dilemmas which alternative moral arrangements can satisfy (MacIntyre, 2006: 152–3), indicts Kantianism as failing the test for being a practical ethic (MacIntyre, 2006: 23).

As a result, non-analytical anarchism shares characteristics of MacIntyre's virtue ethics, namely, rejecting the standard Enlightenment moral positions of consequentialism and deontology. Also both view moral action as involving the transformation of individuals and their social settings. In addition, anarchism and communitarian virtue ethics require a context-dependent understanding (*sophia*) of the manner in which social settings develop and change (MacIntyre, 2006: 155). However, there are two apparent challenges that can be made which suggest areas of disparity between MacIntyre and the anarchism identified here. The first is the legalistic challenge based on MacIntyre's view that the virtues require a consistent adherence to strict social regulation, which appears to be incompatible with anarchism's rejection of the state and state sanction. The second is the question of the biologically determined teleology that is the basis for MacIntyre's description of Aristotle's account of the virtues.

8.6 The legalistic challenge

The first challenge to the thesis that there is a cogent case for a virtue account of anarchism consistent with MacIntyre is based on the view that Aristotelian ethics requires a respect for social norms (*nomos*). These are the fundamental rules which allow societies to develop and function (MacIntyre, 2001: ix; 2006: 151). So for a practice (the venue of virtues) to flourish, certain independently identifiable norms have to be accepted. 'A practice involves standards of excellence and obedience to rules as well as achievement of goods' (MacIntyre, 2006: 190). These laws are not equivalent to the virtues, nor are virtues only practised in relation to these unqualified standards (MacIntyre, 2006: 235). It is necessary but not sufficient to follow this set of prescriptions in accord with the virtues, that is to say, to meet the general principles for communal activity wisely, benevolently and courageously. For example, in setting up any community or project, such as an arts association, a hospital or a radical labour syndicate, certain agreed rules are required that are applicable to all involved, such as protecting the lives of participants, and dealing honestly with other members of the group. However, other values are specific to the function and traditions of these projects, such as the development of compassionate and knowledgeable medical expertise in the case of the healthcare institution, or trustworthy, democratic advice in the case of the union.

The problem charged at anarchists is not with the latter type of immanent values, inherent to the practices (MacIntyre, 2006: 195), but as Clark notes (2007: 78–9), with the notion of enforceable general standards, as it is widely (but wrongly) assumed that this constitutes, or requires, state apparatus, and as such conflicts with anarchism's fundamental rejection of the state. However, such an objection to anarchism is misconceived, according to Clark (2007: 78) and the anarchist anthropologist David Graeber (2004: 65–8), as it mistakes the state for society. For the maintenance of fundamental social principles does not require, *contra* Thomas Hobbes, centralised or institutional arrangements. It is not just theoretically conceivable, but as Kropotkin, Graeber and Clark separately demonstrate, it is practically possible to have communities maintaining the basic principles that allow societies to arise and prosper, in a co-operative, non-hierarchical manner.

Clark draws upon a number of historical and anthropological sources to illustrate his central tenet that the maintenance of functioning, sustainable social networks does not require the presence of a centralised state or permanent structures of dominance. Clark (2007: 109–37) cites the examples of autonomous organisations outside and/or against the state, such as the libertarian militias and communities during the Spanish Civil War and, like the anarchist geographer Kropotkin (1910), he points to non-industrial societies, like the Nuer, to illustrate that sustainable societies do not require a state. Indeed, Clark (2007: 95, 103–7) makes a stronger proposition that centralised states actually inhibit the maintenance of fundamental norms such as the protection of life and basic liberties.

Clark's account of the advantages of anti-state, co-operative formations over contemporary state-based structures echoes MacIntyre's criticisms of the institutional arrangements prioritised by Enlightenment thinking.

> For liberal individualism a community is simply an arena in which individuals each pursue their own self-chosen conception of the good life, and political institutions exist to provide that degree of order which makes such self-determined activity possible. Government and law are, or ought to be, neutral between rival conceptions of the good life of man, and hence, although it is the task of government to promote law-abidingness, it is on the liberal view no part of the legitimate function of government to inculcate any one moral outlook.
>
> (MacIntyre, 2006: 195)

As a result, unlike pre-modern societies with weaker central state functions, post-Enlightenment societies are increasingly run on instrumentalist lines, which strengthen the powers of the bureaucrats who are central to the arbitration of continually arising disputes. It is only in modern societies that we regard the key social players to be split into one or other class of either the 'sovereign individual' or the 'state bureaucrat' (MacIntyre, 2006: 34–5). Instead, MacIntyre, like Kropotkin and Clark, sees practical contrary evidence in pre-modern societies, with weak states, of social institutions maintaining traditions constituted out of virtuous practices (MacIntyre, 2006: 165–6). Unlike Kropotkin and Clark, MacIntyre makes no claims to them embodying anti-hierarchical characteristics, though this possibility is not ruled out in his account. Nonetheless, any objection that anarchism is incompatible with MacIntyre's virtue ethics because of the importance MacIntyre places on the prior maintenance of necessary, but not sufficient, social rules fails because the acceptance of such rules is consistent with anarchism. There is, however, a second challenge to identifying anarchism with virtue theories. Virtue ethics requires a *telos* by which values are judged, and with which to assess competing options. In MacIntyre, as well as in Aristotle, the *telos* is based on an essentialist account of the human subject (MacIntyre, 2006: 54–5). Essentialisms are viewed by contemporary anarchist theorists like Call, May and Newman as inconsistent with anarchism, as it reasserts hierarchy and limits freedom.

8.7 The teleological challenge

In Aristotle's account of the virtues, according to MacIntyre, humans have a specific nature, which provides the *telos* for right actions. The good life is consequently defined in terms of those practices that permit and encourage the full development of these particular human qualities (MacIntyre, 2006: 162). Thus, those without the appropriate characteristics, whether by deficiencies of breeding or external forces that have blunted or destroyed these essential human capacities, are only capable of being inferiors – which for Aristotle includes women, slaves and Barbarians (MacIntyre, 2006: 158–60).

There is much that can be said in reply. One flawed set of replies propose a teleology based on a benign essentialism, in which individuals are essentially good. This is an account often ascribed to anarchism, especially the classical anarchist tradition, both by analytical political philosophers like Jonathan Wolff (2006: 30) and Knowles (2002: 249) and by postanarchists like May (1994: 62–5) and Newman (2001: 38–49). The problem with the benign essentialist theory is twofold. First, it is not the case that it is characteristic of anarchism to assume an essentialism, as Jesse Cohn and Shawn Wilbur (2003) have pointed out. Kropotkin, who is most often associated with benign essentialism, was actually critical of the view, arguing that people have both social and selfish instincts, and that neither is necessarily the main determinant (1992: 32–61). Goldman highlights how social forces can limit and shape human potential, that it is pointless to speak of human nature as the determining force (1969: 62). Malatesta also considers essentialist explanations to be a product of intellectual 'laziness', arguing that instead people have conflicting drives, and that it takes purposive action to generate co-operative arrangements (1984: 73–5).

The second problem with the benign essentialism defence is that it does not resolve the problems inherent within such accounts that they deny (or severely restrict) human agency and freedom, and also maintain social hierarchies, both of which are incompatible with anarchism. Teleological accounts necessarily prioritise those individuals who can best meet these preset, unchangeable standards. By restricting goals to forces beyond human control, teleological accounts curtail the possibility of radical change.

Instead, practical anarchism rejects essentialism. Though this then leaves another problem, for how can the claim be substantiated that anarchism is a virtue ethic of the type described by MacIntyre, if it rejects essentialism and essentialisms are necessary for virtues? If virtue ethics, as MacIntyre suggests, requires a teleology in order to resolve situations in which virtues appear to conflict (MacIntyre, 2006: 202–3), and anarchism rejects essentialism (as a basis for the wider framework or narrative by which social practices and their inherent virtues become intelligible), then this would appear to nullify anarchism's position as a virtue theory. However, this difficulty is resolvable, and in a manner consistent with MacIntyre's approach.

MacIntyre provides a historical examination of the different forms of virtue ethics starting with the Homeric, through the Aristotelian and then the early and later Christian traditions. From this chronological study he concludes that 'one of the features of the concept of a virtue which has emerged [...] is that it always requires for its application the acceptance of some prior account of certain features of social and moral life in terms of which it has to be defined and explained' (MacIntyre, 2006: 186). For instance, in the Homeric tradition a virtue was understood in terms of what enabled individuals to fulfill their social roles; in the Aristotelian one, it was guided by the endpoint of creating the good society in which humanity could properly satisfy its unique biological characteristics; for Christians, it was the training of the human character to meet the model prescribed by divine law (MacIntyre, 2006: 163–8, 186). What all these different accounts of the *telos* have in common is the presence of *a* teleology, not the same teleology. What is more, as MacIntyre's historical account develops, the *telos* develops and changes over time (and geography) as a result of its reciprocal relationship with intersecting practices. Such an account is consistent with practical anarchism.

Consistent anarchists agree with MacIntyre. They share a similar perspective, that the social world is constructed out of intersecting social practices with their own histories and traditions (May, 1994; Morland, 2004: 26; MacIntyre, 2006: 146). The setting for one type of moral practice will have connections to a setting for different types of practice. For MacIntyre, the common elements between the contexts are those that tend towards the same sorts of goal. They are the components of a shared unifying narrative, albeit one capable of change (MacIntyre, 2006: 215–16). Anarchists too view a wider historical narrative being formed by, and forming, social practices. As the postanarchist May explains, 'history is to be understood as a more or less contingent intersection of practices' (1994: 89), where anarchist practices are the methods which challenge hierarchical behaviour (1994: 117).

Anarchism is therefore best understood as a relatively recent historical phenomenon, arriving out of, and in conflict to, the routines of industrial capitalism. A number of historians have identified Wat Tyler and the Peasants' Revolt (Everett, n.d.), Gerard Winstanley's English Civil War Diggers (Woodcock, 1975: 443), the Chartists (Quail, 1978: xi) and the religious radicals of the Medieval period (Marcus, 1989: 91–2; Cohn: 1993) as precursors and anticipators to anarchism. However, anarchism primarily has been a product of, and a response to, the institutions and social and economic relations of industrial liberalism, and in other parts of the globe, as Benedict Anderson (2005) analyses, a response to the corresponding forms of colonialism.

Anarchism is not a homogeneous totality, but is produced in, and by, a network of intersecting practices that initially arose in response to conflicts within late-feudal/early-capitalist communities. Anarchism is thereby formed by the collation of these critical responses to social hierarchies, and thus produces a meaningful narrative of liberation. Thus we see a vast range of practices which contest hierarchy in a prefigurative fashion, yet interconnect to form anarchist narratives. These narratives are open to question and revision but, contemporarily, it is this framework of the oppressed themselves overcoming their subjugation which provides a teleology for current anarchism and is required to understand their tactics and modes of organisation. As a result, the anarchist teleology that informs the settings is a product of, and is produced by, the movement between different practices. Just as MacIntyre notes, the narratives of individual lives interact and build to create different accounts and new meanings, but without these meta-frameworks actions lack significance (2006: 218).

8.8 Conclusion

This chapter has concentrated on describing the main features of anarchism by presenting it in a manner distinct from the main academic ethical accounts. Standard versions, whether in the form of analytical anarchism or in the form of philosophical anarchism, have tended to view anarchism as a subset of liberal, moral theory. The disadvantages of these conceptual approaches are that they overlook the challenge to liberalism that anarchism poses, de-historicise its debates and ignore the particular account of agency and its distinguishing characteristic of adherence to *prefigurative* tactics. Instead, anarchism is best considered as a social virtue theory compatible with the format developed by MacIntyre. While there appear to be some problems with interpreting anarchism as an Aristotelian theory, namely, the importance in virtue theory of respecting important general norms and a teleology based on biological essentialism, such difficulties can be overcome. Respect for the principles necessary for a community to form and develop does not require a permanent, centralised set of hierarchical institutions, nor does a framing teleology have to be external and inflexible. None of this demonstrates that anarchist virtue ethics is superior to all other moral theories, nor without its own methodological and epistemological flaws. Further work is also required to identify which virtues are compatible with practical anarchism (the place, or otherwise, of contentious virtues such as concern for animals, patriotism and modesty). What I hope has been defended is the proposition that a virtue approach to anarchism is coherent and plausible and, in addition, illustrated its advantages over existing accounts of anarchism in the main, contemporary philosophical literature.

Bibliography

J. Adams (2003) *Nonwestern Anarchisms* (npl: Zabalaza Books), also available at: http://www.geocities.com/ringfingers/nonwesternweb.html.
―― (2009) 'Postanarchism in a bombshell', *Aporia Journal*, II, http://aporiajournal.tripod.com/postanarchism.htm, date accessed: 19 June 2009.
Anarchist Federation (1992) 'Direct action', *Organise!*, XXVI: 20.
B. Anderson (2005) *Under Three Flags* (London: Verso).
M. Bakunin (1984) *Marxism, Freedom and the State* (London: Freedom Press).
I. Berlin (1984) 'Historical inevitability' in *Four Essays on Liberty* (Oxford: Oxford University Press).
M. Bookchin (1995) *Social Anarchism or Lifestyle Anarchism* (Edinburgh: AK Press).
M. Brinton (2004) *For Workers' Power* (Edinburgh: AK Press).
L. Call (2003) *Postmodern Anarchism* (Lanham: Lexington Books).
A. Carter (1989) 'Outline of an anarchist theory of history', in D. Goodway (ed.) *For Anarchism* (London: Routledge).
―― (1999) *A Radical Green Political Theory* (London: Routledge).
―― (2000) 'Analytical anarchism: Some conceptual foundations', *Political Theory*, XXVIII(ii): 230–53.
J. Carter and D. Morland (2004) 'Anti-capitalism: Are we all anarchists now?' in J. Carter and D. Morland (eds) *Anti-Capitalist Britain* (Cheltenham: New Clarion Press), 8–28.
S. Clark (2007) *Living Without Domination: The Possibility of an Anarchist Utopia* (Aldershot: Ashgate).
G. Cohen (1978) *Karl Marx's Theory of History* (Oxford: Clarendon).
J. Cohn and S. Wilbur (2003) 'What's wrong with postanarchism?', *From the Libertarian Library*, 8 July 2007, http://libertarian-library.blogspot.com/2007/07/cohn-and-wilbur-whats-wrong-with.html, originally published *Institute of Anarchist Studies* (2003), date accessed: 25 June 2009.

N. Cohn (1993) *The Pursuit of the Millennium* (London: Pimlico).
Commodore Koogie (2005) 'Private parts in the general mayhem' in D. Harvie, K. Milburn, B. Trott and D. Watts (eds) *Shut Them Down* (Brighton: Autonomedia), 127–33.
Corporal Clutter of CIRCA (2005) 'Operation splish splash splosh' in D. Harvie, K. Milburn, B. Trott and D. Watts (eds) *Shut Them Down* (Brighton: Autonomedia), 243–52.
Paul D'Amato (2007) 'Is all organization authoritarian?', *Socialist Worker Online*, 9 March, http://socialistworker.org/2007-1/622/622_10_Authoritarian.shtml, date accessed: 22 June 2009.
R. Dagger (2000) 'Philosophical anarchism and its fallacies: A review essay', *Law and Philosophy*, XIX: 391–406.
J. Elster (1985) *Making Sense of Marxism* (Cambridge: Cambridge University Press).
M. Everett (n.d.) *A Short History of Political Violence* (London: Anarchist Communist Federation).
M. Freeden (1996) *Ideologies and Political Theory* (Oxford: Oxford University Press).
E. Goldman (1969) 'Anarchism: What it really stands for' in *Anarchism and Other Essays* (New York: Dover).
U. Gordon (2006) *Anarchism and Political Theory*, PhD Thesis, Mansfield College, Oxford University, available at http://ephemer.al.cl.cam.ac.uk/~gd216/uri/, date accessed: 22 June 2009.
D. Graeber (2004) *Fragments of an Anarchist Anthropology* (Chicago: University of Chicago Press).
D. Guérin (1970) *Anarchism* (New York: Monthly Review Press).
T. Hobbes (1976) *Leviathan* (Glasgow: William Collins).
E. Hobsbawm (1971) *Primitive Rebels* (Manchester: Manchester University Press).
J. Horton and S. Mendus (1994) 'Alasdair MacIntyre: *After Virtue* and after' in P. Johnston (ed.) *After MacIntyre* (London: Polity), 1–15.
R. Hursthouse (2002) *On Virtue Ethics* (Oxford: Oxford University Press).
IM (2001), 'From riot to revolution', *Black Flag*, CCXXI: 20–4.
P. Johnston (1993) (ed.) *After MacIntyre: A Critical Assessment of the Historical Method of Value Inquiry* (London: Polity).
I. Kant (2008) *The Moral Law: Groundwork to the Metaphysics of Morals* (London: Routledge).
D. Keyt (2005) 'Aristotle and anarchism' in R. Kraut and S. Skultety (eds) *Aristotle's Politics* (Oxford: Rowan and Littlefield), 203–22.
R. Kinna (2005) *Anarchism: A Beginner's Guide* (Oxford: Banbury).
Kolonel Klepto and Major Up Evil (2005) 'The Clandestine Insurgent Rebel Clown Army goes to Scotland via a few other places' in D. Harvie, K. Milburn, B. Trott and D. Watts (eds) *Shut Them Down* (Brighton: Autonomedia), 243–54.
D. Knowles (2002) *Political Philosophy* (London: Routledge).
——— (2007) 'The domain of authority', *Philosophy*, LXXXII: 23–43.
——— (2009) *Political Obligation and the Duties of the Citizen* (London: Routledge).
P. Kropotkin (1910) 'Anarchism', *The Encyclopaedia Britannica*, available online at http://dwardmac.pitzer.edu/Anarchist_Archives/kropotkin/britanniaanarchy.html, date accessed: 18 May 2008.
——— (1992) *Ethics* (Montreal, Canada: Black Rose).
D. Lamb (1997) 'Libertarian socialism: Means and ends', *Animal*, I; available at http://libcom.org/library/libertarian-socialism-dave-lamb, date accessed: 24 December 2009.

V. Lenin (1975) 'Left-Wing' Communism, An Infantile Disorder (Peking, China: Foreign Languages Press).
P. Linebaugh (2006) *The London Hanged* (London: Verso).
J. Locke (1998) *Two Treatises on Government* (Cambridge: Cambridge University Press).
F. Lovett (2004) 'Can justice be based on consent', *Journal of Political Philosophy*, XII(ii): 79–101.
A. MacIntyre (2001) *Whose Justice? Which Rationality?* (Gloucester: Duckworth).
—— (2006) *After Virtue*, 2nd edn (London: Duckworth).
E. Malatesta (1984) *Errico Malatesta – His Life and Ideas*, ed. V. Richards (London: Freedom Press).
G. Marcus (1989) *Lipstick Traces* (London: Secker and Warburg).
T. May (1994) *The Political Philosophy of Poststructuralist Anarchism* (Pennsylvania: Pennsylvania State University Press).
—— (1995) *The Moral Theory of Poststructuralism* (Pennsylvania: Pennsylvania State University Press).
P. McLaughlin (2007) *Anarchism and Authority: A Philosophical Introduction to Classical Anarchism* (Aldershot: Ashgate).
D. Miller (1984) *Anarchism* (London: Dent).
—— (1993) 'Virtues, practices and justice' in P. Johnston, ed. *After MacIntyre* (London: Polity), 245–64.
D. Morland (1997) *Demanding the Impossible?* (London: Cassell).
—— (2004) 'Anti-capitalism and poststructuralist anarchism' in J. Purkis and J. Bowen (eds) *Changing Anarchism* (Manchester: Manchester University Press), 23–38.
S. Nechayev (1989) *Catechism of the Revolutionist* (London: Violette Nozieres Press and Active Distribution).
M. Neocleous (2005) 'Shit, it's the police' in *Radical Philosophy*, CXXX: 48–50.
S. Newman (2001) *From Bakunin to Lacan* (Oxford: Lexington Books).
R. Nozick (1988) *Anarchy, State and Utopia* (Oxford: Basil Blackwell).
O. O'Neill (2002) *Autonomy and Trust in Bioethics* (Cambridge: Cambridge University Press).
K. Popper (1981) 'Prediction and prophecy in the social sciences' in *Conjectures and Refutations* (London: Routledge and Kegan Paul).
J. Purkis and J. Bowen (2004) 'Conclusion: How anarchism still matters' in J. Purkis and J. Bowen (eds) *Changing Anarchism* (Manchester: Manchester University Press).
J. Quail (1978) *The Slow Burning Fuse* (London: Paladin).
H. Steiner and P. Vallentyne (eds) (2001) *The Origins of Left-Libertarianism* (Basingstoke: Palgrave Macmillan).
E. P. Thompson (1991) *The Making of the English Working Class* (Harmondsworth: Penguin).
C. Toner (2006) 'The self-centeredness objection to virtue ethics', *Philosophy*, LXXXI: 595–617.
P. Vallentyne (2001) 'Introduction: Left-libertarianism – A primer', in P. Vallentyne and H. Steiner (eds) *Left-Libertarianism and Its Critics* (Basingstoke: Palgrave Macmillan).
P. Vallentyne and H. Steiner (eds) (2001) *Left-Libertarianism and Its Critics* (Basingstoke: Palgrave Macmillan).

P. Vallentyne, H. Steiner and M. Otsuka (2005) 'Why left-libertarianism is not incoherent, indeterminate, or irrelevant: A reply to Fried', *Philosophy and Public Affairs*, XXXIII(ii): 201–15.

M. van der Linden and W. Thorpe (eds) (1990) *Revolutionary Syndicalism* (Aldershot: Scolar).

S. Villon (2003) 'Post-anarchism or simply post-revolution', originally found at http://www.geocities.com/kk_ab%20acus/other/postanarc%20hism.html, link no longer operative.

C. Wellman (2001) 'Towards a liberal theory of political obligation', *Ethics*, CXI(vi): 735–59.

J. Wolff (2006) *An Introduction to Political Philosophy*, revised edition (Oxford: Oxford University Press).

R. Wolff (1976) *In Defence of Anarchism* (London: Harper Torchbooks).

G. Woodcock (1975) *Anarchism* (Harmondsworth: Penguin).

9
Green Anarchy: Deep Ecology and Primitivism

Elisa Aaltola

Radical environmental discourse often contains anarchic elements. These elements include criticism of authoritarian politics and capitalism and an emphasis on collectivism, individual freedom and self-fulfilment. These anarchic tendencies have increasingly led to the use of the term 'green anarchism'. This chapter investigates two versions of radical environmental discourse, which have included, or have been used to support, ideas familiar to green anarchism: deep ecology and primitivism. The aim is to bring forward their main premises, explore the similarities between the two, examine the criticism directed against them and suggest some possible future directions.

9.1 Deep ecology

Deep ecology is an environmental philosophy which seeks to radically alter the manner in which humans position themselves in relation to the non-human world. Partly resting on the legacy of Ralph Emerson and Henry Thoreau, it aims to reinvent humanity within (rather than outside of) nature. (In this chapter, the term 'nature' will be used to refer to non-human natural entities (in order to reiterate this in the text, occasionally the term 'non-human nature' will be used).) A central theme in deep ecology is 'biospherical egalitarianism', according to which all natural beings and entities are intertwined, and need to be taken equally into account.

The Norwegian philosopher Arne Naess is often referred to as the key thinker within deep ecology. The starting premise in Naess's work is simple. He attacks 'shallow ecology', which concentrates on slight, utilitarian alterations to the Western lifestyle, and argues that 'deep ecology' offers the basis for a more fundamental change, as it seeks to address the primary causes behind environmental problems. Naess maintains that, in order to achieve a more deep-rooted change, attention needs to be placed on ontology: how do we define humanity, non-human nature and the relation between the two? (Naess, 1995). Although deep ecology is intricate, this emphasis on foundational causes and ontology can be viewed as its two core elements.

The intricate nature of deep ecology is evident in the plurality of different viewpoints and principles that are being offered. Perhaps the best introduction to this plurality is the 'Deep Ecology Platform', which Naess wrote together with George Sessions (1984). It stipulates eight key considerations: (1) non-human life has value in itself, (2) diversity is a value in itself, (3) humans can only intervene with diversity in order to satisfy vital needs, (4) the flourishing of non-human life requires a decrease in human population, (5) present human interference with non-human life is excessive, (6) economic, ideological and technological policies need to undergo a fundamental change, (7) we ought to prioritise life quality at the expense of higher standards of living and (8) those who agree with these points ought to seek their actualisation (Naess and Sessions, 1984). The plurality of deep ecology is further emphasised by the fact that this platform is a work in progress – different considerations can be added to it, and each individual is invited to take part in its construction. For Naess, deep ecology is a 'total view', akin to a worldview, which does not depend on any specific set of principles or a grounding philosophy, but rather something that remains open to constant dialogue (a theme that it shares with anarchism). Therefore, it needs to be emphasised that deep ecology is a 'process' rather than a clearly defined philosophy.

Naess offers his own total view in the form of 'Ecosophy T' (named after a Norwegian mountain), only briefly summarised here. It rests heavily on the notions of identification and self-realisation. All natural beings and entities are, in a rather teleological sense, unfolding, as they go through a process of self-realisation. This lays the basis for identification: because other beings and entities are, like human beings, going through a process of self-realisation, humans can identify with them. Identification, again, provides the foundation for expanding the notion of 'self' to also include others, and thus the 'ecological self' is born.

This expanded self-realisation also rests on a prudential consideration: since we are interconnected with other beings (we are all part of the same ecological web), our self-realisation requires the self-realisation of others (the human good requires the good of non-human nature) (Naess, 1989). This process from individual teleology to expanded self-realisation and the ecological self leads to a moral awakening. Perhaps the most noteworthy aspect of the moral awakening is that, within it, moral theory is irrelevant, as are prescriptive normative notions such as 'duties'. Naess uses Kant's term 'beautiful act' to describe the resulting morality that is not performed out of duty, but out of inclination based on an ontological understanding: 'What I suggest is the supremacy of environmental ontology and realism over environmental ethics' (Naess, 1995: 26). He argues that most disagreements about non-human nature do not stem from differences in moral viewpoints (let alone theoretical conflicts), but rather from differences in worldviews (see Katz et al., 2000) and that therefore, rather than environmental ethics, it is environmental ontology that will enable the required changes in the current treatment of non-human nature.

Deep ecology, therefore, is characterised by a plurality of principles and an emphasis on ontology rather than moral theory. To put it simplistically, this ontology suggests that humans are intertwined with, and similar to, non-human nature, and the realisation of this will lead to respect for that nature. Different platform principles will, in practice, give directions to this respect.

Numerous philosophers (such as Warwick Fox, Bill Devall, George Sessions, Alan Drengson and Joanna Macy) have expanded on Naess's theses. However, from the viewpoint of anarchism, perhaps the most interesting formulation comes from Andrew McLaughlin. Rather than concentrating on general, philosophical themes, McLaughlin digs into the political and economic issues behind the current environmental crisis. He claims that the main culprits behind environmental problems are agriculture, industrialisation and capitalism. Agriculture (and domestication in general) defines nature as an entity that is to be altered according to human interest, and within industrialism non-human nature becomes 'an object of domination' (McLaughlin, 1993: 11). Through these two factors, nature is rendered into 'resource', and its inherent value is replaced with instrumental value. Capitalism hits the final nail in the coffin. First of all, global trade effectively nullifies nature, as nature is never global but rather local and contextual (thus, global trade accompanied by global decision-making will, by necessity, overlook nature because its viewpoint does not capture locality). Secondly, within capitalism, the future is irrelevant (financial plans have a short time span), whereas concern for nature requires long-term thinking. Thirdly, non-human nature is finite, and thus cannot accommodate the core principle of capitalism, according to which constant growth is a necessity. Fourthly, capitalism centralises the notion of nature as property.

This renders nature into a commodity and empties it from independent value and meaning. (Whereas Locke still sought to find a justification for the ownership of nature, contemporary thinkers take it for granted – it is thought self-evident that nature should be owned.) Here the logic of the 'consumeristic ethos', which correlates needs with desires and drives hysteric consumption, becomes relevant. It is this ethos that, according McLaughlin, needs to be addressed first (McLaughlin, 1993).

Therefore, some of the basic structures (agriculture, industrialism, capitalism and consumerism) behind contemporary society have led to environmental destruction, and in order to achieve a change, these structures need to be critically scrutinised. According to McLaughlin, natural sciences (that follow the ethos of new science) are also one factor behind the de-valuing of nature, as it renders nature into an indifferent, lifeless and colourless collection of particles without intrinsic value (McLaughlin, 1993). Deep ecology offers an alternative to these problems. It replaces global economics and the consumerist identity with a holistic ontology that emphasises 'interconnected networks' (McLaughlin, 1993: 144). Rather than external manipulators or owners of nature, humans are part of their environments, and understanding this will lead to an ethic which sees independent value in non-human nature.

McLaughlin's take on deep ecology brings forward a political dimension, which offers an obvious similarity between deep ecology and anarchism. This similarity is further highlighted by relatively recent forms of practical politics within the environmental movement, as groups such as Earth First! and Earth Liberation Front (ELF) have combined deep-ecology influences with anarchic elements.

9.2 Primitivism

Primitivism (which goes by many names, such as 'the anti-civilisation movement') argues that the core elements of contemporary civilisation are to blame for current social and environmental problems. Hence, we should forsake civilisation and find alternative ways to exist. The most fruitful alternative is found from the Paleolithic times. Although primitivism is not based solely on environmental concerns (social issues are also brought forward), many authors emphasise environmental considerations.

Perhaps the most influential primitivist thinker, John Zerzan, maintains that the problems faced by contemporary society are the result of two key factors: domestication and mediations. He argues that domestication has reduced humans and non-human nature into entities that have no independent value or agency, and who can be controlled by various forces, such as anthropocentrism or capitalism (Zerzan, 2002). Mediations, such as language, numbers, time and art, have also resulted in the loss of value. They replace what is real and immediate with what is constructed, abstract and detached, and thus alienate humans from themselves and their surroundings. Because they *re*present the reality to us, we lose sight of the 'authentic' reality, and it is particularly this loss of authenticity that leads to a sense of alienation and an inability to draw a distinction between what is real and what is constructed. Moreover, Zerzan (2002: 13) maintains that mediations dominate reality, 'Symbolic categories are set up to control the wild and alien' and argues this to be a particularly significant catalyst behind social and environmental problems (and also psychological problems – a matter which he greatly emphasises).

Zerzan places special emphasis on language; within contemporary society, we live in language, not in the world, and our bodily senses have become ignored as a way of understanding. Here Zerzan refers to ideas familiar from phenomenology and borrows particularly from Merleau-Ponty to argue that language diminishes the richness of perception and leads us further away from direct experience (Zerzan, 2002). Moreover, language creates the impression that reality is formed of concepts that can be manufactured and manipulated, and this leads to an oppressive and instrumentalising relation towards our surroundings.

After his vehement attack on domestication and mediations, Zerzan (2008) urges us to go back to humanity's 'first nature'. First, he argues that it was free from mediation and hence more authentic: 'The communication with all of existence must have been an exquisite play of all the senses, reflecting the numberless, nameless varieties of pleasure and emotion once accessible within us.' Second, he suggests that it was also free from the social and environmental problems faced by contemporary society: 'Pre-agricultural foraging life did not know organised violence, sexual oppression, work as an onerous or separate activity, private property, or symbolic culture' (Zerzan, 2005: 9), and, instead, consisted of 'ample free time, considerable gender autonomy or equality, an ethos of egalitarianism and sharing, and no organised violence' (9). Zerzan is categorical in his defence of the pre-agricultural lifestyle. According to him, the notion of 'civilisation' is based on domestication and mediations, and thus must be abandoned in its entirety. Thus, Zerzan (2002: 119) argues that 'The truly humanitarian and pacific impulse is that which is committed to relentlessly destroying the malignant dynamic known as civilisation, including its roots.'

Other primitivist thinkers include Paul Shepard, John Fillis and Richard Heinberg, all of whom emphasise a loss of authenticity. Shepard places blame specifically on domestication, which, he argues, has not only emptied non-human nature of value, but also rendered human beings static and lifeless, determined by labour and possessions (Shepard, 2005). Fillis follows Zerzan in his emphasis on alienation, but instead of mediation, blames it on technology (Fillis, 2008). Heinberg emphasises psychology and suggests that modern humans are addicts in their elemental need for technology, electricity, luxury and so on, and a lifestyle of constant desire (for more) and fear (of losing what they have).

Addiction feeds denial concerning the cost of the technological drug, and thus the abuse of the environment and people in other parts of the world is ignored. Heinberg refers to the object-relations school in psychology and its emphasis on transitional objects that produce the illusion of safety for children, who have become aware of the separateness of their mother. Modern people remain in this framework of mind and require counselling, fitness regimes, holidays and entertainment in order to cope with their sense of alienation and insecurity. Heinberg does not place blame on specific aspects of civilisation (such as industrialism), but rather on the whole project of civilisation itself, and maintains that even ancient civilisations were defined by 'kingship, slavery, conquest, agriculture, overpopulation, and environmental ruin' (Heinberg, 2005).

Therefore, primitivists argue that social and environmental problems are the results of contemporary civilisation. More specifically, the bases of civilisation – domestication and mediations such as language and technology – are seen as the main culprits as they result in a sense of alienation that empties both non-human nature and humans of value. The only way out of the situation is to forsake civilisation and look back to the history of the human species. Like deep ecology, primitivism is presenting us with an ontology: it is by altering our way of relating to reality, rather than moral or political theory *per se*, that a less damaging existence can be found.

Although primitivism remains rather sketchy, and although its main theses are radical (or even extreme), it has roots in the works of some major thinkers, as Zerzan is particularly keen to point out. One of these is Max Horkheimer, who argued that domination of nature entails domination of human beings and maintained that the loss of value in nature has led to the loss of independent value *per se*, which again has paved the way for mental problems and social rebellion. The result is that only production has value: there is no value outside it, nothing to give us meaning in this 'rationalised irrationality' (Horkheimer, 2005; see also Horkheimer and Adorno, 2002). Another source of influence is Rousseau, who longed for the past era of human existence. Just as the domesticated animal has, in Rousseau's opinion, 'degenerated', so too has the modern human, who is 'weak, fearful and servile', and who was nobler in the state of nature. Agriculture is especially blamed for the current unhappy state of affairs: it leads to loss of equality, emphasis on property, labour, destruction of wilderness, slavery and (in general) misery (Rousseau, 2005). However, whereas contemporary primitivists tend to argue for sociability, for Rousseau it is precisely sociability that is to blame: co-operation with others has led to our demise. Other influences on primitivism include Herbert Marcuse, and to a certain extent Max Weber, and, from fiction, Aldous Huxley's dystopian *Brave New World*.

The links to anarchism should now be evident, particularly in the shared belief that institutional politico-economical structures have led to a crisis. Another possible link is an emphasis on practical politics, which play a significant part in primitivism. However, it would seem that these politics are much more extreme, infrequent and unorganised than within deep ecology. Perhaps unfortunately for primitivism, the Unabomber (Theodore Kaczynski) has come to epitomise this emphasis. Kaczynski, with whom Zerzan has maintained a personal relationship, conducted a mail-bomb campaign in the United States from the late 1970s until the mid-1990s. Although Zerzan is critical of the randomness with which the Unabomber approached violence ('innocents' were harmed and even killed), he finds a 'glint of hope' in this obscure character (Zerzan, 2002). Other primitivists are less keen to support the Unabomber, instead placing an emphasis on direct action that does not involve violence. However, here too the methods can be radical (even if not entirely inconceivable). A popular primitivist author Derrick Jensen states, 'Every morning when I wake up I ask myself whether I should write or blow up a dam. I tell myself I should keep writing, though I'm not sure that's right' (Jensen, 2005: 252).

9.3 Similarities

The similarities between deep ecology and primitivism should now be apparent. First of all, on the more concrete level, many primitivists share a number of sentiments with deep ecology. For instance, Zerzan reminds us tirelessly of environmental problems and argues that civilisations lead to environmental ruin. A focus on ecocentrism is especially common. Heinberg advocates an ecocentric worldview and blames anthropocentrism for the horrific treatment of animals and the scale of environmental destruction (Heinberg, 2005). Also, the idea of holistic self-realisation is widespread. David Watson (2005: 190), for one, talks of the 'articulation of organic unity', and Glenn Parton (2005: 236) argues for 'deep thinking' that will reveal our 'true self'. Therefore, concern for the environment, rejection of anthropocentrism and an emphasis on self-realisation (core aspects of deep ecology) can be found in primitivism.

There are also primitivist elements in some works of deep ecology. For instance, McLaughlin maintains that tribal people are more successful in achieving an ecocentric lifestyle and, as we have already seen, places the blame for environmental problems on the core elements of contemporary civilisation. In its emphasis on experiences of unity with the environment, deep ecology can also implicitly reject the type of mediations that Zerzan is critical of. The model presented by Warwick Fox is of special relevance here. He argues that ontological identification (a form of self-realisation) 'refers to experiences of commonality with all that is brought about through deep-seated realisation of the fact *that* things are' (Fox, 1995: 137). This, he maintains, is not easy to communicate in words – indeed, he suggests that language may hinder self-realisation. Therefore, deep ecology shares, in given works, primitivism's emphasis on the criticism of contemporary civilisation and the mistrust of mediations. At times, the two approaches can be very similar when it comes to locating both the blame and the solution for the current social and environmental situation. For instance, Kirkpatrick Sale (a primitivist) presents a view very similar to that of McLaughlin: it is industrialism, anthropocentrism, globalisation and capitalism that have led to contemporary problems, whereas radical environmentalism may be a solution (Sale, 2005).

On a more general level, the two approaches are bound together via their emphasis on *ontology*. Neither tends to stipulate any clear and sufficiently intricate normative, social or political theories. Primarily, it is via understanding our relation to reality that morally, socially and politically sound ways of existing can be found: ontology comes first, and other viewpoints follow. This reveals another shared element: there is a deep-rooted sense of *realism* at the heart of both movements. They go against the constructivist claim, according to which there is no objective way of understanding reality, by arguing that there is, *if* we alter the way in which we *approach* the world. (However, it has to be noted that the two approaches do not follow standard metaphysics in their stance on realism. Instead of repeating Cartesian dualism between knowing subjects and passive objects, deep ecologists and primitivists maintain on the contrary that we can achieve knowledge, because we are *not* detached from the objects of our knowledge, but rather intertwined with them. The most obvious philosophical links here are Edmund Husserl and Hans-Georg Gadamer, with their emphasis on situated knowledge.) This involves getting rid of anthropocentric mediations and viewing ourselves, not as the constructors of the world, but rather as one part of it – it is 'from within' that reality can be known. This realism is linked to *essentialism*, which stipulates clear identities or categories to different types of beings, entities and phenomena: thus, nature, modernity, primitive peoples, animals and so forth are defined via notions of inherency (for instance, 'civilisation is inherently x'). A further similarity is the emphasis on *human psychology*. It is the individual who is to find her own self and her relation to reality, stripped bare of the influences of any socially constructed identities. (Interestingly, it is via intense individualism that we are to find our ecocentric, holistic self.) Yet another obvious similarity is the *rejection of oppressive mechanisms*. Both human and non-human nature ought to be seen outside hierarchical frameworks that rest on notions of 'control' and 'power', and should be viewed as beings and entities of inherent value.

Finally, both approaches are radically *practical*. As we have seen, direct action is one form of this practicality. Arne Naess used his own body to protect a Norwegian fjord, and Earth First! activists obstruct the building of motorways and power plants by way of direct action. Primitivists follow similar methods, although in a less organised fashion. Thus, similarities also take place on the grassroots level. Zerzan (2005: v) begins his anthology on primitivism with a quote from Earth First! which invites its readers to 'Visualise industrial collapse', so bringing radical environmentalism to the realm of primitivist thinking. *Do or Die*, the publication of Earth First!, argues that from the very beginning the movement wanted not only to conserve wilderness but also to reverse the process of its destruction, thus attacking industrialism, capitalism and other core villains of the contemporary society (Anonymous, 2003).

These two approaches are not only applicable *to* the practical level, but also evolve and actualise *on* the practical level. Here perhaps the most obvious similarity is the belief in 'bioregionalism'. Bioregionalism rests on the idea that communities should be tied to local environments – there is no flying-in imports from far away, dumping one's waste elsewhere or global decision-making that ignores localities. Both movements emphasise decentralised living, using as few resources as possible. However, there may be some fundamental differences; in deep ecology, the role of agriculture and technology is not clear. The moderate form of bioregionalism favoured by Naess would not give up these facets of civilisation altogether, but would only reduce their scale. This would not be enough for Zerzan. According to him, there is no socially and environmentally responsible way of making use of technology, for it is technology itself that leads to social and environmental problems. Therefore, there is a possible difference between the two approaches around the degree to which alternative lifestyles are sought. Deep ecology seeks to introduce a new ontology to civilisation, whereas primitivists seek to replace civilisation with a new ontology.

9.4 Criticisms

A number of criticisms have been advanced against primitivism and deep ecology and though there is significant overlap in these critical analyses, they do not equally apply to both schools. As a result, with regard to the first two sets of criticisms (*underdeveloped moral and political theory* and *mysticism and misanthropy*), I focus my attention on deep ecology, and on the third (*romanticism and bad press*) I focus on primitivism. However, as I indicate, there are basic lines of critique that are appropriate to both deep ecology and primitivism throughout.

9.4.1 Criticisms: Lack of moral and political theory

Eric Katz has argued that, despite its claims to the contrary, deep ecology rests on anthropocentric grounds. Self-realisation, Katz maintains, expands the human ego over the whole of the natural world: in an ultimate feat of anthropocentric egoism, humans swallow up non-human nature by declaring it to be part of the human 'self'. Another sign of egoism is the idea that humans are to protect the non-human natural world because this ultimately serves their own interests – the concern is not other-directed. Katz (2000) maintains that in order to avoid anthropocentrism, ethics (in the form of a clear moral theory) needs to be brought forward. From the viewpoint of ontology, humans will view the world from their own perspective and thus remain egoists, but ethics opens the door for seeing independent value in non-human nature. Val Plumwood (2000) offers a similar criticism. According to her, deep ecology must pay more heed to difference in nature, instead of swallowing everything under the human ego. The type of unity ('holism') that deep ecology underlines cannot accommodate communicative ethics, within which representatives of non-human nature (especially animals) are agents in their own right and have value as they are in themselves, in their difference. Unity implies incorporation, a central aspect of colonialism, which denies the right of the other to be different and independent, and thus one must remain critical of theories that offer unified and expanded notions of self (see also Kheel, 1990). Therefore, the claim is that – due to the lack of emphasis on ethics – deep ecology ends up repeating the type of worldview that it seeks to resist. One cannot fight morally unsound ideologies with ontology alone.

It has also been claimed that deep ecology needs to place more emphasis on political theory. This is because the same ontology can be used to serve various causes: descriptions are always open to adaptation by different political frameworks. To put it simply, the statement that A and B are related can be used to support various agendas. This becomes evident in the criticism presented by Plumwood. She claims that deep ecology's openness to personal interpretation renders it an easy target to be hijacked by oppressive political interest-groups. It can especially be made to accommodate pure capitalism, within which interests are fused and differences rejected. (Although deep ecology has been accused of being open to fascism – perhaps most vocally by Murray Bookchin – Plumwood (2000) finds such criticism old-fashioned and misplaced.) Deep ecology would benefit from paying more attention to political content and context.

Therefore, the charges are that deep ecology remains anthropocentric and does not give adequate regard for moral and political theory. However, it can be defended to some degree. The ecological self is not by necessity an egoistic, anthropocentric self, for identification and holism do not by any necessity imply that difference and independence are rejected. That is, Mary can identify with somebody across the globe and feel that her fate is connected with the fate of that person, but she can still view the other person as being different and independent from herself. To put it simply: giving regard to the viewpoint of another and drawing relations to another are considerations that have to do with form (A is related to B) rather than content (the value of B is A). The notion of an 'ecological self' does pose a risk of unity, but can be interpreted in many ways. One interpretation is that it refers to viewing oneself via others, rather than viewing others via oneself – that is, Mary does not define others by reference to her own ego, but instead defines herself by reference to the well-being of others. Much more needs to be said in order to prove that deep ecology is anthropocentric rather than ecocentric.

Still, critics are right to emphasise the issue of ethics and moral theory. Arguably, normativity is a part of all human action: we are inherently normative creatures. Because of this, categorical divides between ontology and normativity are difficult to draw, and normativity forms a necessary part of ontological notions. Thus, for instance, the careless consumer may define animals via dualistic and mechanistic terms, thereby undermining their cognitive capacities and interests, because she has adopted an ethic within which animals only have instrumental value, or she may happily endorse the destruction of wilderness areas because she feels that nature has no inherent value. Ontologies affect ethics, but ethics also affects ontologies, and hence the two exist as a chiasma (intersection resulting in hybridity) rather than as separate categories. Both deep ecology and primitivism too easily forget this complex relation and overlook ethics, and it is this oversight that presents one of the most significant problems for both. Although deep ecology and primitivism would like a new ontology to lead us to a harmonious existence, it may – without a clear normative content and the back-up of a moral theory – lead to nothing but further problems.

McLaughlin argues that emphasis on moral theory is a 'problem', for such theory is rooted in the very worldview that radical environmentalism seeks to challenge. What is needed is a 'much larger project of radical social change' (McLaughlin, 1993: 172). However, here McLaughlin is overtly generic. Moral theories are heterogenic and nuanced – they cannot all be categorised as anthropocentric. Moreover, standard moral theories do not exhaust the possibilities of moral theory *per se*: there is vast room for new creation. Primitivists and deep ecologists would do well to follow, for instance, the example of environmental ethics, within which value-statements concerning non-human nature place a safeguard against its instrumentalisation.

Criticisms relating to a lack of political theory are also well-placed. Although Naess sees deep ecology as a social movement, and although it includes an activist element, the philosophy tends to exclude sufficiently intricate political and economical arguments, and this threatens to render it somewhat abstract or sketchy (Clark, 2000). Thus, Brian Morris argues that deep ecology would benefit from taking on board concrete social problems such as poverty and exploitation (Morris, 1997), and a similar argument has been made by McLaughlin, who, as seen above, has in his own work sought to link deep ecology with social factors.

A further issue concerns agency. For instance, Bron Taylor (2000) has argued that deep ecologists do not present a sufficient model for social change: how are they to take on the giants of global economy, consumer culture and other hegemonic entities? How, in practice, will deep ecology be actualised? Graham Purchase claims that, as newcomers to organised resistance, eco-activists have not yet understood the power of the multinational corporations, and the need to commit large sections of society to the cause in order to have a hope of fighting such corporations. He suggests that the required agency can be found from anarchism and its syndicalist emphasis on the working classes: it is the ordinary person, at the mercy of the capitalist regime, that needs to be persuaded to fight for the environment (Purchase, 1997).

Although direct action can be effective, it can also quickly become marginalised by the state and the media. If global problems such as those concerning the environment and social inequalities are to be addressed, it is crucial that ways of persuading the general public are found. Therefore, deep ecology needs to pay much more careful attention to how, exactly, its goals can be realised. Much of the criticism mentioned above also applies to primitivism. Arguably even more so than deep ecology, primitivism requires more thorough attention to ethics, political theory and agency.

9.4.2 Criticisms: Mysticism and misanthropy

A tireless advocate of social ecology, Murray Bookchin was also well-known as a vocal critic of deep ecology. Unfortunately, Bookchin (1987, 1995) did not always offer adequate support for his criticism, and hence his depictions have been argued to be 'blatantly unfair' (Clark, 2000). Nonetheless, his criticism does warrant further exploration, although this chapter concentrates particularly on his later criticism of deep ecology.

One of Bookchin's claims was that deep ecology is effected by mysticism and misanthropy. Bookchin argued that it is a part of 'ecomysticism', a 'quasi-religious philosophy that is explicitly anti-humanistic' (Bookchin, 1995: 87), and thought especially horrendous the suggestion that the human population ought to be decreased, or that non-human animals ought to be given equal consideration. Bookchin also argues that instead of Naess, he himself was the original voice for a deep approach. Therefore, Naess's philosophy was 'an old hat' and a 'patently simplistic and singularly unoriginal body of views' that is 'simple-minded' (Bookchin, 1995: 90).

Regarding mysticism, Bookchin was partly on the right track. Some deep ecologists, such as Bill Devall and Fox, draw connections between deep ecology and some form of spiritualism (see Taylor, 2000). However, McLaughlin (1993: 211) argues that deep ecology need not be spiritual – that is, there is nothing in the theory that requires mysticism – and he himself brings forward a take on deep ecology that is free from any spiritual elements. It has to be noted that Naess thought deep ecology to be a balancing act, avoiding both atomistic individualism and organic mysticism (Morris, 1997). Although mysticism is at times evident, then it is by no means a necessary condition of deep ecology. This is another similarity between deep ecology and primitivism, for the latter, too, often includes spiritual elements (Heinberg, 2005), and would benefit from a similar reflection on their relevance.

As it comes to misanthropy, Bookchin based his accusation mainly on the Malthusian statements made by David Foreman, the previous frontman of Earth First!, and as such it is of little relevance to deep ecology in general. The same might be said with regard to primitivism, which Bookchin also attacks on similar grounds, as it is by no means clear that the majority of primitivist thinkers would agree with Zerzan's Unabomber-endorsing ideas, for example. It also has to be noted that the argument for a decrease in human population is by no means necessarily an opinion on human value – statements about quantity are not necessarily statements about quality.

Moreover, deep ecology explicitly endorses human flourishing, and it has little to do with the type of 'throw the surplus out of the life-boat' mentality that Bookchin seems to have in mind. Quite the contrary, deep ecologists emphasise human interests: for instance, McLaughlin maintains that deep ecology wants people to reach their 'best potential' (McLaughlin, 1993: 182, 202) via a decrease in the population, and reminds us that the best way to achieve this decrease is to provide a decent living standard for all. As it comes to equality between species, Bookchin is also off the mark. Rejection of speciesism does not mean rejection of human value: humans are not excluded, but rather others are brought within the realm of normative consideration. McLaughlin reminds us that various forms of oppression (such as racism, sexism and domination of nature) intertwine: 'Concern for any oppression requires concern for all oppression' (McLaughlin, 1993: 223). Therefore, it can even be argued that – due to both historical and theoretical commonalities – rejection of speciesism is necessary for social equality.

It is useful to acknowledge the context from which Bookchin presented his criticism. Although Bookchin criticised dualism and anthropocentrism, he also emphasised the special nature and value of humanity in a manner that seemed to repeat or imply these very frameworks. Thus, he maintained that the belief in human superiority has been the basic theme of 'nearly all sophisticated civilisations' (Bookchin, 1995: 8) and he also talked of the 'immense divide' between humans and the rest of nature – he even claimed that humans are 'fundamentally' and 'sharply distinguished' from the rest of nature (125) and that de-centring humans is 'cultural and social barbarism of frightening proportions' (105).

The apparent reason behind the latent anthropocentrism and dualism was the significance Bookchin placed on the human capacity to alter her environment: whereas animals adapt, humans innovate, which has enabled humans to progress from the 'first nature' of biological evolution to the 'second nature' of social evolution – a progress that allows humans to actively change the world for the better, a dream of social ecology (18). Bookchin himself recognised the possible contradiction in his position and sought to correct it by maintaining that there is a difference between 'duality' and 'dualism': however, this seems to erase the problem only on a semantic level (see Bookchin, 2005). In his belief in human supremacy and cultivation, Bookchin seems to belong to the club of modernists who emphasise human superiority and progress while these factors play key roles in many social and environmental problems. Bookchin emphasised the human ability to alter nature, but in the Lockean model, it is precisely altered nature that becomes human property (and ultimately a commodity). This paradoxical situation (both attacking and supporting anthropocentric and dualistic frameworks) takes away some credibility from Bookchin's criticism of deep ecology.

9.4.3 Criticisms: Romanticism and bad press

Unsurprisingly (taking into account his emphasis on 'second nature' and future progress), Bookchin is no more sympathetic towards primitivism. He asserts that primitivists have 'grossly distorted our understanding of the lives and cultures of aboriginal peoples by attributing to them superhuman, paradisiacal dimensions' (Bookchin, 1995: 120). Primitivism is romantic and naïve, and bears a negative effect on aboriginal people by downplaying their social problems.

Whereas before tribal people were told they were 'savage', now they are, in line with 'primitivist arrogance', told that they should not develop. In Bookchin's opinion, the reality of the pre-historic people was anything but idyllic. They struggled to make ends meet, their societies were plagued by oppression and hierarchies and their lives were very short. Due to the immediacy of their own needs, pre-historic people could not take non-human interests into account and therefore they altered their environments drastically in order to serve their own needs and treated animals cruelly rather than 'spiritually' (120). Similar criticism is offered by Brian Oliver Sheppard (2008), who argues that following the primitivist agenda would mean mass annihilation of humans due to such things as the loss of medicine and enhanced crop production. Most importantly, since we have very little knowledge of the lives of the pre-historic people, the primitivist depiction of the Paleolithic times remains no more than a fantasy.

Primitivists have responded by arguing that the bygone days were not as grim as suggested. They claim that physical health in the pre-historic times used to be less dire than often thought, and they add to this the claim that the greatest killers in the contemporary world are created by Western lifestyles. Zerzan (2005) emphasises the correlation between modern civilisation and mental problems, maintaining that depression, high suicide rates, anxiety and so on are the results of the former. Moreover, he claims that his views are not romantic or naïve, but are rather based on evidence from archaeology and anthropology. However, this part of the debate comes down to scientific expertise: in order to pick sides, we need more data.

To move on to the second point of criticism, the response by primitivists is that they do not discriminate against contemporary tribal people, as they include these people and Westerners in the rejection of civilisation. Still, it is difficult to avoid the impression that romantic notions of tribal people are common in primitivism. For instance, Sale argues that tribal societies consisted of great cohesion, harmony, freedom from crime, few needs (easily satisfied) and a lot of spare time – in contrast, contemporary society is described as that of atomic bombs, toxic waste, traffic jams, crime and unemployment (Sale, 2005).

These black-and-white dichotomies suggests that primitivists are not realistic about environmental and social issues: they blame everything on 'civilisation' without recognising the evidence that indicates that even those outside civilisation may abuse the environment and each other. Here generalisations play a role. Zerzan tends to unify 'primitives' under one banner and makes sweeping statements that cover 2 million years. Not enough attention is placed on diversity and the negative aspects of pre-historic times: characterising them as Eden is neither believable nor fruitful.

Although it is important to avoid creating utopian images of the future (such as that offered by Bookchin), it is equally important to avoid creating overtly nostalgic images of the past. This leads to a related problem, which also has a bearing on deep ecology (and which is often cited in relation to anarchism). Taylor finds it problematic to assume that people are 'naturally' co-operative to the degree required by anarchic bioregions and fears that bioregionality would struggle to keep in check the selfish and the powerful: 'Unless bad people all become good, there is no solution to violence other than some kind of government to restrain the evil few' (Taylor, 2000: 282).

Primitivism has also come under attack by certain anarchists. Sheppard separates primitivism sharply from anarchism and calls it quite simply 'rubbish' (Sheppard, 2008: 2). He points out that whereas anarchists wish to eliminate the state and give the means of production to the hands of the people, primitivists want to get rid of production itself. This, in Sheppard's opinion, is a grossly mistaken view. For instance, it is not technology in itself that is harmful, but the manner in which it is distributed and controlled. Thus, Sheppard claims, anarchists seek to establish a 'true civilisation', whereas primitivists wage a war on mistaken premises; he goes so far as to suggest that primitivists are 'flakes and crazies', who have had a harmful impact on the manner in which anarchism is presented in the media. Instead of Noam Chomsky, the media wants to interview eccentric primitivists, and thus deflects the discussion away from rational arguments. Therefore, anarchism is marginalised as a sector of lunacy. The 'Unabomber' is a typical example of the high media profile given to the 'crazies'.

Does Sheppard's criticism have any merit? It has to be noted that Sheppard is presenting a rather naïve understanding of technology and other 'infrastructures' of civilisation. Technology is not just a tool, to which humans can give any meaning they wish, but also an entity, which lays the basis for given types of meanings. The claim that technology (rather than just the distribution or products of technology) brings about alienation is common: already Walter Benjamin suggested that the 'aura' of things is lost in mechanical reproduction, and Jean Baudrillard brought this claim further by arguing that via reproduction and simulation, the 'real' is replaced by the 'hyper-real'.

It is simplistic to claim that all that is needed is a change in power-relations concerning matters such as industrialism or technology, for much more scrutiny needs to be placed on the type of meanings that these elements of contemporary society tend to encourage. One could argue that, despite its own over-simplifications, this is the merit of primitivism: it brings forward the problems related to the very human innovations that some (like Bookchin) celebrate somewhat uncritically. However, it also has to be noted that there is some truth to Sheppard's criticism, for the types of meanings different infrastructures encourage depend partly on the types of meanings society at large celebrates. Infrastructures do not exist in a social vacuum, but rather gain their meaning and implications within particular social contexts. Primitivists seem to be, again, guilty of generalisations that overlook the complexities behind different core aspects of civilisation. Technology is not inherently 'bad', but it invites negative implications only within specific social, political and economical circumstances.

With regard to Sheppard's second point of criticism, one has to be careful not to repeat contemporary society's tendency to label most things radical as 'crazy'. Sheppard is talking of primitivists with the same contempt as those believing in the *status quo* talk of anarchism, and this runs the risk of repeating the belief in the monopoly of ideology. However, there is some truth to the claim that primitivism can play a part in the marginalisation of anarchistic thinking. Radical but reasonable ideas are rarely given space in the media, whereas radical but bizarre ideas are often eagerly broadcast. They are not viewed as criticism, but entertainment, and serve to stereotype and undermine those who have more substantial arguments to present. This suggests that primitivists need to (again) place attention on the social context – this time, that context concerns the broader consequences of a highly mediated public image.

Some of the claims made by primitivists remain unreflective. Particularly, the criticism directed against mediations would benefit from a more thorough exploration. The obvious argument against the criticism is that language in particular is a capacity that is intrinsic to humanity. Following Ludwig Wittgenstein, we are deeply lingual beings, and there is no way out from language. Language may distort and deceive, but it is also one backbone of our relation to reality, including primitivist thinking. It is important to bring forth non-lingual forms of relating and understanding the surrounding world, but a wholesale rejection of mediation needs to be replaced with a nuanced reflection concerning epistemology. This, again, points towards the simplistic nature of (at least some) primitivist thinking. In order to become a serious political philosophy, primitivism needs to pay more thorough attention to its grounding premises.

One final criticism is that it is unrealistic to expect modern people to become tribal. However, a fruitful take on the matter brings forward not a total adoption of Paleolithic lifestyle, but rather reflection on contemporary society. Thus, Heinberg (2005) argues that the issue is not 'going back', but rather 'getting back on track' (Heinberg, 2005), and McLaughlin maintains that the point is not to travel back in time, but rather to 'raise a critical framework within which we can reconsider the question of what human progress really means, and thus consider deeply the kind of future we should create' (McLaughlin, 1993: 90).

9.5 General criticisms

The points of criticism above have been specific, either in their scope or in their target. But what of the more general comments that could be made in regard to the two versions of green anarchy?

First of all, attention needs to be placed on the risk of simplification – a term used frequently in the above text. Both deep ecology and primitivism tend to (although particularly in deep ecology there are notable exceptions) offer broad outlines rather than precise, nuanced philosophies and, in doing so, become vulnerable to over-simplification. This simplification takes various forms, one of which is an emphasis on dichotomies. The philosophies bring forward different juxtapositions: civilisation–pre-historic time, mediation–freedom, individual–ecology and so forth. These taxonomies suggest a categorical normative content to them; for instance, civilisation is 'bad'. Both (although, again, primitivism more urgently than deep ecology) would benefit from further theoretical exploration and clarification.

The emphasis on dichotomies goes together with an emphasis on a 'grand narrative' that describes the descent of humanity and focuses on single causalities (such as 'agriculture' or 'language'). As is often the case with grand narratives, heterogeneity and ambiguity are given less regard than they deserve. From the perspective of poststructural theory, these forms of simplification render the two approaches dubious. Ironically, like Bookchin, deep ecology and primitivism risk being staunchly modern in their approach, if they underline dichotomies and grand causalities, and both would benefit greatly if the complexity of reality were taken more carefully into account.

Interestingly, Zerzan seems to be aware of the possibility of poststructural criticism and addresses it by launching an attack on postmodern thinking. He argues that postmodernism is 'moral cowardice' with 'zero degree of content' (Zerzan, 2005: 3): it remains superficial, plural, fragmented and uninterested in origin, history or agency – moreover, it is value-denying and full of promises of endless possibilities, just like consumerism itself. In effect, it is a product of the consumerist society, and as such cannot be taken seriously. Furthermore, it provides a poor map for the type of moral change that the looming environmental catastrophe requires, for 'Little or nothing is compelling, authentic, or makes a difference' (Zerzan, 2002: 110). Borrowing from Frederick Jamieson, Zerzan maintains that 'Postmodernism is what you have when the modernization process is complete and nature is gone for good' (Zerzan, 2008). The result is that nothing can be opposed, since 'reality' is a social construction.

Zerzan's criticism does strike a chord. As has been noted, the postmodern view does resemble the consumerist cultural context out of which it has been born. It is especially reluctant to talk about ethics, and thus, postmodern environmental philosophy can be obscure in its approach to the crucial question: 'What should we do?' Nothing is of inherent value, and one may wonder whether such a philosophy can offer any promise from the viewpoint of non-human nature that suffers precisely because of the belief that everything is expendable. However, saying this, it has to be noted that Zerzan offers a rather one-sided view on postmodern philosophy. Much of postmodernism has been highly critical of anthropocentrism, technology, industrialism and the current treatment of non-human nature (for a critical overview, see Calarco, 2008). More importantly, a critique of the postmodern approach does not salvage deep ecology and primitivism from the problem of simplification. Whether one accepts postmodernism or not, the two theories still require more specification and gradation.

The most significant point of criticism is the lack of clear normative and political elements. Although the two theories offer normative and political claims and implications (again, deep ecology fairs significantly better than primitivism in this regard), comprehensive normative and political theories remain largely absent. The most obvious reason for this stems from the emphasis given to ontology: norms and politics are implicitly or explicitly argued to be secondary in relation to an ontological understanding of our place in reality. However, this hierarchy needs to be re-thought.

First of all, as suggested above, normative and political beliefs affect ontological notions: thus, for instance, facts and values exist as a chiasma rather than as clearly separate categories. The ontologies brought forward by both deep ecology and primitivism will, therefore, include normative and political dimensions, even if these are not explicated. Secondly, even if this inter-relatedness between ontology, ethics and politics is not accepted, it is still evident that philosophies with radical normative and political implications cannot sustain themselves without a direct and thorough exploration of the frameworks on which they are relying. More meticulous attention on these frameworks would also protect the two approaches from the criticism mentioned above – they would not have to resort to simplifications, if moral and political viewpoints enabled them to draw clear conclusions even from a complex and ambiguous reality.

Moreover, the ontologies brought forward by deep ecology and primitivism require more specification. Here one valuable direction for both approaches is phenomenology. For instance, Edmund Husserl (1983) emphasised empathy, values and intuition as direct forms of understanding that enable one to perceive other beings as fellow subjects rather than as mere physical bodies – for him, they are 'our primary form of experience of others, as others' (Smith, 2007: 228). These elements also enable the acknowledgement of inter-subjectivity, which is a crucial concept for Husserl. When we experience the world, we understand that others experience it too, that it is there for everyone (hence, when looking at an object, we realise that it is also for others to see: I understand that the manifold of perspectives towards a given object also includes the perspectives of other beings). I am not alone in the world, but rather surrounded by other agentive beings.

Although intuition, values and empathy are crucial forms of knowledge, and although reality ought to be viewed via inter-subjectivity, the contemporary world fails to acknowledge the relevance of these factors. Quite famously, Husserl felt that there was a disparity between these forms of everyday experience ('the life-world') and mathematised science, which seeks to understand reality via rigid, theoretical formulas. This leads to alienation, within which we ultimately view ourselves and others in a disconnected, mathematised manner, and thus a 'crisis' is born. Maurice Merleau-Ponty brought forward similar themes.

According to Merleau-Ponty, uncommunicative and alienating knowledge leads to objectification and loss of particularity. Bodily perception and mutuality, on the other hand, pave the way for recognising that we are inter-related, co-habiting beings: 'It is precisely my body which perceives the body of another, and discovers in that other body a miraculous prolongation of my own intentions, a familiar way of dealing with the world' (Merleau-Ponty, 2002: 412). Again, objectifying knowledge is replaced with a more direct, bodily understanding that allows for inter-subjectivity. A further reference is Henri Bergson, whose 'process philosophy' maintained that understanding is best achieved via intuition that follows the heterogeneity of the lived reality (which he again defined as 'duration'). Bergson (1992) argued that concepts abstract and categorise reality without being able to truly grasp it, and that only intuition would enable us to understand what surrounds us in its capacity to dwell in, to be a part of, those surroundings. Central to all this is the situatedness of human beings: we are part of the lived reality, not detached agents whom can achieve rational objectivity. Therefore, situated knowledge and an understanding of inter-subjectivity are strong themes. The similarities to deep ecology and primitivism are obvious. On the one hand, situated knowledge offers a framework for the criticism of mediations offered in primitivism; on the other hand, the notion of inter-subjectivity presents deep ecology with new possibilities for developing the ideas of ecocentricity, inherent value and self-realisation. Deep ecology has seen numerous valuable attempts to incorporate phenomenology in the form of 'ecophenomenology' (for a particularly fruitful approach, see Langer, 2004). However, too many of these attempts are rather specific and concentrate on given authors, in particular, Heidegger (for an example, see Zimmerman, 1983), rather than the broader ramifications that phenomenology could offer. Moreover, although primitivists, and Zerzan in particular, make some references to phenomenology, these have remained very superficial and are in need of more systematic investigation. Therefore, phenomenology offers some important themes to explore further in the search for a more intricate ontology.

A further notion that might be helpful here is 'solidarity', brought forward by Plumwood. According to Plumwood (2000: 67), solidarity refers to 'Positioning the self *with* or in support of the other' and involves recognising the heterogeneity, multiplicity and value of other beings. If we extend the scope of solidarity to include non-agentive entities (such as natural phenomena) and emphasise its normative and political nature (solidarity posits value in the other being and suggests a politics within which the other is not distanced or assimilated, but rather viewed via both difference and respect), it becomes a perfect tool for both deep ecology and primitivism. It would offer a new ground for the deep ecologist to argue for ecocentric concern, and for the primitivist to explore non-hierarchical social arrangements. Most importantly, the notion of solidarity would combine ontology, ethics and politics in a manner that would enable one to avoid some of the criticism mentioned above: it holds the promise of bringing together ontological relations, normative consideration and political awareness. Along with phenomenology then, the concept of solidarity offers another useful direction for green anarchy to take.

9.6 Conclusion

Deep ecology and primitivism share many themes and offer strong and interesting criticisms against contemporary consumerist society.

However, their normative, ontological and political undercurrents have to be further explored and explicated. This would open the door for a more grounded radicalism that could more poignantly question the current brutal and ignorant treatment of human beings, the environment and non-human animals. The positive and much-needed contribution of both deep ecology and primitivism has been the willingness to offer criticism of anthropocentric consumerism – the next step is to give this criticism more theoretical clarity (this applies particularly strongly to primitivism, which is considerably less vigorous in its approach than deep ecology). Therefore, although green anarchy brings forward extremely valuable claims relating to the value and treatment of the environment and non-human animals, it will benefit from further theoretical scrutiny. One direction for such scrutiny is phenomenology (already to some extent explored in deep ecology), and another is the notion of 'solidarity', which offers a way to combine ontological, normative and political concerns.

Bibliography

Anonymous (2003) 'The birth of Earth First!' *Do or Die* X: 4–5.
Z. Bauman (2005) 'Modernity and the Holocaust' in J. Zerzan (ed.) *Against Civilisation* (Los Angeles: Feral House).
H. Bergson (1992) *The Creative Mind* (New York: The Citadel Press).
M. Bookchin (1987) 'Social ecology versus deep ecology: A challenge for the ecology movement', *Green Perspectives: Newsletter of the Green Program Project* IV–V.
—— (1995) *Re-Enchanting Humanity: A Defense of the Human Spirit Against Anti-Humanism, Misanthropy, Mysticism and Primitivism* (New York: Cassel).
—— (2005) *The Ecology of Freedom: The Emergence and Dissolution of Hierarchy* (Edinburgh: AK Press).
M. Calarco (2008) *Zoographies: The Question of the Animal* (New York: Columbia University Press).
J. Clark (2000) 'How wide is deep ecology?' in E. Katz, A. Light and D. Rothenberg (eds) *Beneath the Surface: Critical Essays in the Philosophy of Deep Ecology* (London: MIT Press).
J. Fillis (2008) 'What is primitivism?' *Primitivism*, http://www.primitivism.com/what-is-primitivism.htm, last accessed: 15 August 2008.
W. Fox (1995) 'Transpersonal ecology and the varieties of identification' in A. Drengson and Y. Inoue (eds) *The Deep Ecology Movement* (Berkeley: North Atlantic Books).
R. Heinberg (2005) 'Was civilization a mistake?' in J. Zerzan (ed.) *Against Civilisation* (Los Angeles: Feral House).
M. Horkheimer (2005) 'Eclipse of reason' in J. Zerzan (ed.) *Against Civilisation* (Los Angeles: Feral House).
M. Horkheimer and T. Adorno (2002) *Dialectic of Enlightenment* (Stanford: Stanford University Press).

E. Husserl (1983) *Ideas Pertaining to a Pure Phenomenology and to a Phenomenological Philosophy: Studies in the Phenomenology of Constitution* (Dordrecht: Kluwer).
D. Jensen (2005) 'Actions speak louder than words' in J. Zerzan (ed.) *Against Civilisation* (Los Angeles: Feral House).
E. Katz (2000) 'Against the inevitability of anthropocentrism' in E. Katz, A. Light and D. Rothenberg (eds) *Beneath the Surface: Critical Essays in the Philosophy of Deep Ecology* (London: MIT Press).
E. Katz, A. Light and D. Rothenberg (2000) 'Introduction' in E. Katz, A. Light and D. Rothenberg (eds) *Beneath the Surface: Critical Essays in the Philosophy of Deep Ecology* (London: MIT Press).
M. Kheel (1990) 'Ecofeminism and deep ecology: Reflections on identity and difference' in I. Diamond and G. Orenstein (eds) *Reweaving the World: The Emergence of Ecofeminism* (San Francisco: Sierra Club Books).
M. Langer (2004) 'Merleau-Ponty and deep ecology' in D. Moran and L. Embree (eds) *Phenomenology: Critical Concepts in Philosophy* (London: Routledge).
A. McLaughlin (1993) *Regarding Nature: Industrialism and Deep Ecology* (New York: State University of New York Press).
M. Merleau-Ponty (2002) *Phenomenology of Perception* (London: Routledge).
B. Morris (1997) 'Reflections on deep ecology' in M. Bookchin, G. Purchase, B. Morris and R. Aitchley (eds) *Deep Ecology and Anarchism: A Polemic* (London: Freedom Press).
A. Naess (1989) *Ecology, Community and Lifestyle* (Cambridge: Cambridge University Press).
────── (1995) 'The shallow and the deep, long-range ecology movement: A summary' in A. Drengson and Y. Inoue (eds) *The Deep Ecology Movement* (Berkeley: North Atlantic Books).
A. Naess and G. Sessions (1984) 'Deep ecology platform: Foundation for deep ecology', Deep Ecology Foundation, http://www.deepecology.org/platform.htm, date accessed: 10 August 2008.
G. Parton (2005) 'The machine in our heads' in J. Zerzan (ed.) *Against Civilisation* (Los Angeles: Feral House).
V. Plumwood (2000) 'Deep ecology, deep pockets, and deep problems: A feminist ecosocialist analysis' in E. Katz, A. Light and D. Rothenberg (eds) *Beneath the Surface: Critical Essays in the Philosophy of Deep Ecology* (London: MIT Press).
G. Purchase (1997) 'Social ecology, anarchism and trades unionism' in M. Bookchin, G. Purchase, B. Morris and R. Aitchley (eds) *Deep Ecology and Anarchism: A Polemic* (London: Freedom Press).
J. Rousseau (2005) 'Discourse on the origins of inequality' in J. Zerzan (ed.) *Against Civilisation* (Los Angeles: Feral House).
K. Sale (2005) 'Rebels against the future: Lessons from the Luddites' in J. Zerzan (ed) *Against Civilisation* (Los Angeles: Feral House).
P. Shepard (2005) 'Nature and madness' in J. Zerzan (ed.) *Against Civilisation* (Los Angeles: Feral House).
B. Sheppard (2008) *Anarchism vs. Primitivism* (London: Active Distribution).
W. D. Smith (2007) *Husserl* (London: Routledge).
B. Taylor (2000) 'Deep ecology and its social philosophy: A critique' in E. Katz, A. Light and D. Rothenberg (eds) *Beneath the Surface: Critical Essays in the Philosophy of Deep Ecology* (London: MIT Press).

D. Watson (2005) 'Civilization in bulk' in J. Zerzan (ed.) *Against Civilisation* (Los Angeles: Feral House).
J. Zerzan (2002) *Running on Emptiness: The Pathology of Civilization* (Los Angeles: Feral House).
―――― (ed.) (2005) *Against Civilisation* (Los Angeles: Feral House).
―――― (2008) 'Language: Origin and meaning', *Primitivism*, http://www.primitivism.com/language.htm, date accessed: 15 August 2008.
M. Zimmerman (1983) 'Toward a Heideggerean *ethos* for radical environmentalism', *Environmental Ethics*, V(ii): 99–131.

10
Listening, Caring, Becoming: Anarchism as an Ethics of Direct Relationships

Jamie Heckert

> 'cause I know there is strength
> in the differences between us
> and I know there is comfort
> where we overlap.
>
> (Ani DiFranco)

Anarchism is notoriously difficult to define. It has been referred to as an ideology, a discourse (Williams, 2007), a political culture (Gordon, 2008), a utopian philosophy and even a 'definite trend' in the history of humankind (Rocker, cited in Chomsky, 2005: 9). And that is just among its supporters. Here, I want to add to this polyvocal effort to understand and explore anarchism with a complementary notion: that of anarchism as an ethics of relationships. Ecological and social, embodied and symbolic, interpersonal and interspecies, of class and race and gender and nation, anarchist ethics apply to relationships of all sorts.

Of course, ethics are always concerned with relationships. Sometimes, however, they are prescriptive, scripting in advance the right way to relate. In this sense, ethics are imagined to precede social relations, whereby that potentially messy and emotionally challenging work of actually relating is imagined to have already been achieved. There are established rules, procedures, protocols or principles to be followed – a social contract to which we have already consented without being asked our desires (Brown, 1995). An action can thus be judged, by those claiming moral/juridical authority, as right or wrong, ethical or unethical, moral or immoral, legal or illegal according to a story which preceded the act. An anarchist ethic of relationships might work otherwise.

Anarchy does not mean simply opposed to the *archos*, or political leader. It means opposed to *archē*. Now, archē, in the first instance, means *beginning*, origin. From this it comes to mean a *first principle, an element;* then *first place, supreme power, sovereignty, dominion, command, authority*; and finally a *sovereignty, an empire, a realm, a magistracy, a governmental office.*

(Tucker, 1897: 112, his emphasis)

My proposal here is an ethics with neither origin nor conclusion, ethics which are continually produced in the present, in being present. Ethics here are not simply about relationships: distant, objective and cool. They are born of relationships, of relating: directly, intersubjectively and warmly. An intimate process which never ends:

> The theoretical and practical progress of Justice is such that we cannot detach ourselves from it in order to see its end. [...] we will never know the end of Right, because we will never cease creating new relations among ourselves.
> (Proudhon, 1930: 328; trans. Jesse Cohn)

Anti-state, anti-capitalist, anti-racist, anti-sexist, anti-hierarchical, anti-authoritarian: anarchism and other forms of radical politics are criticised for being anti-everything, begging the question, what is anarchism for? I was once challenged for posing a similar question at an activist and intellectual gathering (*Hack the Knowledge Lab*, Lancaster University), by someone who was 'tired of anti-anti'. So, before rushing into what values anarchism affirms, I want to recognise the power and importance of anti-, of no. From the anti-fascist 'no pasaran' of the Spanish Civil War and beyond to the 'fuck off' of anarcho-punk, saying no to domination in whatever form it appears is absolutely crucial in undermining its power. To say no, first, is to carve out a space to say maybe, yes or even 'many yeses' (Kingsnorth, 2003). I see this, too, in an interview from the research project where I first began to think of anarchism as an ethics of relationships. 'Erica' was talking about how she reclaimed her sexuality after a history of childhood sexual abuse:

> My first really sexual experience was to decide not to have sex. To just say 'no' to sex and it came out of fear and out of confusion and out of all sorts of shit but actually it was really affirming and sexual and

made me feel really sexy because I realised that I couldn't really say 'yes' to sex without knowing what it was like to say 'no'.

(Heckert, 2005: 145)

My concern, shared with others (such as Sullivan, 2007), is that the no can be imagined to be unconnected to any yes. Caught up in the addictive numbness of resentment (Nietzsche, 1969), nihilism offers an enticing substitute for an empowering anarchism which has space for both yes and no. Just as a no without a yes denies the possibilities of life, a yes without a no denies the possibilities of choice.

The yes which does not know how to say no (the yes of the ass) is a caricature of affirmation. This is precisely because it says yes to everything which is no, because it puts up with nihilism it continues to serve the power of denying – which is like a demon whose every burden it carries. The Dionysian yes on the contrary, knows how to say no: it is pure affirmation, it has conquered nihilism and divested negation of all autonomous power. But it has done this because it has placed the negative at the service of the powers of affirming. To affirm is to create, not to bear, put up with or accept.

(Deleuze, 2005: 175)

Part of my project, in this chapter, then is to hear the yes behind the no (Kashtan, 2002). For anarchism, with all of its anti-s, 'is an affirmative force that breaks the chains of domination through revolt only in order to better affirm, in the very movement of rupture, another possibility, another composition of the world' (Colson, 2001: 33; trans Cohn). In anarchist critiques of speaking for others and in practices of collective organising, I hear a radical commitment to listening. In offering challenges to institutionalised domination and in demonstrating the power of mutual aid, I hear a radical commitment to care. In undermining the false futures of neoliberalism and stories of the 'end of history' and in practices of individual and collective empowerment and transformation, I hear a radical commitment to becoming.

I see interpreting anarchism as an ethics of direct relationships as consistent with anarchist traditions where the state is viewed as 'a relationship between human beings, a way by which people relate to one another' (Landauer, 2005: 165), characterised by being 'watched, inspected, spied upon, directed, law-driven, numbered, regulated, enrolled, indoctrinated, preached at, controlled, checked, estimated, valued, censured, commanded' (Proudhon, 1923: 293–4), a social relationship which cannot be 'blown up' (Anonymous, 1990), but can be destroyed 'by entering into other relationships, by behaving differently to one another' (Landauer, 2005: 165). Anarchism is offered as affirming alternative relationships to those of state (and equally, to intertwined hierarchical relationships including capitalism, patriarchy, heteronormativity and colonialism). Furthermore, it does so in a way which recognises the capacity of individuals and groups to change those relationships: 'That power is a relationship [...] and not something metaphysical or otherwise beyond the grasp and control of human individuals, is clearly understood by anarchist thinkers' (Brown, 1996: 149).

Approaching anarchism as an ethics of relationships supports longstanding anarchist feminist criticisms of how gendered patterns of domination continue within anarchist milieux by refusing to draw a line between personal and political relationships; or, as Deleuze and Guattari (1988: 213) write, 'every politics is simultaneously a macropolitics and a micropolitics.' Refusing to acknowledge borders between the micro and the macro, the personal and the political, the social and the psychological, anarchism as an ethics of relationships is consistent, too, with postcolonial critique.

> [Colonialism's] most important area of domination was the mental universe of the colonised, the control, through culture, of how people perceived themselves and their relationship to the world.... To control a people's culture is to control their tools of self-definition in relation to others.
> (Ngugi wa Thiong'o, cited in West, 2007: 67; see also, Reinsborough, 2003; de Angelis, 2005)

Placing the emphasis on relationships, then, may offer a basis for letting go of the individualism associated with certain constructions of masculinity and whiteness that are carried into radical anti-racist and anti-sexist movements (starr, 2006; Winnubst, 2006). Understanding anarchism as an ethics of relationships might also explain how anarchist critique encompasses economic, erotic, emotional, ecological and aesthetic relationships as well as a focus on what is narrowly constructed as the political. In doing so, it may bridge the supposedly unbridgeable, offering a common ground where the lifestyle anarchist and the social anarchist (Davis, 2010), the luddite and the hacker (Gordon, 2008), the class warrior and the queer permaculturist may find mutual understanding, if not necessarily agreement. In this logic of affinity (Day, 2005), anarchism recognises that security comes not from the fascist desire for sameness, or the unity of the state (Rocker, 1937; Dean and Massumi, 1992), but through connections which recognise and affirm difference as well as commonality.

Finally, this understanding of anarchism is an eminently practical one. While anarchist discourses frequently prioritise organisation (e.g., in communities and in workplaces), I am in agreement with Donna Haraway (2003: 20) when she argued that 'the "relation" is the smallest possible unit of analysis,' and consequently, a place to start. It seems to me that both individual empowerment and collective organising depend fundamentally on relationships: with self, with other beings, with the land. And anarchism offers a history of thought in practice on the character of sustainable, empowering and egalitarian relationships. As the eco-feminist and anarchist philosopher Chaia Heller (1999: 93) once wrote,

> if capitalism is a set of *social* relationships based on exploitation, regularization, alienation, and commodification, then the antidote to capitalist rationalization is a new relationality, an empathetic, sensual, and rational way of relating that is deeply cooperative, pleasurable, and meaningful.

Yet how often are the relationships in groups put aside to focus on abstract, macropolitical questions? How many anarchist projects have struggled or even fallen apart disastrously because of relationship difficulties (an example being Hansen, 2002)? Or, to put it another way, what else is anarchism but an invitation to the joys and pains of relating to each other in deeply egalitarian ways? In this chapter, I hope to offer some helpful thoughts on the very practical question of organising.

Nurturing autonomy in communities, workplaces, ecosystems and homes, it seems to me, necessarily involves getting on with others who experience the world differently. Things fall apart or come together through relationships. In this way, anarchist politics does not need to hold itself against those dominant, and dominating, terms of a 'culture of evaluation' (Weaver, 2008): success and failure, particularly where success refers to a global revolution abolishing all systems of domination and failure refers to all else. Instead, an emphasis on relationships prioritises the small steps of everyday life, making anarchy accessible without being watered down, not so much gradualist or reformist as *emergent* (Chesters, 2003; Chesters and Welsh, 2006). Likewise, this emphasis on relationships maintains anarchy as alive (Gordon, 2008) without being limited to *anarchists*; anarchism, in this sense, might be understood as an appreciation of (and desire for) the anarchy which in various ways and to varying degrees already exists: as nature (Kropotkin, 2009; Jones, 2009), as ontology (Bey, 1994), as human culture (Barclay, 1990; Graeber, 2004) and as an everyday part of life hidden when we focus on domination as definitive of reality (Ward, 1982; Shukaitis, 2009). Anarchy is alive and well, and it is everywhere.

My methodology in coming to tell this story of anarchism as an ethics of direct relationships is, among other things, ethnographic.

> When one carries out an ethnography, one observes what people do, and then tries to tease out the hidden symbolic, moral, or pragmatic logics that underlie their actions; one tries to get at the way people's habits and actions make sense in ways that they are not themselves completely aware of. One obvious role for a radical intellectual is to do precisely that: to look at those who are creating viable alternatives, try to figure out what might be larger implications of what they are (already) doing, and then offer those ideas back, not as prescriptions, but as contributions, possibilities – as gifts.
>
> (Graeber, 2004: 11–12)

Listening, caring, becoming. These are the anarchist ethics I have seen, heard, felt, tasted. They are also the ethics I have desired. Perhaps this chapter contains not only histories of anarchist thought and an ethnography of the present but also 'an archaeology of the future' (Le Guin, 1988: 3).

10.1 Listening

> The capacity to give one's attention to a sufferer is a very rare and difficult thing; it is almost a miracle; it is a miracle. Nearly all those who think they have the capacity do not possess it.
>
> (Simone Weil, quoted in Rosenberg, 2003: 92)

For anarchists, a critique of representation is 'something absolutely fundamental: the indignity of speaking for others' (Deleuze, 1977; see also, May, 1994; Sullivan, 2005; Tormey, 2006). In anarchist discourse, this is expressed as an ethical commitment to people being involved as directly as possible in making the decisions that affect their lives. It might also be expressed as the dignity of listening to others, the dignity of being listened to.

This process might begin with learning to listen to oneself, to the authority of one's own experience, one's own knowledge, one's own body. Indeed, it is essential in learning to question others' claims of authority.

> In the matter of boots I refer to the authority of the bootmakers; concerning houses, canals or railroads I consult that of the architect or engineer. For such or such special knowledge I apply to such or such a savant. But I allow neither the bootmaker nor the architect nor the savant to impose his authority upon me. I accept them freely and with all the respect merited by their intelligence, their character, their knowledge, reserving always my incontestable right of criticism and censure.
> (Bakunin, cited in Kinna, 2005: 70)

This sentiment is echoed strongly in anarcha-feminist discourse where women support each other to resist patriarchal claims of authority, whether in relation to health (see Gordon and Griffiths, 2007; Griffiths and Gordon, 2007; Lisa, 2008) or notions of what constitutes the political or the revolutionary (examples include Dark Star, 2002; Jeppesen, 2004; Ackelsburg, 2005; Jose, 2005; Davis, forthcoming).

Learning to listen to oneself might be seen to constitute a practice of direct action, a counter-practice to a culture in which many of us have learned to doubt ourselves, to believe ourselves lesser (or greater) than others. This may also be understood as prefigurative – a means which is an end in itself. Listening is also a becoming. By listening to oneself, I do not mean to become caught up in the stories of the mind – the tales of how things really are, of who you really are and of what is possible. I suggest caution towards these narratives – they are simply stories, simply points of view (e.g., Stainton Rogers and Stainton Rogers, 1997; Chödrön, 2002). Coming to believe that they are unquestionably true inhibits one's capacity to listen, to empathise, to care. There are always other stories, other ways to see. No, I refer here to a deeper listening – a listening to one's own body, to sensations and desires, to pleasure and pain, to breathe and perhaps even to a stillness within that lies behind thought and feeling (Adyashanti, 2006). For domination, too, exists 'in a more subtle psychological sense, of body by mind, of spirit by a shallow instrumental rationality' (Bookchin, 2003: 4). And I know, the more deeply I listen to myself, the more I am able to listen to others, to be open to their stories, their points of view, to craft together revolutions great and small (Rosenberg, 2003).

The capacity to listen to others is, it seems to me, integral to the radically libertarian, egalitarian and participatory forms of organisation promoted and practised in anarchism. Liberty to express one's own thoughts, feelings and desires (verbally or through other forms of behaviour) without listening with care to the thoughts, feelings and desires of others is more consistent with the macho individualism of capitalism than the social libertarianism of anarchism. Likewise, the equality under the law of liberal democracy only requires very shallow forms of listening (such as ballot counting, lobbying and petitioning) in contrast to the deep listening desired, if not always found, in horizontal methods of organising. And in anarchism as participatory culture, where everyone is invited to make their contributions to decision-making and to co-creating the structures of social life, participants ideally learn to listen to each other in order to work and play together (such as McDonald, 2002; Le Guin, 2004; Sitrin, 2006). It is this ethic of listening which keeps anarchism fresh and alive, like the Zapatismo which is one of its contemporary sources of inspiration.

> The idea of a listening revolution turns preconceived notions of struggle on their head. Zapatismo throws political certainty to the wind, and out of the shape-shifting mist it grasps change; change not as a banal revolutionary slogan, but as actual process. Change as the ability of revolutionaries to admit mistakes, to stop and question everything.
>
> (Jordan, 2004: 484)

Rather than relying on fixed structures and rigid thinking, anarchism perhaps then involves developing a comfort with uncertainty (Chödrön, 2002).

Finally, many currents of anarchism, contemporary and historical, are inspired by a deep recognition of the interdependence of humankind with the rest of the ecosystems of which we are only ever a part. This is sometimes expressed as learning to listen to the land. For pagan, permaculturist and/or primitivist anarchists, this may have a very literal meaning. Influential writers such as Derrick Jensen (2000) and Starhawk (2004) have described their deepening sense of connection with land and life through listening to plants and non-human animals — something which might be considered insane in Eurocentric discourses of pathologisation (i.e., labelling difference as illness). Jensen and Starhawk, among others, reverse this discourse, arguing that indigenous cultures have always listened to the land, that it is the dominant culture that is insane in its refusal to do so. Similarly, many anarchists are inspired by permaculture – an ethical design system for creating permanent agriculture and permanent culture inspired by the understandings of natural systems developed by indigenous peoples. It is a practical method of producing abundance despite capitalism's efforts to produce scarcity. Like anarchism, ecology is a fundamentally cooperative effort, and, as permaculturist Patrick Whitefield (2007: 414) writes,

> We can only co-operate with a person or a place if first we listen to them. I use the word listening here in its broadest sense, to include all the ways we can learn about places and people, not just those which involve our ears.

10.2 Caring

> [Human beings suffer from] a nostalgia for which there is no remedy upon earth except as is to be found in the enlightenment of the spirit – some ability to have a perceptive rather than an exploitative relationship with his [sic] fellow creatures.
>
> (Bakunin, quoted in Tifft and Sullivan, 1980: 2)

Whether expressed as class solidarity (Franks, 2006), mutual aid (Kropotkin, 2009) or love (Horrox, 2009; Christoyannopoulos, 2010; Davis, forthcoming), anarchism involves an ethic of care. I use this term advisedly, aware of the ways in which control over others, including institutionalisation, can be exercised under the guise of care. It is in this patronising sense that disability activists, for example, have been critical (Sposaro, 2003; Hughes et al., 2005; Shakespeare, 2006). Similarly, an anarchist ethic of care rejects paternal notions of development: 'If you come only to help me, you can go back home. But if you consider my struggle as part of your struggle for survival, then maybe we can work together' (Q. Australian aboriginal woman in People's Global Action, 2008). I remember how shocked I felt the first time I heard an anarchist say, 'I don't support charity.' I have since come to recognise how the dynamics by which charity, imposed notions of development and certain practices called care continually act to produce hierarchical relationships, separating the giver from the receiver. An anarchist ethic of care, therefore, is one which emphasises equality, mutuality, embodiment and interdependence – similar in many ways to certain contemporary feminist formulations (Beasley and Bacchi, 2007).

The practice of this ethic of care might, once again, begin with the self. In purely practical terms, an uncared-for self is unlikely to be able to practise sustainable and mutual forms of care. To prioritise care for others over care for the self, or indeed to imagine that they are separable, is to sidestep mutuality, perhaps out of certain cultural norms of the strong and independent individual, and to ensure burnout (Jones, 2007). For Foucault, with whom a number of thinkers see a great affinity with anarchism, care of the self is a practice of freedom. In the antiquity which he studied, it was this practice by which one constituted oneself an ethical subject, ethical in relationships with others and with regard to questions of social organisation. Before his death he was unable to turn to the question of how one might apply this practice in response to current patterns of domination. However, on the subject Foucault (1987: 14) said,

> I have the impression that in the political thought of the 19th century – and we might even have to go beyond, to Rousseau and Hobbes – the political subject has been thought essentially as subject to law, either in naturalist terms or in terms of positive law. In turn, it seems to me that the question of an ethical subject does not have much of a place in contemporary political thought.

The ethical subject, that of anarchist (anti-)political philosophy, who is not subject to law, may only come into existence through care of the self. This care of the self is simultaneously a care for others; this is the interdependent self, the relational self, the ecological self whose needs are intertwined with the needs of other beings.

Anarchist ethics emphasise the care for others, often crossing borders of species, citizenship and any supposed line between 'us' and the 'more-than-human world' (Abram, 1997). This may be expressed through valuing some practices of relationship over others. Note, for example, Uri Gordon's contrasting of permaculture with capitalism.

> The permaculture ethic of 'care for the land and the people', transposed into broader cultural terms, would involve facilitating that self-development of the plant or the person, the garden or the community, each according to its own context – working with, rather than against, the organic momentum of the entity cared for. Whereas in monoculture (or industry, or existing social relations) what is

sought after is the opposite – maximal control and harnessing of natural processes and labour power.

(2008: 137)

In capitalist stories, resources are inherently scarce and it is not possible for everyone's needs to be met. In anarchist stories, scarcity is precisely the effect of capitalism, of the enclosure of resources. The same applies to care; what patterns of social relations produce an apparent scarcity of love, intimacy, understanding and empathy? In this story, only some of us are good, deserving of love and respect; or, in other words, capitalism involves a moral economy of personhood (Skeggs, 2004). Some are bad, undeserving, unworthy. We might invert this story of bourgeois morality, instead claiming that the oppressed are good and the oppressors bad (what Nietzsche refers to as a slave morality). Rosenberg (2003) offers an alternative, questioning the purpose of moral judgement entirely and working to undermine moral hierarchies through micropolitical practice and through the development of sociocracy (a model for a self-governing society which has affinities to, and overlaps with, anarchist approaches). Is moral judgement always at the same time an unacknowledged expression of pain for life-serving desires (e.g., freedom or equality) unmet or of pleasure for those which are fulfilled? What is the insistence on moralising but a strategy for denying pain (and thus pleasure), resorting instead to abstraction (what Nietzsche calls *ressentiment*)?

Drawing on Nietzsche's argument, the feminist philosopher Wendy Brown has suggested that the disempowering strategy of a state-centred politics of recognition may well be an effect of this simultaneous denial of, and holding on to, pain: 'politicised identities generated out of liberal, disciplinary societies, insofar as they are premised on exclusion from a universal ideal, require that ideal, as well as their exclusion from it, for their own perpetuity as identities' (1993: 398). I suspect the same may apply to anarchist identities. Like Newman, my interest is in 'an anarchism without ressentiment' (2004: 124). Letting go of pain, resentment and judgement may offer the basis of a compassionate anarchist ethic, sidestepping the disempowering effects of identities and politics defined by inequality, by unfreedom. Pleasures and pains, values and desires expressed directly may be easier for others to hear than the authority-claims of morality, thus further facilitating relationships (Rosenberg, 2003). This compassionate spirit infuses much, though certainly not all, of anarchist discourse. I see it here in this critique of prison by American anarchist Voltairine de Cleyre (2004: 154).

I think that within every bit of human flesh and spirit that has ever crossed the enigma bridge of life, from the prehistoric racial morning until now, all crime and all virtue were germinal. Out of one great soul-stuff are we sprung, you and I and all of us; and if in you the virtue has grown and not the vice, do not therefore conclude that you are essentially different from him whom you have helped to put in stripes and behind bars.

Instead of a punitive 'justice' system, anarchist criminology emphasises restorative justice:

> [J]ustice done restoratively requires that participants continually remain open to each other's concerns, ideas, needs, feelings, desires, pain and suffering, so that each can see the other not as a resource to be used or exploited or as an object to be derided or scorned, but as he or she is, similar to oneself, a person engaged in an unending struggle to become human, with dignity [...]. When such collaboration takes place, we experience the beginnings of a restorative community, of a political economy of peace and democracy.
> (Sullivan and Tifft, 2001: 30; see also Tifft and Sullivan, 1980; Rosenberg, 2004; Gaarder, 2009)

This ethos of care for others is not limited to a critique of prisons, but is found throughout anarchist politics: in animal liberation, deep ecology, feminist health projects, anti-militarism, class struggle, queer liberation, No Borders activism and beyond.

10.3 Becoming

> Anarchists have often compared this open cooperative social structure to a biological organism. Organisms are living beings which evolve of their own free will through a process of perpetual becoming that is unbounded and non-deterministic. Similarly, an anarchist society emulates this openness through a harmonious social structure that is free, dynamic, and ever-evolving.
> (Antliff, 2008: 6)

One of the most frequent responses to anarchist ideas is that they sound good in theory, but can never work. People are just not like that – caring, cooperative and egalitarian. For anarchist theorists, among other social scientists and philosophers of course, this human nature argument is suspect.

> Surely our understanding of the nature of man [sic] or of the range of viable social forms is so rudimentary that any far-reaching doctrine must be treated with great scepticism, just as scepticism is in order when we hear that 'human nature' or 'the demands of efficiency' or 'the complexity of modern life' requires this or that form of oppression and autocratic rule.
> (Chomsky, 2005: 119)

One might well ask two questions in response to a human nature argument: (1) how is it that people come to perceive each other as predominantly or essentially hierarchical and competitive? (2) What is it about particular macro-level patterns of social relations (such as the state, capitalism and patriarchy) that support or encourage particular traits (such as obedience, competition and domination)?

In relation to the second question, anarchists have developed more sophisticated arguments than simply suggesting that the official political economy and all other mechanisms of control could be abolished in a moment allowing human nature to be free to express its natural cooperative instincts, free of repression (Clark, 2007; Morland, 1997).

> The problem is not of trying to dissolve [relations of power] in the utopia of perfectly transparent communication, but to give one's self the rules of law, the techniques of management, and also the ethics, the ethos, the practice of self, which would allow these games of power to be played with a minimum of domination.
> (Foucault, 1987: 18)

Rather than an event of liberation, social revolution towards possible anarchist futures might be understood better as a becoming – the process by which people learn self-management (autonomy).

Autonomy, too, is a becoming:

> Autonomy is not a fixed, essential state. Like gender, autonomy is created through its performance, by doing/becoming; it is a political practice. To become autonomous is to refuse authoritarian and compulsory cultures of separation and hierarchy through embodied practices of welcoming difference [...]. Becoming autonomous is a

political position for it thwarts the exclusions of proprietary knowledge and jealous hoarding of resources, and replaces the social and economic hierarchies on which these depend with a politics of skill exchange, welcome, and collaboration. Freely sharing these with others creates a common wealth of knowledge and power that subverts the domination and hegemony of the master's rule.

(subRosa Collective, 2003: 12–13)

Both the macro-level patterns of social order desired (such as anarchy or autonomy) and the individuals who both constitute and are constituted by the social order are processes. The anarchist is made, not born. As Carole Pateman points out, 'participation develops and fosters the very qualities necessary for it; the more individuals participate the better able they become to do so' (1970: 42–3). More recently, non-hierarchical ecological politics have also drawn on this ethic of empowerment through direct participation, direct action.

> Power-to must involve participation, but not any kind of participation: it is only when it is active and constructive that it meets needs effectively. Empowerment is a process of self-organisation and self-realisation – a process, because it is passed on through co-operation between different empowered agents. Through co-operation, we can build whole empowered societies.
>
> (Begg, 2000: 141)

Once again, empowerment of the individual is intertwined with empowering relationships – there is no division between the personal and the political. The question of whether or not people are immediately capable of self-organisation without rigid structures of control is, then, perhaps not the most relevant one. Anarchists, instead, might ask: what do people need to learn, what do I need to learn, to practice, to become more capable? How can we support each other in those practices, in that learning?

To return to the question of perception, one of the reasons I have emphasised listening to the self, care of the self, is precisely because it seems to me that these are what enable both a broader perception of *what is* and a wider imagination of *what is possible*. How quickly we have learned to draw conclusions about the state of the world, the state of human nature, to come to believe those stories as unquestionable truths. The practice of anarchy, of autonomy, necessitates a certain open-mindedness – otherwise, it becomes a new dogma, a new institutionalisation of knowledge/power (as discussed by Crimeth Inc., 2002; also see Foucault, 1980). Anarchists have taken up numerous strategies in order to nurture this open-mindedness. Radical pedagogy (such as Suissa, 2006; Latif and Jeppesen, 2007) and mental health projects (raised by The Icarus Project, 2009), film making (Porton, 1999, 2009), storytelling (Le Guin, 2004, 2009; Killjoy, 2009), street theatre and other forms of cultural activism (Duncombe, 2002; Grindon, 2008; Shepard, 2009) and, of course, anarchist philosophy all work to nurture a sense of imagination, an openness to possibilities.

Imagination has long been important to anarchism (Shukaitis, 2009). For those who particularly emphasise the inseparability of mind and body, a flexibility of imagination and emotion is deeply intertwined with a flexibility of muscle and ligament. Thus, anarchist practices of becoming also include yoga, tai chi, dance, football and other forms of movement and play. These practices alter perception not only of what is possible but also of what already exists. As Anaïs Nin once wrote, 'We see the world as "we" are, not as "it" is; because it is the "I" behind the "eye" that does the seeing' (Quoted in Institute of General Semantics, 2009). Changing ourselves changes our perception of 'reality' and, consequently, what might be realistic.

10.4 Conclusion: Being and becoming

> The state is a relationship between human beings, a way by which people relate to one another; and one destroys it by entering into other relationships, by behaving differently to one another. [...] we are the state – and are it as long as we are not otherwise, as long as we have not created the institutions that constitute a genuine community and society of human beings.
>
> (Landauer, 1910/2005: 165)

What characterises this condition, this relationship between human beings, that we might call the state? Is it, at least in part, a fear of intimacy, a fear of life? Is this the contrast Landauer offers when he posits community as other than the state? Community, not as idealised vision of perfect harmony and easy relationships – relationships of production and reproduction, of work and family, of culture and knowledge. No, not this. Community, rather, as living experience, always involving the pleasures and pains of intimacy. Community as a vibrant network of relationships, of relating to each other as equals (May, 2009), as subjects not objects, as co-creators, as fellow beings who are always becoming.

And the state? The state is that condition, that relationship, that strategy of trying to make something happen (Scott, 1998). Rules and regulations, standards and measures, blueprints and judgements, the state is the relationship that is trying too hard to get it right and in doing so prevents the very intimacy desired. The state is the mind intruding on the body: the dancer getting in the way of the dance, the seducer, fancying himself the lover yet never experiencing love, the protector of the weak (Brown, 1995), denying himself the pleasures of weakness – of receiving care, of surrendering to a life which is so much more than just himself and his armour. I do not say this to judge the dancer, the seducer, the protector; if I do, I judge myself at the same time. Instead, I might simply grieve. For the state, as a simultaneously micro-political and emergent macro-web of social relations, is a multitude of opportunities for intimacy lost.

To listen, to care, involves an awareness of presence, of being which is not caught up in thought, in judgement. When judgement arises, compassionate listening may be able to hear the feelings and desires which underlie the judgement. It is this which allows for connection, for relationship (Rosenberg, 2003). This is an intimate form of direct action. The non-authoritarian philosophy of J. Krishnamurti may be helpful here. He questions the place of thought in relationships – are we relating to a living, breathing and changing self/other or to the image of the self/other in the mind? For him, 'relationship is direct, not through an image' (2005: 23). Letting go of the image, of the need to draw conclusions about who we/they are, relationship is to Krishnamurti the key to freedom because it creates an alternative to violence and to authority.

> Obviously there must be authority as long as community is based on violence. Is not our present social structure based on violence, on intolerance? The community is you and another in relationship; and is not your relationship based on violence? Are you not ultimately out for yourself? Is not our present relationship based on violence – violence being the process of self-enclosure, isolation? Is not our daily action a process of isolation? And since each one is isolating himself [sic], there must be authority to bring about cohesion, either the authority of the state, or the authority of organised religion.
>
> (1997: 19)

Like Foucault and many anarchists before and since, Krishnamurti points out the problem is not simply the state as institution, but also the individualism upon which the state and other forms of domination depend. If, as Krishnamurti suggests, *being present* is precisely what enables direct relationship, enables a letting go of individualism, then this may be the continual practice from which the becoming-revolution springs.

Acknowledgements

Written with warm thanks to the supportive efforts of Matt Wilson, Benjamin Franks, Anthony McCann, Jesse Cohn and an anonymous reviewer, and to the students of *Social and Political Movements* at the University of Edinburgh (2006–07) and the organisers and participants of *Practical Utopias and Utopian Practices*, University of Bristol, and the *Anarchist Studies Network Conference*, University of Loughborough (both 2008), where I presented earlier versions of this chapter.

Bibliography

D. Abram (1997) *The Spell of the Sensuous: Perception and Language in a More-Than-Human World* (New York: Vintage Books).
M. Ackelsburg (2005) *Free Women of Spain: Anarchism and the Struggle for the Emancipation of Women* (Oakland/Edinburgh: AK Press).
Adyashanti (2006) *True Meditation* (Louisville, CO: Sounds True).
Anonymous (1990) *You Can't Blow Up a Social Relationship: The Anarchist Case Against Terrorism* (Tucson, AZ: See Sharp Press).
A. Antliff (2008) 'Open forum and the abstract imperative: Herbert Read and contemporary anarchist art', *Anarchist Studies*, XVI(i): 6–19.
H. Barclay (1990) *People Without Government: An Anthropology of Anarchy* (London: Kahn and Averill).
C. Beasley and C. Bacchi (2007) 'Envisaging a new politics for an ethical future: Beyond trust, care and generosity – towards an ethic of "social flesh" ', *Feminist Theory*, VIII(iii): 279–98.
A. Begg (2000) *Empowering the Earth: Strategies for Social Change* (Foxhole: Green Books).
H. Bey (1994) *Immediatism* (Oakland/Edinburgh: AK Press).
M. Bookchin (2003) *The Ecology of Freedom: The Emergence and Dissolution of Hierarchy* (Warner, NH: Silver Brook Press).
L. S. Brown (1996) 'Beyond feminism: Anarchism and human freedom' in H. Ehrlich (ed.) *Reinventing Anarchy, Again* (Oakland/Edinburgh: AK Press).
W. Brown (1993) 'Wounded attachments', *Political Theory*, XXI(iii): 390–410.
―――― (1995) *States of Injury: Power and Freedom in Late Modernity* (Princeton: Princeton University Press).
L. Call (2002) *Postmodern Anarchism* (New York/Oxford: Lexington Books).

G. Chesters (2003) 'Shapeshifting: Civil society, complexity and social movements', *Anarchist Studies*, XI(i): 42–65.
G. Chesters and I. Welsh (2006) *Complexity and Social Movements: Multitudes at the Edge of Chaos* (London: Routledge).
P. Chödrön (2002) *Comfortable with Uncertainty: 108 Teachings on Cultivating Fearlessness and Compassion* (Boston, MA: Shambhala).
N. Chomsky (2005) *Chomsky on Anarchism* (Oakland/Edinburgh: AK Press).
A. Christoyannopoulos (2010) *Christian Anarchism: A Political Commentary on the Gospel* (Exeter: Imprint Academic).
S. Clark (2007) *Living Without Domination: The Possibility of an Anarchist Utopia* (Farnham: Ashgate).
D. Colson (2001) *Petit Lexique Philosophique de L'anarchisme de Proudhon à Deleuze* (Paris: Librairie Générale Française).
CrimethInc. (2002) 'Why we're right and you're wrong (Infighting the good fight)' *Harbinger*, IV, http://www.crimethinc.com/texts/harbinger/infighting.php, date accessed: 1 October 2009.
Dark Star Collective (2002) *Quiet Rumours: An Anarcha-Feminist Reader* (Oakland/Edinburgh/London: AK Press/Dark Star).
L. Davis (forthcoming) 'Love and revolution in Le Guin's *Four Ways to Forgiveness*' in J. Heckert and R. Cleminson (eds) *Anarchism & Sexuality: Ethics, Relationships and Power* (London: Routledge).
—— (2010) 'Social anarchism or lifestyle anarchism: An unhelpful dichotomy'. *Anarchist Studies*, XVIII(i): 62–82.
R. Day (2005) *Gramsci Is Dead: Anarchist Currents in the Newest Social Movements* (London: Pluto Press).
M. de Angelis (2005) 'Zapatismo and globalization as social relations', *Humboldt Journal of Social Relations*, XXIX(i): 179–203.
V. de Cleyre (2004) *The Voltairine de Cleyre Reader* (Oakland/Edinburgh: AK Press).
K. Dean and B. Massumi (1992) *First and Last Emperors: The Absolute State and the Body of the Despot* (New York: Autonomedia).
G. Deleuze (1977) 'Intellectuals and power: A conversation between Michel Foucault and Gilles Deleuze' in D. Bouchard (trans.), D. Bouchard and S. Simon (eds) *Language, Counter-Memory, Practice* (Ithaca: Cornell University Press). Also available online at http://libcom.org/library/intellectuals-power-a-conversation-between-michel-foucault-and-gilles-deleuze, date accessed: 2 May 2008.
—— (2005) *Nietzsche and Philosophy* (New York/London: Continuum).
G. Deleuze and F. Guattari (1988) *A Thousand Plateaus: Capitalism and Schizophrenia* (London: Athlone).
S. Duncombe (ed.) (2002) *Cultural Resistance Reader* (London: Verso).
M. Foucault (1980) *Power/Knowledge*. C. Gordon (ed.); C. Gordon, L. Marshall, J. Mepham and K. Soper (trans.) (Brighton: Harvester Press).
—— (1987) *The Final Foucault* (Cambridge, MA: The MIT Press).
B. Franks (2006) *Rebel Alliances: The Means and Ends of British Anarchisms* (Oakland/Edinburgh: AK Press).
E. Gaarder (2009) 'Addressing violence against women: Alternatives to state-based law and punishment' in R. Amster, A. Deleon, L. Fernandez, A. Nocella and D. Shannon (eds) *Contemporary Anarchist Studies: An Introductory Anthology of Anarchy in the Academy* (London: Routledge).

M. Goldberg (2005) *Telling Mythologies: Pasts and Possible Futures in Activist Literature* (Self-published MSc thesis: Centre for Human Ecology), http://www.myshelegoldberg.com/academic/goldberg_thesis.pdf, date accessed: 3 May 2008.

T. Gordon and B. Griffiths (2007) 'How to manage your own health' in Trapeze Collective (ed.) *Do It Yourself: A Handbook for Changing Our World* (London: Pluto Press).

U. Gordon (2008) *Anarchy Alive! Anti-Authoritarian Politics from Practice to Theory* (London/Ann Arbor: Pluto).

D. Graeber (2004) *Fragments of an Anarchist Anthropology* (Chicago: Prickly Paradigm Press).

B. Griffiths and T. Gordon (2007) 'Why society is making us sick' in Trapeze Collective (ed.) *Do It Yourself: A Handbook for Changing Our World* (London: Pluto Press).

G. Grindon (2008) *Aesthetics and Radical Politics* (Newcastle-on-Tyne: Cambridge Scholars Publishing).

A. Hansen (2002) *Direct Action: Memoirs of an Urban Guerrilla* (Oakland/Edinburgh: AK Press).

D. Haraway (2003) *The Companion Species Manifesto: Dogs, People, and Significant Otherness* (Chicago: Prickly Paradigm Press).

J. Heckert (2005) *Resisting Orientation: On the Complexities of Desire and the Limits of Identity Politics* (Self published PhD thesis, University of Edinburgh), http://sexualorientation.info/thesis/, date accessed: 5 October 2009.

C. Heller (1999) *Ecology of Everyday Life: Rethinking the Desire for Nature* (Montreal: Black Rose Books).

J. Horrox (2009) *A Living Revolution: Anarchism in the Kibbutz Movement* (Oakland/Edinburgh: AK Press).

B. Hughes, L. McKie, D. Hopkins and N. Watson (2005) 'Love's labours lost? Feminism, the disabled people's movement and an ethic of care', *Sociology*, XXXIX(ii): 259–75.

Icarus Project, The (2009) http://theicarusproject.net/, date accessed: 5 October 2009.

Institute of General Semantics (2009) http://generalsemantics.org/, date accessed: 5 October 2009.

D. Jensen (2000) *A Language Older than Words* (London: Souvenir Press).

S. Jeppesen (2004) 'Seeing past the outpost of post-anarchism', http://auto_sol.tao.ca/node/77, date accessed: 5 October 2009.

P. Jones (2007) *Aftershock: Confronting Trauma in a Violent World: A Guide for Activists and Their Allies* (Herndon, VA: Lantern Books).

—— (2009) 'Free as a bird: natural anarchism in action' in R. Amster, A. Deleon, L. Fernandez, A. Nocella and D. Shannon (eds) *Contemporary Anarchist Studies: An Introductory Anthology of Anarchy in the Academy* (London: Routledge).

J. Jordan (2004) 'The sound and the fury: The invisible icons of anticapitalism' in D. Solnit (ed.) *Globalize Liberation: How to Uproot the System and Build a Better World* (San Francisco, CA: City Light Books).

J. Jose (2005) '"Nowhere at home", not even in theory: Emma Goldman, anarchism and political theory', *Anarchist Studies*, XIII: 23–46.

I. Kashtan (2002) 'Hearing the "yes" in the "no."' The Centre for Nonviolent Communication, http://www.cnvc.org/en/what-nvc/articles-writings/hearing-yes-no/hearing-yes-no, date accessed: 5 October 2009.

M. Killjoy (2009) *Mythmakers and Lawbreakers: Anarchist Writers on Fiction* (Oakland/Edinburgh: AK Press).

P. Kingsnorth (2003) *One No, Many Yeses: A Journey to the Heart of the Global Resistance Movement* (London: Simon and Schuster).

R. Kinna (2005) *Anarchism: A Beginner's Guide* (Oxford: Oneworld).

J. Krishnamurti (1997) *Krishnamurti: Reflections on the Self* (Chicago: Open Court Publishing Company).

—— (2005) *Facing a World in Crisis: What Life Teaches Us in Challenging Times* (Boston: Shambhala).

P. Kropotkin (2009) *Mutual Aid: A Factor of Evolution* (London: Freedom Press).

G. Landauer (1910/2005) 'Weak statesmen, weaker people', *Der Sozialist* in R. Graham (ed.) *Anarchism: A Documentary History of Libertarian Ideas: From Anarchy to Anarchism (300CE–1939)*, Volume 1 (Montreal: Black Rose Books).

A. Latif and S. Jeppesen (2007) 'Toward an antiauthoritarian antiracist pedagogy' in S. Shukaitis and D. Graeber (eds) *Constituent Imagination: Militant Investigations, Collective Theorization* (Oakland/Edinburgh: AK Press).

U. Le Guin (1988) *Always Coming Home* (London: Grafton).

—— (2004) 'Telling is listening' in *The Wave in the Mind: Talks and Essays on the Writer, the Reader, and the Imagination* (Boston: Shambhala).

—— (2009) 'A message about messages' in *Cheek by Jowl Talks & Essays on How & Why Fantasy Matters* (Seattle: Aqueduct Press).

Lisa (2008) *Threads* (Glasgow: self-published).

T. May (1994) *The Political Philosophy of Poststructuralist Anarchism* (University Park: Pennsylvania State University Press).

—— (2009) 'Anarchism from Foucaults to Rancière' in R. Amster, A. Deleon, L. Fernandez, A. Nocella and D. Shannon (eds) *Contemporary Anarchist Studies: An Introductory Anthology of Anarchy in the Academy* (London: Routledge).

K. McDonald (2002) 'From solidarity to fluidity: Social movements beyond "collective identity" – The case of globalised conflicts', *Social Movement Studies*, I(ii): 109–28.

D. Morland (1997) *Demanding the Impossible?: Human Nature and Politics in Nineteenth-Century Social Anarchism* (London: Continuum).

S. Newman (2004) 'Anarchism and the politics of ressentiment' in J. Moore with Spencer Sunshine (eds) *I Am Not a Man, I Am Dynamite! Friedrich Nietzsche and the Anarchist Tradition* (New York: Autonomedia).

F. Nietzsche (1969) *On The Genealogy of Morals* (New York: Vintage).

C. Pateman (1970) *Participation and Democratic Theory* (Cambridge: Cambridge University Press).

People's Global Action (2008) *PGA Bulletin* I, https://www.nadir.org/nadir/initiativ/agp/en/pgainfos/bulletin1.html, date accessed: 3 May 2008.

R. Porton (1999) *Film and the Anarchist Imagination* (London: Verso).

—— (2009) *Arena: On Anarchist Cinema* (San Francisco, CA: PM Press).

P.-J. Proudhon (1923) *General Idea of the Revolution in the Nineteenth Century* (London: Freedom Press).

——— (1930) *De la Création de l'Ordre dans l'humanité ou principes d'organisation politique*, Volume 1 (Paris: Rivière).

P. Reinsborough (2003) 'De-colonizing the revolutionary imagination,' *Journal of Aesthetics and Protest*, I(ii), http://www.journalofaestheticsandprotest.org/1/de_colonizing/index.html, date accessed: 5 October 2009.

R. Rocker (1937) *Nationalism and Culture* (London: Freedom Press).

M. Rosenberg (2003) *Nonviolent Communication: A Language of Life* (Encinitas, CA: PuddleDancer Press).

——— (2004) *We Can Work It Out: Resolving Conflicts Peacefully and Powerfully* (Encinitas, CA: PuddleDancer Press).

J. C. Scott (1998) *Seeing Like a State: How Certain Schemes to Improve the Human Condition Have Failed* (New Haven: Yale University Press).

T. Shakespeare (2006) *Disability Rights and Wrongs* (London: Routledge).

B. Shepard (2009) *Queer Political Performance and Protest* (London: Routledge).

S. Shukaitis (2009) *Imaginal Machines: Autonomy and Self-Organization in the Revolutions of Everyday Life* (London: Minor Compositions).

M. Sitrin (2006) *Horizontalism: Voices of Popular Power in Argentina* (Oakland, CA: AK Press).

B. Skeggs (2004) *Class, Self, Culture* (London: Routledge).

M. Sposaro (2003) 'Anarchism and blindness', InfoShop News, http://news.infoshop.org/article.php?story=03/05/28/2994545, date accessed: 5 October 2009.

W. Stainton Rogers and R. Stainton Rogers (1997) 'Does critical social psychology mean the end of the world?' in T. Ibáñez and L. Íñigues (eds) *Critical Social Psychology* (London: Sage).

Starhawk (2004) *The Earth Path: Grounding Your Spirit in the Rhythms of Nature* (San Francisco: Harper).

a. starr (2006) 'Grumpywarriorcool: What makes our movements white?' in S. Best and A. J. Nocella, II (eds) *Igniting a Revolution: Voices in Defence of the Earth* (Oakland/Edinburgh: AK Press).

subRosa Collective (2003) 'Introduction: Practicing cyberfeminisms' in M. Fernandez, F. Wilding and M. Wright (eds) *Domain Errors! Cyberfeminist Practices* (New York: Autonomedia).

J. Suissa (2006) *Anarchism and Education: A Philosophical Perspective* (London: Routledge).

D. Sullivan and L. Tifft (2001) *Restorative Justice: Healing the Foundations of Our Everyday Lives* (Monsey, NY: Willow Tree Press).

S. Sullivan (2005) 'An other world is possible? On representation, rationalism and romanticism in social forums', *Ephemera*, V(ii): 370–92, http://www.ephemeraweb.org/journal/5-2/5-2ssullivan.pdf, date accessed: 3 May 2008.

——— (2007) ' "Viva Nihilism!" On militancy and machismo in (anti-) globalization protest' in R. Devetak and C. Hughes (eds) *The Globalization of Political Violence: Globalization's Shadow* (London: Routledge).

L. Tifft and D. Sullivan (1980) *The Struggle to Be Human: Crime, Criminology, and Anarchism* (Sanday: Cienfuegos Press).

S. Tormey (2006) ' "Not in my name": Deleuze, Zapatismo and the critique of representation', *Parliamentary Affairs*, LIX(i): 138–54.

B. Tucker (1897) *Instead of a Book: By a Man Too Busy to Write One: A Fragmentary Exposition of Philosophical Anarchism* (New York: B. R. Tucker).

C. Ward (1982) *Anarchy in Action* (London: Freedom Press).
K. Weaver (2008) Personal Communication, 8 July 2009.
R. West (2007) *Out of the Shadow: Ecopsychology, Story, and Encounters with the Land* (London: University of Virginia Press).
P. Whitefield (2007) *The Earth Care Manual: A Permaculture Handbook For Britain and Other Temperate Climates* (East Meon, Hampshire: Permanent Publications).
L. Williams (2007) 'Anarchism revived', *New Political Science*, XXIX(iii): 297–312.
S. Winnubst (2006) *Queering Freedom* (Indianapolis: Indiana University Press).

11
A Well-Being Out of Nihilism: On the Affinities Between Nietzsche and Anarchist Thought

Jones Irwin

> 'the will to system is a lack of integrity'
> Nietzsche, *Twilight of the Idols*

11.1 Introduction

Friedrich Nietzsche's *On The Genealogy of Morals* (Nietzsche, 1967) polemically deconstructs the history of Western moralisms and demonstrates much of their underlying hypocrisies and implicit power plays. In this measure, at least this part of Nietzsche's philosophical project can be seen as anarchistic, and analogous to the critique which Mikhail Bakunin (Bakunin, 1977c) puts forward of the residual power relations in the Marxist attempt at an emancipatory project. For Nietzsche, the incongruity is that the philosophies which most claim to be virtuous and moral are those which precisely most emasculate their own hidden and malevolent will-to-power (Nietzsche, 1967); Bakunin, Proudhon (Proudhon, 1877) and Goldman (Goldman, 1977) would say exactly the same of the self-proclaimed 'revolutionary' philosophies.

In this chapter, I will take cognisance of this tendency to contestation – a *de jure* suspicion of authority as authority and especially when it presents itself as supposedly benevolent and good. Within a general anarchist tradition, the value of authority *per se* is contested (Bakunin, 1977a) and this can provide a crucial framework for understanding key elements of Nietzsche's own work. However, tensions in the affinity between Nietzschean thought and anarchism are also evident on both sides. From an anarchist perspective, certain motifs within Nietzsche's texts, such as the 'Eternal Return' or the 'Will to Power' (Nietzsche,

1967), would seem to risk a falling back into metaphysics or mysticism while, from a Nietzschean perspective, the moral, or sometime religious, imperative of anarchism (Read, 1977) might be subjected to the same critique Nietzsche applies to other forms of ethics. The chapter will conclude with a reflection on how this debate is played out in a more contemporary setting, with reference to recent work on the affinities between (neo-) anarchism and (neo-Nietzschean) poststructuralist thinking (May, 1994; Newman, 2001).

11.2 Understanding anarchism

As Alexander Moseley has commented, 'much political philosophy is invested in confusing the logic and implications of competing theories, and anarchism particularly feels the brunt of misrepresenting descriptions of and deployment of its term as a description of nihilism and chaos' (Moseley, 2008: 117). George Woodcock, in his essay 'Anarchism: a historical introduction', outlines a general definition of anarchism more sensitive to the specificity of anarchist political ideology; 'what we are concerned with, in terms of definition, is a cluster of words which in turn represents a cluster of doctrines and attitudes whose principal uniting feature is the belief that government is both harmful and unnecessary' (1977: 11). Studying the etymology here is instructive: '[...] a double Greek root is involved: the word *archon* meaning a ruler, and the prefix *an*, indicating without; hence anarchy means the state of being without a ruler' (11).

Anarchism is thus the philosophy (or *a* philosophy) which contends that government is the source of most of our social troubles and that there are viable alternative forms of voluntary organisation. And, by further specificity, the anarchist is the person who sets out to create a society without government. Society must become a closely knit fabric of voluntary relationships. This has significant implications both for the nature of anarchist political organisation and for the nature of anarchist thought, with regard to the possibility of having a systematic view of the world. Proudhon, for example, rejected all forms of political organisation, including the idea of a political party when he was elected to the Constituent Assembly of France during the Revolution of 1848 and also the very idea of a constitution: 'I have voted against the Constitution because it was a Constitution' (quoted in Woodcock, 1977: 14). In a letter to Karl Marx written in 1846, Proudhon, while cordially supportive of Marx's political 'aims', nonetheless states a philosophical reservation: 'I believe it is my duty, as it is the duty of all socialists, to maintain for some time yet the critical or dubitive form... in short, I make profession in public of an almost absolute economic anti-dogmatism' (Proudhon, 1977). Proudhon goes on to warn Marx of the 'dream of indoctrinating the people'.

Thus, it has never been possible to talk of anarchism as a philosophical or political system of the same kind as, for example, Marxism or even Communism. Anarchism is, by definition, protean and subject to radical forms of self-deconstruction and critique. Although we can say this of most ideological or political philosophies (at least in the twenty-first century), it is perhaps the vehemence and radicality of such self-critique and also the simultaneous suspicion of ultimate or final categorisation which mark anarchism out as a distinctive mindset and political practice. To this extent, one might say that anarchism is paradigmatically philosophical, if one takes Plato's original definition of *philosophia* as an endless 'orexis' (striving) for truth rather than an exact possession of it. If philosophy is congenitally suspicious of final conclusions, then so too is anarchism, and this would seem to connect anarchism and philosophy in a quite unique way. As we will see below, Nietzsche's own specific understanding of philosophy (while differing radically in other ways) is surprisingly in line with Plato's, when it comes to the need for endless self-questioning and *elenchus* (refutation). This will thus also bring Nietzsche close to the motivational wellsprings of anarchism.

In this context, Woodcock makes a significant reference to another early Greek philosopher, Heraclitus, a thinker simultaneously influential on both Plato and Nietzsche: 'the anarchist is really a natural disciple of the Greek philosopher Heraclitus, who taught that the unity of existence lies in its constant change. "Over those who step into the same river", said Heraclitus, "the waters that flow are constantly different"' (Woodcock, 1977: 16). Woodcock goes on to draw out the implications for the relationship between anarchism and the philosophical project: 'the image is a good one for anarchism, as it has been and as it remains, since it conveys the idea of a doctrine with many variations, which nevertheless moves between the banks of certain unifying principles' (16). To provide more depth to this analysis, I will look in more detail at essays from two specific anarchist thinkers from the tradition, Bakunin and Goldman, while bringing the movement more up to date with an analysis of an essay by Murray Bookchin on the May '68 'revolution' and its contemporary relevance, as Bookchin has been a key figure in the resurgence of interest in anarchism since the 1970s.

Briefly, it is instructive to mention here the intra-anarchist arguments between Bookchin (1995) and, in particular, his book *Social Anarchism* or *Lifestyle Anarchism* on the one side, which attacks Hakim Bey for 'irrationalism', and Bey and Bob Black's (1997) defence of Bey (1985) on the other. These arguments relate to the future direction and framework for twenty-first-century anarchist thought. My own view is that both sides could gain more from developing connections between their work (of which there are many).

Mikhail Bakunin is a paradigmatic figure for anarchism insofar as he demonstrates the fundamental antagonism between anarchism and other forms of socialist or communist thought (an antagonism which exists despite all the simultaneous affinities between the two). This antagonism was to have catastrophic implications for anarchism in the Spanish Civil War, but this tension is already explicitly prefigured in Bakunin's (1977c) essay 'Perils of the Marxist State'. As Woodcock notes, from the early 1870s, Bakunin and his followers prophesied quite accurately that the Marxist failure to understand that power is psychologically, as well as economically, based would lead to a recreation of the state in new form.

A revolution that did not get rid of authority would lead to an even more pervasive power, a rigid oligarchy of officials and technocrats constituting a Marxist political order (Woodcock, 1977: 38). Sharing with Marx a vehement critique of theology and religion ('a theological lie which invented the idea of original sin to destroy the consciousness of individual worth'), Bakunin (1977b) also seeks to completely disentangle the intrinsic relationship between church and state. Bakunin (1977b: 83), like Marx, rejects the idea of individual free will in favour of an idea of the natural sociability of humanity. Where Bakunin diverges radically from Marx, thus delineating the anarchist divergence from Marxism as an overall ideology, is in relation to their respective interpretations of power and the state. For Bakunin (1977c: 142), 'the state, like the church, is a great sacrificer of living men' and, for all the claims to the contrary, the Marxist state (or 'Mr Marx's popular state') will be no different: 'in Mr Marx's popular state, we are told, there will be no privileged class at all' (142). Bakunin begs vehemently to differ:

> There survives in his state everything that contributes to the truly despotic and brutal nature of all states... it will be the reign of scientific intelligence, the most aristocratic, despotic, arrogant and scornful of all regimes; there will be a new class, a new hierarchy of real and pretended scholars; and the world will be divided into a minority that rules in the name of science and a vast ignorant majority; then, let the mass of the ignorant look out! (143)

Bakunin's last word on the Marxist state reiterates the problems associated with the organisation of such a political structure, pointing to its complicity with the very reactionary forms of the traditional state which, it is being claimed, are being revolutionised, while also pointing to the inevitable failure of the overall project into the future: 'there is the same employment of armed forces, the last argument of all threatened political powers, against the masses who, tired of always believing, hoping, accepting and obeying, rise in rebellion' (143). There will, therefore, be 'rebellion' *contra* 'Mr Marx's popular state', as soon as the 'masses' realise that this Marxism is just bluffing, just another form of authoritarianism in disguise. Bakunin thus anticipates the fundamental weaknesses, as well as the ultimate fundamental (and catastrophic) failure, of the Marxian political and philosophical project, from an anarchist perspective.

It is important to note here that Bakunin, in rejecting the statist model of Marxism, is not rejecting the value of authority as such, although he is fundamentally contesting this value. Rather, he is pointing to the inevitable misuse of 'corruption' of power and authority, in systems of the Marxist type. As Woodcock (1977: 137) notes, 'to proceed through the use of power towards the abolition of power in Marx's theory of transitional dictatorship of the proletariat is an impossibility, a paradox that refuses to resolve itself.' In his essay 'What is Authority?' (Bakunin, 1977a), Bakunin makes clear, however, that this does not rule out the use of authority in all cases. Crucially, anarchism and the value and practice of authority are not mutually exclusive. What we are concerned with here is rather what might be termed *a failure of authority*. As Bakunin (1977a: 312–13) observes in this essay, 'do I reject all authority? Far from me such a thought [...]. I listen to them freely [...] reserving always my incontestable right to criticism and censure.' Bakunin rejected a single, fixed authority and proposed a continual exchange of mutual and voluntary authority (313–14).

Emma Goldman's (1977) essay, 'The Failure of the Russian Revolution', captures both the radicality and the refusal of dogmatism characteristic of anarchist thinking and is also instructive for our purposes in the measure to which it concludes with an affirmative reference to Nietzsche's key notion of a 'transvaluation of all values'. To begin, Goldman (1977: 155) makes a stark contrast between the aims of the 'political party' and the 'revolution'. Whereas the political party sought to maintain its power 'by all means at hand', the aims and tendencies of the revolution were diametrically opposed to those of the ruling political party: 'the revolution had an entirely different object; and in its very character it was the negation of authority and centralisation' (155). Far from being some avoidable or accidental fate, therefore, the failure of the Russian Revolution was tied to the very principles of the socialist ideology which sought to put the revolution into practice. In its authoritarianism and statist mentality, 'it was Marxism, however modified, which killed the Russian Revolution' (155). Written in 1924, this anarchist critique of Marxism reiterates the very specific points of Bakunin, who wrote before the revolution. Crucially, however, here in 1924, Goldman remains optimistic for anarchism, if not for socialism: 'but this by no means involves the death of the libertarian idea' (155).

In what Woodcock (1977: 137) refers to as a 'Nietzschean touch', Goldman (1977: 158) identifies the future of anarchism not with 'the replacement of one class with another' but with 'rather the fundamental transvaluation of values' (158). Goldman is suggesting here a complete revolution in the way we think about life and morality. This is an implicit reference to Nietzsche's original notion of the 'transvaluation of values' which he introduces in the Preface to *On The Genealogy of Morals* (Nietzsche, 1967), which I discuss in more detail in the next section. The Nietzschean tonality is maintained in her development of this idea:

> [R]evolution is the negation of the existing, a violent protest against man's inhumanity to man with all the thousand and one slaveries it involves [...]. It is the herald of NEW VALUES [...] ushering in a transformation of the basic relations of man to man, and of man to society [...]. It is first and foremost, the TRANSVALUATOR, the bearer of new values. It is the great TEACHER of the NEW ETHICS.
> (Goldman, 1977: 161; Goldman's emphasis)

This is heady stuff, and it represented the rallying cry for the development of an even stronger and more engaged 'movement' of anarchism, which was to tragically run aground in Spain. 'The anarchist movement died in Spain when General Francisco Franco marched into Barcelona,' notes Woodcock (1977: 45), and goes on 'but the anarchist idea did not die and has risen like a phoenix.' Written in 1977, these words remain true today, as the 'anarchist idea' continues to enthral and inspire a newer generation. Woodcock refers to the eclectic legacy of this ideology, which itself drew from eclectic earlier anarchist sources such as the Surrealists, Oscar Wilde and Mallarmé. One can speak, for example, of Erich Fromm and Wilhelm Reich in psychology, with their 'heretical Freudian teachings' (48), of Paulo Freire, Ivan Illich and 'a new type of education which would enable men to accept but also to endure freedom', of Huxley's calling for political forms which would be 'Kropotkinesque and co-operative' (52) and, of course, one can refer to George Orwell. But perhaps the key event here in the rejuvenation of anarchism was the May '68 movement, in Paris and beyond.

I would like to conclude this section by looking at Murray Bookchin's (1977) essay on the May '68 movements, 'Paris, 1968'. Faced first with Emma Goldman's (1977: 153–62) radical critique of the Russian Revolution as descending into a 'scheme of mutual deceit' and then with the almost fatal attacks on the anarchist movement not simply from the Right but also from the hard Left during the Spanish Civil War, little hope seemed to remain of any kind of political or even philosophical possibility for anarchism in the second-half of the twentieth century. But as Bookchin's article makes clear, 'Paris, 1968' redirected a whole series of anarchist themes and problems. Against the attempt to align with Marxism, the guiding aims of the revolutionaries have changed: 'the motive forces of revolution today are the quality of everyday life, the demand for the liberation of experience, the attempt to gain control over one's destiny' (Bookchin, 1977: 257). Indeed, the antagonism between anarchists and Marxists, already clearly evident in our earlier discussions of Proudhon, Bakunin and Goldman, respectively, returns to haunt the attempted unification of revolutionary movements in 1968. Once again, as Bakunin had elaborated almost a hundred years before, it was a problem of 'hierarchy' and 'authority'. As Bookchin (1977: 261) notes, 'what distinguishes the anarchists and Situationists from the others is that they worked not for the seizure of power but for its dissolution.'

It is ironic given Bookchin's later criticisms of 'lifestyle anarchism' that he here (in an article originally written in 1974) chooses to delineate a key paradigm shift in revolutionary content and meaning, from the earlier history of revolutionary movements: 'the problems of survival, scarcity and renunciation had changed into those of life, abundance and desire; experience itself' (Bookchin, 1977: 264). This, written in the same year as the French publication of *Anti-Oedipus* (Deleuze and Guattari, 2004), is positively Deleuzian-Guattarian. The revolution must connect to the 'realisation of desire and freedom' and the proletariat are extended to include 'everyone who felt dispossessed, denied and cheated of life [...] in a process of alienation' (Bookchin, 1977: 262). If one were to interpret Marxism more 'existentially', one might see Bookchin here as close to the kind of 'cultural Marxism' of Marcuse (2002) or Gramsci (1988). But Bookchin is as clear as his anarchist predecessors as to his distance from the latter. Once more, with Marxism, it is a question of the 'political organisms' (i.e., the political parties) becoming 'ends in themselves'. Moreover, there is a problem with the 'self' in more traditional (or nonanarchist) approaches to revolutionary action. The monopolistic emphasis on the party or even the vanguard (however much this is meant to constitute a transitional phase) in a sense 'removes' the self from the process of revolution. This desubjectivication (or *objectification*) is fatal for the revolutionary process according to Bookchin: 'to remove the self from the process is to vitiate the revolution's liberatory goals, social liberation can only occur if it is simultaneously self-liberation, if it involves the highest degree of individuation and self-awakening' (Bookchin, 1977: 264). This would seem to be an implicit critique of Althusserianism, a critique connected to the failure of the latter (Buchanan, 2008) to account for the contingency and simultaneous subjectivity of the May '68 developments.

What makes May '68 extraordinary for Bookchin is its attempt not to reconsolidate power, or to exchange one class dictatorship for another, but its attempt to create a situation in which 'power is dissolved.' Again, for Bookchin, this transformation is aesthetic and experiential (and subjective) before it is anything else: 'an expansion of personal experience and freedom almost aesthically congruent with the possibilities of our time' (Bookchin, 1977: 264). And moving on from '68 (and its ultimate failure, as well as all its minor triumphs), Bookchin is also clear on the task in hand: 'the primary responsibilities of the revolutionary today are to deal unequivocally with the ideological movements that seek to control the revolutionary process' (265). Once more, anarchism finds itself defined very much in vitriolic opposition to not simply its right-wing but precisely its left-wing (counter-revolutionary) opponents.

11.3 Nietzsche on authority, nihilism and morality

One interesting and significant parallel between Nietzsche's philosophy and anarchist thought relates to the confusion of both these thought-systems with the philosophy of nihilism. As Alexander Moseley (2008: 117) has commented, 'the political philosophy of anarchism should not be confused with the moral doctrine of nihilism.' He goes on: 'nihilism is the rejection of all moral and political values... anarchism rejects government and privileged institutions, but it does not necessarily reject the need for rules and a moral order' (117). In Nietzsche's work, what he refers to as the 'problem of nihilism' is intrinsically related to Nietzsche's interpretation of Christianity. Earlier, I referred to Mikhail Bakunin's critique of religion and the very notion of God. Bakunin shares with

Marx a vehement critique of theology and religion ('a theological lie which invented the idea of original sin to destroy the consciousness of individual worth') and seeks to completely disentangle the intrinsic relationship between church and state (Bakunin, 1977b). This critique of religion and theology connects Marx, Bakunin and Nietzsche, but it should be pointed out that it does not describe all forms of anarchism. As Woodcock notes, religion (and especially mysticism) has often been the wellspring of anarchist thought and action; perhaps the most prominent case of a 'religious anarchism' is that of the English anarchist Herbert Read which he outlines forcibly in 'Anarchism and the Religious Impulse' (Read, 1940).

Nietzsche, while vehemently critical of religion, is nonetheless also cognisant of Read's (1940) claim that the 'ethos' of religion provides a social meaningfulness, which is a 'necessity'. Nietzsche disagrees that religion is necessary, but he takes account of the problems associated with creating a meaningful society without religion, in his very notion of 'nihilism'. Nietzsche's problem is that nihilism – the breakdown of any values or meaning in which one can trust – is constituted *both* by religion, insofar as Christianity falsifies the world, and by the very downfall of religion which leaves a moral and epistemological vacuum. Indeed, one might say that this is the same nihilism which we have seen Bakunin and Goldman describe in relation to the decline of faith in socialism or Marxism. In the corresponding case of religion, for Nietzsche, the existence of God *and* the death of God are thus both aspects of nihilism. Moreover, the destructiveness of philosophy itself, what Plato (Plato, 1990) called its tendency to *elenchus* (refutation) and what Nietzsche refers to as 'philosophising with a hammer', accelerates or contributes to disbelief in God, and thus philosophy (and here specifically Nietzsche's own philosophy) can be said to be an aspect of the problem of nihilism which he is seeking to address.

The Japanese Buddhist philosopher Kieji Nishitani (1990), in his text translated as *The Self-Overcoming of Nihilism*, has addressed this specific issue in Nietzsche's work, but his analysis has relevance more generally in relation to the threat of nihilism and the dangers that philosophy faces of being complicit with such nihilism. As Moseley (2008: 117) notes, anarchism itself runs this risk so acutely that it has often been accused of being indistinguishable from nihilism. For Nishitani (1990), it is the simultaneous nihilism and anti-nihilism in Nietzsche which is so significant – on his interpretation, Nietzsche undergoes the experience of nihilism so thoroughly that it finally overcomes itself.

For Nishitani, Hegel's phenomenology represents the last great ruse of the West before a breakdown in order and harmony but those philosophers, most prominently Nietzsche, who face up to the attendant crisis in values and meaning, can be said to be nihilistic in a positive sense. Nishitani defines nihilism as 'a sign of the collapse of the social order externally and of spiritual decay internally – and as such signifies a time of great upheaval' (Parkes, 1990: xviii). However, nihilism also stands for the honest appraisal by the modern philosopher of his/her own predicament. Nietzsche acknowledges this as his own self-image in a note from *The Will To Power*, describing himself as 'the first consummate nihilist in Europe, who has himself already lived nihilism through to the end in himself – who has it behind him, beneath him, outside of him' (Quoted by Nietzsche in Nishitani, 1990: 3), and also describes an 'experimental philosophy, as I live it, [which] tentatively preempts the very possibilities of fundamental nihilism' (Quoted by Nietzsche in Nishitani, 1990: 2). Thus while Nietzsche is aware that his diagnosis speeds up the process of nihilism as a breakdown in values, he nonetheless sees this foregrounding of the 'death of God' as a possible escape from nihilism to what he will later refer to as a 'transvaluation of all values'.

It is *On The Genealogy of Morals* (Nietzsche, 1967) which takes up this challenge of a 'transvaluation of all values' most courageously. It is a phrase we have already seen Emma Goldman use in response to the 'failure of the Russian revolution'. Anarchism and Nietzsche thus share not simply a critique of nihilism but an attempt to put forward a constructive alternative to meaninglessness. However, both sides are keen to avoid the 'dogmatism' of which Proudhon speaks; as Nietzsche puts it, in *Twilight of the Idols*, 'the will to system is a lack of integrity.' In the *Genealogy* (Nietzsche, 1967), Nietzsche undertakes this analysis from the point of view of the development or 'origin' of morality. As with his critique of religion, Nietzsche seeks to undo the widespread assumption that morality of 'good and evil' cuts nature at the joints, the idea that it is ahistorical and indispensable. Rather, in presenting us with a genealogy of morality, Nietzsche is precisely historicising the moral notions of good and bad, good and evil. To this extent, he is excavating the *arche* or principle of origination of ethics. By historicising this *arche* (which is usually hidden), he is in effect practising an *an-anarchism*, a deconstruction of that which is assumed as the unquestioned foundation of civilisation and culture.

In *On The Genealogy of Morals*, Nietzsche (1967: 36ff.) traces the distinction between 'good' and 'evil' to the development of what he terms 'slave morality'. From a historical perspective, this category of ethics is loosely associated with the development of a Judeo-Christian ethic (Nietzsche, 1967: 33 – 'with the Jews there begins the slave revolt in morality'). It is opposed in principle to the development of a parallel ethic, Nietzsche's (28ff.) so-called 'noble morality' that is linked to Hellenism. Whereas 'slave morality' is said to posit an opposition between good and evil, noble morality posits an opposition between good and bad (33). As Norman (1983) has noted, these categorisations are not accurate from a strictly historical perspective, but they do provide a useful framework within which to understand the genealogy of the ethical as such. For our purposes, two main points are worthy of note in terms of this genealogical analysis. First, the opposition, which is posited between good and evil (Nietzsche, 1967: 36). Initially this movement took its cue from Judaism but it has now developed to envelop culture as a whole: 'The slave revolt in morality: that revolt which has a history of two thousand years behind it and which we no longer see because it – has been victorious' (33).

Second, in Essay 1 (and developed in Essay 2) Nietzsche (1967: 36ff.) links this emphasis on condemnation with his concept of *ressentiment* – rather than being based on affirmation, slave morality is from the beginning reactive in essence:

> [T]he slave revolt in morality begins when *ressentiment* itself becomes creative and gives birth to values: the *ressentiment* of natures that are denied the true reaction, that of deeds, and compensate themselves with an imaginary revenge [...] in order to exist, slave morality always first needs a hostile external world; it needs, physiologically speaking, external stimuli in order to act at all – its action is fundamentally reaction. (36)

Here, Nietzsche traces the anxiety over 'evil' to the negative emotions of envy and self-abnegation (33ff.). Contrasted with this slave morality is the apparently superior and healthier noble morality that has the alternative binary of good/bad in place instead of the good/evil opposition (28ff.). Noble morality consists in a positive affirmation of goodness instead of a condemnation of 'bad'. Indeed, Nietzsche notes a definite 'benevolence' in the attitude expressed by the noble towards the bad:

> One should not overlook the almost benevolent nuances that the Greek nobility, for example, bestows on all the words it employs to distinguish the lower orders from itself; how they are continuously

mingled and sweetened with a kind of pity, consideration, and forbearance...the 'well-born' *felt* themselves to be the 'happy'; they did not have to establish their happiness artificially by examining their enemies, or to persuade themselves, *deceive* themselves, that they were happy (as all men of *ressentiment* are in the habit of doing). (36ff.)

In terms of this fundamental Nietzschean opposition, therefore, 'evil' has a most pejorative status as the product of *ressentiment* and slave morality. Historically speaking, Nietzsche's claim is that the dominance of noble morality has given way to the ubiquity of its opponent. The slaves, and their preoccupation with 'evil', have become the new masters. Nietzsche reinforces this historical genealogy with an acute psychological analysis. Modern humanity is a being of *ressentiment*, preoccupied with condemnation and reaction, incapable of authentic responsibility and action. Nietzsche's self-appointed mission appears to be the liberation of modern man from such a predicament. Here, he looks to a 'man of the future':

> This man of the future, who will redeem us not only from the hitherto reigning ideal but also from that which was bound to grow out of it, the great nausea, the will to nothingness, nihilism; this bell-stroke of noon and of the great decision that liberates the will again and restores its goal to the earth and his hope to man; this Antichrist and antinihilist; this victor over God and nothingness – *he must come one day*. (95ff.)

Again, it is clear that 'nihilism' is *the* problem for Nietzsche here. This problem is radically reinforced by the fact that what is meant to counter nihilism ('morality') is nihilistic *par excellence*. This is precisely the human and philosophical predicament we find ourselves in. Nietzsche's 'man of the future' is unequivocally posited as a liberator, simultaneously, from the hegemony of slave morality and from the ethos of 'evil'. To quote from another of Nietzsche's texts, this future will be *'beyond good and evil'*.

11.4 Neo-Nietzscheanism and contemporary anarchism

What has come to be termed as 'neo-Nietzscheanism' (Taylor, 1994) constitutes a specific strand of postmodern thought (Drolet, 2004) and involves the more contemporary development of Nietzsche's critique of morality and authority, which we have described above. As with Nietzsche's own attempt to critique nihilism, the problem is that neo-Nietzscheanism is itself seen by many as part of the problem of nihilism (Taylor, 1994). In a short essay written in 1887 just before the *Genealogy*, entitled 'European Nihilism' (Nietzsche, 2006), Nietzsche tackles this complex issue of meaninglessness and its connection both to his own philosophy and to that of his opponents. This essay helps us to better understand what brings Nietzsche's thought and anarchism closer together while also differentiating them more closely from those philosophies which they oppose, and which oppose them. Nietzsche gives the lie to those who would present his own thinking (or indeed that of anarchism) as involving some kind of will-to-destruction. 'Who will prove to be the strongest in this? The most moderate, those who have no need of extreme dogma, those who do not only concede but love a good measure of chance and nonsense, those who can conceive of man with a significant reduction in his value without thereby becoming small and weak' (Nietzsche, 2006: 389). This, in my view, could serve as a definition of anarchism. Its proximity to the thought of Proudhon, Bakunin and Goldman is striking.

The same accusatory logic projected against neo-Nietzscheanism is also applied incessantly to anarchism (Moseley, 2008: 117). In both cases, the supposed 'nihilism' is said to be a paradigm which rejects the normativity of morality in favour of 'ill-being' or what Freire has termed 'necrophily' (Freire, 1972). This 'hatred of life', or destructive will, is then contrasted with a valued notion of well-being, or 'flourishing'. The revival of interest in and respect for the concept of 'well-being' in philosophy can be traced from the growing influence of a specific group of neo-Aristotelian philosophers in the latter part of the twentieth century, especially the works of Alastair MacIntyre and Martha Nussbaum (MacIntyre, 1981; Nussbaum, 1986). Understanding the reasons for the divergence between neo-Nietzscheanism and neo-Aristotelianism can help us to better understand what I am claiming is the specific contribution which Nietzsche and his philosophical descendants have made to our understanding of nihilism and its remedy.

Again, I claim that there is much in common here between neo-Nietzscheanism and anarchism. The struggle over the concept of 'well-being' is in many respects also a quintessentially anarchist struggle. Against the traditionalists (here, the neo-Aristotelians), who claim that their version of interpretation provides the fundamental ground for well-being and its interdependency with morality, the neo-Nietzscheans, alongside the anarchists, want to claim the reverse. Nietzsche argues that the very concept of morality and well-being has been dogmatically defined by those in 'authority', that it is a definition which requires historicisation and a philosophical genealogy and that precisely through such a genealogical reading, a different possibility of both well-being and ethics opens up. This has been the consistent refrain throughout all our readings of Proudhon, Bakunin, Goldman, Nietzsche and Bookchin (and we hear it also, for example, in Lyotard and Deleuze) – our opponents do not have a monopoly on the possibility of ethics or authentic politics or authentic well-being.

Nietzscheanism or anarchism reject the traditional (or even radical, as in the case of Marxian) definitions of what constitutes morality or well-being. This does not thereby imply, or entail, nihilism on their part. Often so-called 'virtue' can be a front for the maintenance of the *status quo* and a protection of vested interests. Paul Ricoeur refers to this aspect of Nietzsche's work as emblematic of his being a 'master of suspicion'. This last point pushes us towards a more positive possibility within the postmodernist philosophy.

This suspicion of amoralism has coloured readings of Jean-François Lyotard, one of the most interesting theorists to have developed Nietzsche's philosophy. Lyotard's work too has interesting affinities with anarchist thought, and like Nietzsche and anarchist philosophy, Lyotard's work has often been interpreted as 'nihilistic', the result of misreadings of his most famous work (although not necessarily his best), *The Postmodern Condition*. *The Postmodern Condition* and other significant Lyotardian texts which preceded and succeeded it are *not* advancing a nihilistic affirmation of late. This is especially clear if we look back to Lyotard's texts which were influential during May 1968, both those texts which led up to the event and were part of its rhetoric and those texts which commented on '68, in the aftermath. Lyotard's significant involvement at the University of Nanterre as a lecturer (alongside Henri Lefebvre in Sociology) in the '68 events, before and after, is little known and itself emblematic of his political affiliations and concerns, concerns which are consistent across his eclectic *oeuvre*, early to late (for a further development of Lyotard's thought, see Irwin, 2008a).

The possibility of a radical politics based on differently orientated well-being highlights very clearly a key (perhaps *the* key) complementarity between neo-Nietzscheanism and neo-anarchism. It is this connection, among others, which has led thinkers such as Todd May (May, 1994) and Saul Newman (Newman, 2001) to highlight the advent of what they term a 'poststructuralist anarchism'. Benjamin Franks has also pointed to the fundamental affinities between such recent developments and 'the anarchist ideal' (Franks, 2006: 154ff.). Rather than such a philosophy being a recipe for nihilism, it may also be seen as offering the possibility of a critique of the blind spots within the discourse of neo-Aristotelianism or the more generalised discourse of well-being. To this extent, neo-Nietzscheanism and (neo-) anarchism may be arguing less for an end to well-being than for the advent of a more authentic well-being (Irwin, 2008b). In this measure, both can be seen as emphasising a crucial (and often underestimated) dimension of the work of their forebears.

Nonetheless, we should not neglect the points of tension between both these traditions of thought. With reference to Nietzsche's aforementioned critique of humanism, strength of character is there seen as undermining of epistemological certainty and dogmatism. This is undoubtedly a shared perspective between Nietzsche and anarchism.

However, while Nietzsche can certainly be described as critical of humanism (even as 'anti-humanist'), many of the earlier anarchist thinkers are often viewed as still believing in a 'human essence'. Newman, for example, traces a tendency towards an 'essentialist' perspective on human nature in Bakunin and Kropotkin (Newman, 2001: 37ff.). For Newman, it is perhaps Max Stirner who comes closest to Nietzsche in the anarchist tradition, insofar as he also undertook a vehement critique of the residual humanism in the earlier anarchist movement. We know, of course, that Stirner was an influence on Nietzsche's thinking, although the connection is not often made in this relation to Stirner's anarchism (as the latter's relation to anarchism was itself problematical) (Newman, 2001: 55ff.).

Other points of tension concern Nietzschean 'doctrines' such as the 'Eternal Return' and the 'Will to Power' (Nietzsche, 1967) (and their conflict with anti-dogmatism in anarchism) and a certain tendency towards a mystical or religious perspective in anarchists such as Herbert Read (and their conflict with Nietzsche's anti-religious critique). Certainly, there are some grounds for disagreement in these contexts. However, in the first case, a closer inspection of Nietzsche's two most famous 'doctrines' reveals that they are hardly antithetical to the main wellsprings of anarchist philosophy. In an important essay ('Nietzsche and Metaphysical Language'), Michel Haar (1990: 3) recognises the 'Will to Power' and 'Eternal Return' conceptions (alongside the 'Overman') as 'surely the most comprehensive of Nietzsche's far ranging themes...for they condition his reflections on nature, art, religion, morality, psychology and history.' However, although these seem to be 'metaphysical' doctrines and thus inimical to anarchist thinking, Haar shows convincingly that, despite appearances, Nietzsche's three most central ideas are anti-metaphysical, through and through. The 'Will to

Power' idea is described by Haar as being synonymous with 'plurality and complexity itself' (1990: 8), in the measure to which Nietzsche disagrees with there being any unitary will. 'There is no will but rather a plurality of elementary wills – which is to say unconscious impulses, forever in conflict, alternately imposing themselves and subordinating themselves' (10).

The conception of 'Eternal Return' in Nietzsche's texts is somewhat more enigmatic but it can help us to make sense of possible tensions between a Nietzschean critique of religion and a specific kind of religious impulse which we find in anarchist thinkers such as Herbert Read (although others, such as Bakunin and Stirner, are more univocally antireligious). One way into this argument is to suggest that it is not so much religion as such which Nietzsche opposes as a very particular 'moralisation' of religion (Nietzsche, 1967) by Christianity and Judaism, among others. Moreover, one can argue that the notion of 'Eternal Return' is still a religious notion of sorts. Haar, for example, in arguing that the essence of this notion is to affirm the passing of *time as time* and to avoid lamentation, nostalgia or regret, states the following:

> How does this doctrine take hold? In the same way that religion does, a religion with no hell, without sin and without error. This doctrine establishes, as any religion does, a tie with the divine understood as a totality and a unity of self and world. Divinity is not synonymous with that of perfection, it is rather synonymous with absolute affirmation embracing imperfection itself.
> (Haar, 1990: 29)

It is arguable that Herbert Read might see just such an understanding of the 'Eternal Return' as compatible with his own mystical anarchism, thus bridging the supposed chasm between Nietzsche and religiously inflected anarchist variants. Its emphasis on 'imperfection' (and the latter's affirmation) brings it close to Stirner's critique of humanist perfectionism. Similarly, its notion of a 'totality and unity of self and world' is not far removed from the very 'humanism' which we were citing as a possible tension between Nietzsche, on the one side, and Bakunin and Kropotkin, on the other. In the end, however, it should not be a matter of seeking to flatten or repress, of seeking to horizontalise, the irreducibility and singularity of each of these thinkers and traditions of thought. To return to a thinker of a kind of original anarchism, Heraclitus, we can say that 'conflict (*polemos*) is justice.' Perhaps the great fertility of the Nietzsche–Anarchism dialogue, in the contemporary world, derives from exactly the vehemence of both its agreements *and* its disagreements.

Bibliography

L. Althusser (1994) 'Ideology and ideological state apparatuses (Notes towards an investigation)' in S. Žižek (ed.) *Mapping Ideology* (London: Verso).
Aristotle (1976) *Ethics* (London: Penguin).
M. Bakunin (1977a) 'What is authority?' in G. Woodcock (ed.) *The Anarchist Reader* (Glasgow: Fontana).
―――― (1977b) 'Church and state' in G. Woodcock (ed.) *The Anarchist Reader* (Glasgow: Fontana).
―――― (1977c) 'Perils of the Marxist state' in G. Woodcock (ed.) *The Anarchist Reader* (Glasgow: Fontana).
G. Bataille (1988) *Visions of Excess: Selected Early Writings* (Minnesota: University of Minnesota Press).
B. Baugh (2003) *French Hegel: From Surrealism to Postmodernism* (New York: Routledge).
H. Bey (1985) *CHAOS: The Broadsheets of Ontological Anarchism* (New York: Grim Reaper).
B. Black (1997) *Anarchy After Leftism* (Birmingham: CAL Press).
M. Bookchin (1977) 'Paris, 1968' in G. Woodcock (ed.) *The Anarchist Reader* (Glasgow: Fontana).
―――― (1995) *Social Anarchism or Lifestyle Anarchism: An Unbridgeable Chasm* (Stirling: AK Press).
P. Bourdieu and T. Eagleton (1994) '*Doxa* and common life: An interview' in S. Žižek (ed.) *Mapping Ideology* (London: Verso).
I. Buchanan (2008) *Deleuze and Guattari's Anti-Oedipus* (London: Continuum).
R. Day (2005) *Gramsci Is Dead: Anarchist Currents in the Newest Social Movements* (London: Pluto).
G. Debord (2000) *Society of the Spectacle* (London: Rebel Press).
G. Deleuze and F. Guattari (2004) *Anti-Oedipus* (London: Continuum).
J. Derrida (1977) 'The end(s) of man' in *Margins of Philosophy* (Chicago: Chicago University Press).
N. Dolby and G. Dimitriadis (2004) *Learning to Labour in New Times* (London: RoutledgeFarmer).
M. Drolet (2004) *The Postmodernism Reader: Foundational Texts* (London: Routledge).
T. Eagleton (2003) *Figures of Dissent* (London: Verso).
B. Franks (2006) *Rebel Alliances: The Means and Ends of Contemporary Anarchisms* (Edinburgh: AK Press).
P. Freire (1972) *Pedagogy of the Oppressed* (London: Penguin).
E. Goldman (1977) 'The failure of the Russian revolution' in G. Woodcock (ed.) *The Anarchist Reader* (Glasgow: Fontana).
A. Gorz (1982) *Farewell to the Working Class: An Essay on Post-Industrial Socialism* (London: Pluto Press).
A. Gramsci (1988) *The Antonio Gramsci Reader: Selected Writings 1916–1935* (London: Lawrence and Wishart).

S. Hall and P. Cohen (eds) (1993) *Resistance Through Rituals: Youth Subcultures in Post-War Britain* (London: Routledge).
M. Haar (1990) 'Nietzsche and metaphysical language' in D. Allison (ed.) *The New Nietzsche: Contemporary Styles of Interpretation* (Massachusetts: MIT Press).
I. Illich (1971) *Deschooling Society* (London: Marion Boyars).
J. Irwin (2008a) 'Re-politicising education – interpreting Jean-François Lyotard's *The Postmodern Condition* in a contemporary context' in C. Kavanagh (ed.) *Yearbook of the Irish Philosophical Society 2008* (forthcoming).
——— (2008b) 'Philosophical questioning of the normativity of well-being' and 'intellectual analysis and youth culture: Cultural studies and educational well-being' in M. O'Brien (ed.) *Well-Being and Post-Primary Schooling: A Review of the Literature and Research* (Dublin: NCCA).
H. Lefebvre (2002) *Critique of Everyday Life: Foundations for a Sociology of the Everyday*, Volume 2 (London: Verso).
J. F. Lyotard (1990) *The Postmodern Condition* (London: Routledge).
A. MacIntyre (1981) *After Virtue* (Notre Dame: University of Notre Dame Press).
J. Macquarrie (1972) *Existentialism* (New York: Penguin).
H. Marcuse (2002) *One-Dimensional Man: Studies in the Ideology of Advanced Industrial Society* (London: Routledge).
T. May (1994) *The Political Philosophy of Poststructuralist Anarchism* (Pennsylvania: Pennsylvania University Press).
A. Moseley (2008) *An Introduction to Political Philosophy* (London: Continuum).
S. Newman (2001) *From Bakunin to Lacan: Anti-Authoritarianism and the Dislocation of Power* (Plymouth: Lexington).
F. Nietzsche (1967) *On The Genealogy of Morals* (New York: Vintage).
——— (2004) *On the Future of Our Educational Institutions* (Indiana: St Augustine's Press).
——— (2006) 'European nihilism' in K. Ansell-Pearson and D. Large (eds) *The Nietzsche Reader* (Oxford, Blackwell).
K. Nishitani (1990) *The Self-Overcoming of Nihilism* (New York: SUNY).
R. Norman (1983) *The Moral Philosophers* (Oxford: Oxford University Press).
M. Nussbaum (1986) *The Fragility of Goodness* (Oxford: Oxford University Press).
G. Parkes (1990) 'Introduction' in K. Nishitani (ed.) *The Self-Overcoming of Nihilism* (New York: State University of New York).
Plato (1990) *The Republic* (London: Penguin).
P.-J. Proudhon (1877) 'To Karl Marx' in G. Woodcock (ed.) *The Anarchist Reader* (Glasgow: Fontana).
J. Rancière (1991) *The Ignorant Schoolmaster: Five Lessons in Intellectual Emancipation* (Stanford: Stanford University Press).
H. Read (1977) 'Anarchism and the religious impulse' in G. Woodcock (ed.) *The Anarchist Reader* (Glasgow: Fontana).
C. Taylor (1994) 'The politics of recognition' in A. Gutmann (ed.) *Multiculturalism: Examining the Politics of Recognition* (Princeton, NJ: Princeton University Press).
R. Vaneigem (2006) *The Revolution of Everyday Life* (London: Rebel Press).
P. Virilio (2000) *Art and Fear* (London: Continuum).
G. Woodcock (1977) 'Anarchism: A historical introduction' in G. Woodcock (ed.) *The Anarchist Reader* (Glasgow: Fontana).
S. Žižek (2006) *Lacan* (London: Granta).

12
Are Postanarchists Right to Call Classical Anarchisms 'Humanist'?

Thomas Swann

The core feature of the postanarchist critique of older anarchisms is the claim that they subscribe to a position which assumes the existence of a specific human nature. Saul Newman (who I will take as representative of postanarchism) writes (2001: 38): 'Anarchism is based on a specific notion of human essence. For anarchists there is a human nature with essential characteristics.' In this chapter, I aim to develop a framework within which this claim can be assessed. Postanarchism has come under criticism for what many regard an ill-informed view of classical anarchisms. Authors such as Jesse Cohn (2002), Shaun Wilbur (with Cohn, 2003) and Benjamin Franks (2007) argue that classical anarchisms incorporate a more complicated picture of the human individual which rejects the essentialism encountered in the one-dimensional image the postanarchists accuse it of. Indeed, as Sasha Villon (2003) writes, 'Newman constructs this essentialist "anarchism" as a straw man in order to knock it down and to put his postanarchism in its place.' However, many of the attempts to reassert the relevance of classical anarchisms in the wake of the postanarchist attack have been based on selecting quotations from classical anarchist writers that display non-humanist leanings, in a similar manner that postanarchists selectively quote the same writers to highlight the humanist content of classical anarchisms.

I intend, in this study, not to further quote from Godwin, Proudhon, Stirner, Bakunin or Kropotkin to determine whether or not different classical anarchisms are guilty of humanism or not. Instead, I want to propose a method for determining whether the ethical theories the various schools of classical anarchism adhere to display the features sufficient for them to be called humanist. This will involve taking classical anarchism not as a set of quotations but as a number of ethical and political theories sharing a family resemblance. Franks (2007: 134) writes that 'anarchism does not require a metaphysical fixed certainty, which postanarchism assigns it – and therefore postanarchism's anti-essentialist critique of anarchism is redundant.' The task of this chapter then is to suggest how such a claim could be properly evaluated. In order to do so, I will begin in the first section by providing a clarification of what is meant by humanism in the present context, arriving at a definition which is appropriate for assessing the claims of postanarchism, as shown in the second section.

The third section of the chapter will then present the different ethical theories that are present within the classical anarchist tradition of political thought. This will yield divisions between consequentialist anarchism, deontological anarchism, virtue-based anarchism and egoist anarchism. I hope, in this section, to show how consistent political theories based on certain ethical positions can (or cannot, as the case may be) accurately be described as humanist. This method, I argue, is appropriate to enabling an assessment of postanarchism's criticism of classical anarchisms as being guilty of subscribing to humanism. One of the conclusions I draw in this chapter is that the postanarchism of Newman, based as it is on Stirner's egoism, also entails an essentialism and so can be described as humanist.

12.1 A general definition of humanism

Humanism is an incredibly vague term and commonly subject to imprecise and improper use. In light of this, I will begin by clarifying how I use the term in the present context. The definition of humanism I want to apply in this chapter is one that comes mainly from the continental tradition of philosophy, but will draw some aspects from a related debate in analytic philosophy. As Kate Soper (2001: 116) highlights, humanism can be understood in continental philosophy as a commitment to essentialism with respect to 'human nature'. For the humanist, all members of the set of human beings are members of that set because they share some intrinsic property: every human being has a shared essence. In addition to this, there is the assumption that the set of human beings has members; that there are entities that are human beings (in the most common articulation, all *Homo sapiens*). Based on this, a definition of humanism can be put as follows:

> Humanism: a theory (or set of theories) that holds (or that the members of which hold) that every human being displays some property

(or properties) that is (are) essential to their identity as a human being.

The first thing I want to appropriate from analytic philosophy is some of their terminology which I believe clarifies this definition of humanism. Generally speaking, analytic philosophy has not seen the same use of the term 'humanism'; as Soper notes, within this tradition humanism refers more to a position encompassing atheism, a confidence in human powers of determination over divine or supernatural ones and a faith in progress and the perfectibility of humanity (Soper, 1986: 13; 2001: 115–16). However, analytic philosophers of mind and metaphysics, beginning with P. F. Strawson (1959), have approached the subject of identifying conditions for an entity being considered a 'person'. In everyday life, human beings are thought to be entities with certain biological and metaphysical properties, such that every human being displays both a certain general physical constitution and some non-physical elements such as being sentient. The introduction of the term 'person' in this debate is meant to highlight that two entities are in fact identifiable and distinguishable: the physical body and the non-physical (or metaphysical) person (Frankfurt, 1971: 6). It is because the term 'person' refers only to the metaphysical entity commonly labelled 'human' that I will henceforth use it here (this is not to say that continental philosophers do not make the distinction, only that the analytic terminology is, I would suggest, most appropriate). The other terminological feature that the continental humanist can benefit from, I think, is the notion of 'sufficient conditions', because when the humanist speaks of the essence of human beings/persons she proposes an approach that takes there to be some conditions that are enough for some entity to be considered a human being/person. The definition of humanism can then be reformulated to take these changes into account:

> Humanism: a theory (or set of theories) that holds (or that the members of which hold) that every person displays some condition (or conditions) that is (are) sufficient for personhood.

As I am appealing to a continental use of humanism, I will only deal with those conditions which are present in the continental debates around humanism. This means discarding a number of conditions that are identified by analytic philosophers such as being the subject of conscious states or having second-order desires (Strawson, 1959: 87–116;

Frankfurt, 1971). Despite this, there is some overlap between the conditions for personhood found in analytic philosophy and those essential characteristics of human beings written of by continental thinkers. Daniel Dennett (1979: 269–71), in the former camp, picks out several conditions which humanism takes as sufficient (1978: 285). Two of these find resonance in the continental tradition. These are:

(1) Rationality: all persons are capable of employing norms of correct reasoning in their thinking.

(2) Self-consciousness: all persons are aware of themselves as persons to which 'I'-thoughts refer.

In addition to these, Harry Frankfurt (1971: 14–17) argues for another condition for personhood that is rejected by Dennett but which, according to Soper (2001: 116–17), is a feature of the continental use of humanism:

(3) Free will: all persons have the capability to think and act in a voluntary way.

One final condition that will be included as sufficient for personhood in a humanist theory is specific to continental philosophy (Soper, 2001: 116):

(4) Teleology: that there is a purpose or goal for all persons that ought to be pursued by them.

To elaborate in any great detail on these four conditions for personhood would be outside the scope of this chapter. I avoid a prolonged discussion of the logical relationships between the conditions simply because it is an unnecessary deviation from the present course. If an entity is assumed in a theory to be rational, this may entail that that entity is also held to be self-conscious, or free in will; but whether or not this is the case, it makes no difference to the fact that the theory can be properly described as humanist, and to argue for such dependence (or interdependence) between conditions should be kept to works focusing on metaphysics or philosophy of mind (see Dennett, 1978). However, some minimal remarks are necessary if I am to proceed to a discussion of humanism in the context of the ethical theories of classical anarchism.

Firstly, it should be noted that the definition of rationality should be taken as broad enough to account for any form of reasoning in which the entities in question apply certain norms that are thought to be correct. The particular form this rationality takes in specific instances is of no importance. What is important, however, is that for this definition to apply, it must be recognised that in a theory where rationality is attributed to actors, it is necessary that one form of rationality be considered correct, with other norms of reasoning being, for one reason or another, deemed irrational. In other words, in a humanist theory that assumes rationality, all persons display the same mode of reasoning, or at least a capability for this mode of reasoning, and where this is thought to be the only proper mode of reasoning. Furthermore, this reasoning must be seen in relation to action such that the rational deliberation is causally responsible for the action of the entity.

Secondly, when an actor is said to be self-conscious, that actor must simply be able to act and think in relation to some entity which is identical to the actor and where this identity is recognised by the actor. Perhaps an example will help to illustrate this notion. A famous experiment carried out by animal psychologists is the 'mirror test', whereby a coloured mark is placed on an animal's forehead and the animal is sat in front of a mirror. Some animals (chimps, elephants and dolphins) are able, once they are familiar with mirrors, to acknowledge that the image in the mirror is an image of them and try to remove the mark by rubbing their forehead (obviously dolphins cannot rub their foreheads so the observations are based on other behaviours (Reiss and Marino, 2001)). This shows that the entity doing the acting (removing the mark) is recognised as the entity acted upon (having the mark on its forehead). The important point to make here regarding self-consciousness is that as the term is used in relation to humanism, it is a self-reflective disposition, not a physical entity. So, a self-conscious entity is one that has conscious states which relate to itself, as itself. This is the same as saying that a self-conscious entity will be one that has 'I'-thoughts, for instance, 'I am in pain,' 'I believe the sun will rise tomorrow' and so on. Interestingly, this (as is potentially the case with the other conditions too) expands the set of persons to include animals other than *Homo sapiens*, and so personhood should not be seen as necessarily restricted to one species. Indeed, A. J. Hamilton (n.d.), in a rare use of a continental meaning of humanism within analytic philosophy, defines his 'philosophical humanism' as applying equally to chimps.

Free will is a fairly intuitive concept in that for an agent to be free on this account she must be able to act and think in a manner of her own volition. Teleology, however, does deserve some elaboration. A distinction can be made between 'prefigurative' and 'non-prefigurative' teleological positions. By a prefigurative teleological position, which is what is intended in the definition above, it is meant one whereby agents pursue their natural end in a manner judged appropriate in reference to this end. In other words, 'the means used are supposed to encapsulate the values desired in their preferred goals' (Franks, 2008: 137). A non-prefigurative teleological position, on the other hand, holds that the action determined appropriate to achieve a certain end or goal need not encapsulate the values of this goal. This is the type of teleology that consequentialist theories of action subscribe to. It may be argued that a non-prefigurative teleology (or *poiesis*) can prescribe a course of action in which the goal, happiness or pleasure, for example, are inherent in the act. However, in this case, the goal of the action remains distinct from the act. While the pleasure is immediately experienced on acting, it is nonetheless not a characteristic of the act; it is, rather, a consequence. In prefigurative teleology (*praxis*), the goal is inherent in the act itself in such a manner that the acting itself is the goal: the end of action is to be acting in a certain way. Therefore, when a humanism is said to be teleological, it is when the persons referred to have some end towards which they ought to act, but where that action must also embody the values of the end in question.

12.2 Humanism and postanarchism

As indicated above, this is the most adequate articulation of humanism as it is used within continental philosophy, but what justifies the use of the above general definition in the current chapter? Given that the purpose of this chapter is to present a framework for assessing whether the claims of postanarchist writers with regard to classical anarchism's commitment to humanism are sound, it is appropriate to adopt a general definition within which the particular definition used by those postanarchist authors can be located.

So what does Newman say about humanism? To begin with, he defines essentialism with respect to human beings as 'the idea that beneath surface differences, there lies one true identity or character' (Newman, 2001: 13), and while this narrows the definition to too great an extent (including only Platonic distinctions between particular appearances and universal reality), a belief in human nature with certain characteristics does underwrite the position, thus displaying essentialism understood as above. Furthermore, he elaborates on this essentialism to highlight some (though not all) of the sufficient conditions for personhood outlined previously. For example, he writes that the humanist position insists that it is an 'essential kernel of humanity that [human beings] must live up to' (Newman, 2001: 61). This encapsulates teleology: the notion of 'living up to' something essential implies a natural end that can and ought to be achieved. With the further addition of claims of rationality to Newman's use of humanism (2001: 65), he can be said to critique a humanism which holds that persons display rationality and teleology as constituent parts of their human essence. Free will is neither explicitly nor implicitly mentioned by Newman, and neither is self-consciousness, so these should not be included in an account of the postanarchists' use of humanism. What I will call the 'postanarchist definition of humanism' (not, of course, suggesting that all postanarchists support such a position) can be stated as follows:

> Postanarchist definition of humanism: a theory (or set of theories) that hold (or that the members of which hold) that every person displays both (1), rationality, and (4), teleology.

Newman and other postanarchist writers (May, 1994; Adams, 2003) make the claim that classical anarchisms subscribe to the position labelled postanarchist humanism above, that is, they include as a part of their philosophical and political theories a firm belief in persons displaying the essential characteristics of rationality and teleology. For example, applying the charge of essentialism, Newman (2001: 38) writes, '[a]narchism is based on a specific notion of human essence. For anarchists there is a human nature with essential characteristics.' Furthermore, 'morality is the essence of man. It is innate to human nature, an essential part of human subjectivity' (Newman, 2001: 40). Here, then, goodness is equated with that which is the natural essence of human beings, and history is understood as those organisms' development towards 'a state of humanity, in which man can finally see himself as fully human' (Newman, 2001: 37).

12.3 The ethics of classical anarchism

Rather than providing a clear definition of classical anarchism, which is a notoriously difficult project (Franks, 2007: 128), I will simply note a family resemblance between a number of political theories which may or may not have used the term 'anarchist' in a self-referential way and which were founded and initially developed in the period that began with the French Revolution and ended with the turn of the twentieth century. This range, which is further narrowed by the exclusion of non-European thought, includes writers such as William Godwin, Pierre-Joseph Proudhon, Max Stirner, Mikhail Bakunin and Peter Kropotkin. As for the classification of different schools of thought within classical anarchism, I opt here for an approach that accounts for the differences in ethical belief, following the recent work of Franks (2008), Paul McLaughlin (2007) and Nathan Jun (2009). However, while McLaughlin (2007: 30–1) and Jun (2009: 508–9) characterise classical anarchisms as sharing a form of scepticism towards claims of authority in ethical matters (which is not the same as scepticism about the possibility of ethical knowledge) or outright rejection of the coercive practices that may follow such claims, I will follow the path laid by Franks, who argues that 'different traditions of anarchism can be partly identified through their adoption of distinctive ethical traditions' (Franks, 2008: 136). While I am not suggesting here that classical anarchisms are reducible to ethical theories I do hope to assess one important part of this tradition. There are four ethical theories which are represented within the classical anarchist canon: consequentialism, deontology, virtue ethics and egoism, or, rather, egoistic virtue ethics. Consequentialism, deontology and egoism will receive very brief treatment here, allowing for an extended (though still far too sweeping) discussion of virtue ethics, which, I suggest, has been the most influential in classical anarchist thought. This section, it should be noted before going any further, does not represent any definite conclusions but should be taken as an example of how the above definition and models of humanism could be applied to the ethical theories found in the various classical anarchisms.

The method applied in this section will make use of the definition of humanism presented above in such a way as to determine whether classical anarchisms are conditional on this essentialism of human nature. Given that the focus of the definition of humanism is on sufficient conditions for personhood, the object of interest is the picture of the 'moral actor' demanded by each ethical theory. Each of these positions is taken as a normative one in which certain actions are prescribed to actors, and, as such, those actors have to be able to act according to those prescriptions. Thus, the ethical theories under consideration here can only be judged consistent if they incorporate an image of a moral actor who displays properties necessary for following the normative commands they entail. This should make the relevance of the above discussion of personhood apparent. If an ethical theory is conditional on a moral actor displaying metaphysical properties including one or more of

(1) rationality, (2) self-consciousness, (3) free will and/or (4) teleology, then the ethical theory can be described as humanist.

Before considering each of the ethical theories in turn, something must be said of the categorisation of classical anarchism I have presented here. Given that the postanarchists rarely distinguish between different schools of thought within anarchism, it may need clarification as to why I have chosen to focus solely on classical anarchism, to the exclusion of later additions to the anarchist tradition. As with the rationalisation of the definition of humanism in the previous section, it is within this definition of classical anarchism where the postanarchist use of the term can be located. Indeed, Newman (Evren et al., 2005) says as much: 'my account of anarchism is by no means comprehensive. [...] I was trying to explore a certain political logic at the heart of classical anarchist theory and to show how this ran into certain conceptual limitations.' While the picture of classical anarchisms given here aims to be somewhat more systematic than that contained in the postanarchist literature, I want to stress that it is still open to debate and, ultimately, correction. As has been argued in anarchist scholarship (Jun, 2009: 515–17), classical anarchist writers rarely produced clearly argued philosophical manuscripts, writing instead texts aimed at educating and inspiring peasants, workers and other oppressed groups to revolutionary action.

12.3.1 Consequentialism

An important distinction can be drawn between consequentialism as it has been most influential within moral philosophy and consequentialist reasoning. Consequentialist reasoning is that whereby a qualitatively distinct goal is to be achieved by certain means that are judged, for one reason or another, appropriate. What I want to discuss here, however, is a consequentialism in which the quantity of a certain good is to be maximised in the outcome of actions. A formal definition may be as follows (this and following definitions of deontology, virtue ethics and egoism are taken or adapted from Rosalind Hursthouse (1996)):

> *Consequentialism*: An action is right *iff* (if and only if) it promotes the best consequences.

Consequentialism, in its utilitarian form (where the best consequences are defined as those in which happiness is maximised), is represented in the classical anarchist tradition by Godwin: '[t]he true standard of the conduct of one man towards another, is justice. Justice is a principle which proposes to itself the production of the greatest sum of pleasure or happiness' (1971: 14). Consequentialism demands a maximising impression of rationality, one that bears close resemblance to that attributed to the *Homo economicus* of liberal economics. As John Tomer (2001: 282) writes, 'he has the ability to create mental images of possible goods and the satisfaction they provide as well as the ability to calculate precisely concerning these possible satisfactions.' Therefore, the moral actor on which this maximising consequentialism is dependent qualifies as a person: she must display rationality. As such, consequentialism can be properly described as humanist.

12.3.2 Deontology

Alan Ritter (1969: 66–7) describes Proudhon as adhering to a deontological ethics in which emphasis is put on whether or not acts are in line with certain inviolable laws, rather than on the desired ends of action. While reference to a form of virtue ethics can be found in his work (McLaughlin, 2007: 71–4), Proudhon does put great emphasis on rights and duties, arguing that individuals have a duty to follow certain rules of nature (1970: 282–3). He writes, for example: 'we need labour in order to live. To do so is both our right and our duty.'

> *Deontology*: An action is right *iff* it is in accordance with a correct moral rule or principle.

Traditionally, any ethics which bases itself on one or more moral laws appeals to some kind of essentialism, be it of an intuitionist or a rationalist variety, to explain how individuals are able to apprehend moral axioms. Furthermore, the very notion of action being judged in terms of their being in accord with a correct rule would necessitate that moral actors are able to think and act rationally. According to the definition of rationality above, in which persons are able to reason according to norms and where such reasoning influences their action, the moral actor of deontology would be a prime example. Therefore, along with consequentilaism, deontology requires a rational moral actor, and as this moral actor thus qualifies as a person, the theory is humanist.

12.3.3 Virtue ethics

As Franks (2008: 137; Chapter 8) notes, an ethical approach based on virtue can be found in much of the classical anarchist thought that developed from a Young-Hegelian background. This is seen in the writings of Bakunin and is present as well in Kropotkin's work. Before elaborating on this, it is worth drawing out a distinction between traditional virtue ethics and that which is visible within the writings of certain classical anarchists. Traditionally, an ethics of virtue, which takes its inspiration from Aristotle, centres on the notion that moral actors ought to act virtuously, or exercise the virtues. Virtues are commonly defined as traits of character that, when manifest in an agent's actions, constitute for the agent a proper or purposeful manner of existing. Virtue theory, then, determines how agents should act not in accordance with desired ends or acts, but rather in so much as their actions display a character that is deemed desirable.

> *Virtue ethics*: An action is right *iff* it is what a virtuous agent would characteristically (i.e. acting in character) do in the circumstances.

According to this, a virtuous agent is one who has fulfilled the determined purpose of living: reached a state of *eudaimonia* or flourishing (Hursthouse, 1996: 23). The keystone of traditional virtue ethics is a belief in a teleological human nature. In P. M. S. Hacker's (2007: 134) words, '[f]lourishing is doing well in a form of life [...and] in the activities characteristic of the form of life.' This 'form of life' is synonymous with the *psuchē* of Aristotle: 'the "principle" of life that makes it the kind of being it is' (Hacker, 2007: 22).

Kropotkin's virtue ethics differs from this traditional account, but is more similar to it than that of Bakunin, which will be discussed below. It is often stated that Kropotkin asserts sociability as a prime virtue that human beings ought to express. However, for Kropotkin, the instinct to cooperate does not constitute a virtue as cooperation is not the content of the actions of a virtuous agent, but the background for the possibility of virtuous action in general: sociability is a 'broad necessary foundation' (Kropotkin, 2004: 5). Against social Darwinists, Kropotkin (1970: 96) argues that in evolution it is cooperation, not competition, which provides species with the behaviours necessary for survival:

> The more thoroughly each member of the society feels his solidarity with each other member of the society, the more completely are developed in all of them those [...] qualities which are the main factors of all progress[. ...] Without mutual confidence no struggle is possible; there is no courage, no initiative, no solidarity – and no victory!

Here, Kropotkin describes some of the virtues that an actor will express in order to secure the survival of her community or species (in primitive times and in animals), or of life in general (in civilised humanity) (Kropotkin, 2004: 209). Survival (in a certain 'good' mode of living) constitutes an end that is shared by all actors and ought to be achieved, making teleology a property that moral actors necessarily display, and thus providing a sufficient condition for personhood. Kropotkin can thus be described as a humanist.

The distinction between Bakunin's virtue ethics and both the traditional account and that of Kropotkin can be highlighted by examining the roots Bakunin's ethics has in the thought of G. W. F. Hegel. Allen Wood (1990: 31) calls Hegel's ethics a 'self-actualisation' theory, its starting point being the conception of a certain self or identity to be exercised or actualised, to be embodied and expressed in action. The theory selects the actions to be performed and the ends to be pursued because they are the actions and ends of that kind of self. The difference between this and traditional virtue ethics lies, however, in Hegel's understanding of this self that is fulfilled in self-actualisation.

Rather than asserting the existence of a nature common to persons, Hegel argues for 'historicised naturalism' (Wood, 1990: 33) whereby the identity being expressed by agents is historically constructed through a dialectical process such that agents come to manifest a universal Spirit (*Geist*). This may be confusing for readers who are not familiar with Hegel's philosophical project, but what should be noted is that under this conception of self-actualisation, the virtuous character is something that is malleable and will alter from historical epoch to historical epoch (Knowles, 2002: 73). As Hegel (1952: §150) writes, '[v]irtue is the ethical order reflected in the individual character so far as that character is determined by its natural endowment.' The virtuous character is not an attribute of persons, but of a universal Spirit that acts through them, so to speak.

Like other Young-Hegelian philosophers, Bakunin transforms Hegel's philosophy in a number of ways. What he retains, however, is this notion of self-actualisation and historical naturalism (McLaughlin, 2002: 48–9, 190–1) and so can be said to subscribe not to a traditional virtue ethics, but to one similar to that of Hegel. Indeed, Bakunin writes,

> [W]e are absolutely the slaves of [natural and social] laws. [...] In his relation to natural laws but one liberty is possible to man – that of recognizing and applying them on an ever-extending scale *in conformity*

> with the object of collective and individual emancipation or humanization which he pursues.
>
> (1973: 128–9, italics added)

How, then, is this account of virtue ethics, based as it is on dialectical, historical naturalism (McLaughlin, 2002: 33), to be viewed in relation to humanism? Bakunin's account could be said to subscribe to teleology, as it does prescribe a natural end that human beings ought to actualise. However, the *telos* present in his historicist virtue theory is not one that emanates from some given property of human beings and so cannot be located within the definition of teleology I use here. While free will is not necessarily precluded by determinism in general (Frankfurt, 1971: 20), it is also true that the moral actor demanded by this type of virtue ethics does not require free will to act ethically, and so neither is this a necessary property. It is not a requirement that an agent choose to act as a virtuous agent would. Similarly, it is not necessary that the moral actor reason in any sense about the actions being undertaken; they simply have to be undertaken, and so while rationality is included in the forces that determine agency, it is not a property of the closed minds of persons.

In addition, I would argue that self-consciousness also be rejected as a necessary property held by the moral actor in this virtue ethics. Again, for the virtuous character to be actualised, the agent acting need not be consciously aware of herself as an acting agent. As such, Bakunin's virtue ethics does not necessitate a commitment to humanism, as the moral actor need not display any of the conditions sufficient for personhood. Properties that are displayed by moral actors are not properties of that entity but are manifested properties of the universal Spirit (in Hegel) or Nature (in Bakunin) that develops through the dialectical progression of history. It is this, among other things, that leads R. B. Fowler to include classical anarchists within the natural law tradition (Fowler, 1972: 750).

12.3.4 Egoism

Rather than representing a wholly distinct ethical theory, egoism (as I use the term here) instead encompasses egoistic versions of the three main ethical positions. The egoistic varieties of consequentialism and deontology will not be discussed here. Instead, I will focus on egoistic virtue ethics, which is more noticeable among classical anarchisms. Egoistic virtue ethics would be one in which rather than the *telos* of the agent's life being inherent to persons or to material or ideal conditions, the goal of the agent's life and the virtues that express such a goal are determined by the agent, independent of any (alleged) commonality. Furthermore, this virtuous life is subject to be changed by that agent at any time.

> *Egoistic virtue ethics*: An action is right *iff* is it what a freely determined virtuous agent would characteristically (i.e. acting in character) do in the circumstances.

For example, Stirner (1912: 483) writes, 'I am unique. [...] I set myself to work, and develop myself, only as this. I do not develop man, nor as man, but as I, I develop – myself.' While Newman argues that such an ethical position rejects any essentialism, taking Stirner to be referring to a self 'which is empty, undefined, and contingent' (Newman, 2001: 67), others (Cohn, 2002; Glavin, 2004) note a commitment to free will in Stirner's account of the moral actor. Furthermore, self-consciousness would seem to be a similarly necessary property.

To see more clearly why this latter claim is true, it is perhaps helpful to elaborate on why free will is a necessary property. As Newman (2001: 60) writes, 'it is up to the individual to create something out of this [nothingness] and not be limited by essences.' Clearly, there is a distinction here between the empty ego (character) and the individual (moral actor). In egoistic virtue ethics, the moral actor acts on this character to shape it in a certain way. Now, this does not in itself necessitate free will in a moral actor, only a causal primacy of moral actor over character; the moral actor could be acting in a determined way. However, such a deterministic account of an egoistic virtue ethics would be to present something quite unlike the egoistic virtue ethics of Stirner. Egoistic virtue ethics demands that the moral actor freely choose the virtuous character, and so free will is an obvious condition. In addition, egoistic virtue ethics also requires that this distinction between the moral actor and the character be recognised. This could be reconciled with a view that denied self-consciousness, because crucially the moral actor is acting upon something that is distinct from itself. However, the elaboration of self-consciousness in the previous section indicated the requirements for self-consciousness: that an actor be aware of relating to herself in thought. The presence of 'I'-thoughts, where the object referred to in the thought is the same as the subject having the thought, is indicative of this. Stirner's egoistic virtue ethics is founded upon the notion of a moral actor who is correctly aware both of herself *and* of herself as free. In light of this, while the teleological content of the moral actor may be undetermined, egoistic virtue ethics can also be said to be a humanist theory, in that the moral actor required by it must be both self-conscious and free.

12.4 Conclusion

What I have attempted to outline and put into practice in this chapter is a method for assessing the soundness of the postanarchist criticism of classical anarchisms. The claim that is made by authors such as Newman is that as a political theory of resistance, '[anarchism] demands a pure place of revolution, and it finds it in natural essence, in an essential human subjectivity' (Newman, 2001: 39). My approach has been to arrive first at a definition of humanism (one that is sufficiently conditional on a claim that persons display one or more of rationality, self-consciousness, free will and/or teleology) and then suggest how classical anarchisms may or may not be described as humanist under such a definition. This latter task has only been included here as an example of an application of this analytic method, but I would suggest that it can be taken as presenting some (albeit tentative) conclusions as to the accuracy of the postanarchist critique. By dividing classical anarchisms into a number of ethical theories found present in the writings of several authors, I have shown that in no case is the postanarchist claim strictly true. Newman, for example, argues that older anarchisms display a commitment to an agent who is both rational and teleological. Consequentialism, deontology, Kropotkin's virtue ethics and egoism all subscribe to a humanism, but ones in which rationality and teleology do not coincide. Consequentialism and deontology both demand a rational agent, and Kropotkin requires a teleological one. Egoism, in opposition to postanarchist claims about it, is also humanist in its insistence on free will and self-consciousness. So, while the strict postanarchist claim is not valid for these, a wider charge of humanism can be levelled. Bakunin's virtue ethics is the only position that withstands description as humanist, although in this case a reduction to historical necessity is required, and this is something the postanarchists, as evidenced in their critique of Marxism, would be equally unhappy with (Newman, 2001: 32). Franks' (2006: 114; 2008: 147–8) recent introduction of a non-essentialist virtue ethics may overcome these reductionist qualms, especially as '[i]t views goods as being inherent to social practices' (Franks, 2008: 137). However, Franks' approach is not an ethical justification of anarchism, but an ethics that is relevant to anarchist practices. It tells us how to behave properly as anarchists, but not why we ought to behave as anarchists in the first place.

Before closing, I want to address the issue of the originality of the postanarchist critique. McLaughlin (2007: 167) notes that anarchists early in the twentieth century dealt with the issue of fixed human essentialism, and there is nothing new in the postanarchist critique. Indeed, Errico Malatesta (1977: 267), in the 1930s, criticises Kropotkin for his optimistic interpretation of natural law. I close with the following quotation:

> If it is true that the law of Nature is harmony, I suggest one would be entitled to ask why Nature has waited for anarchists to be born, and goes on waiting for them to triumph in order to rid us of the terrible destructive conflicts from which mankind has always suffered.

Bibliography

J. Adams (2003) 'Postanarchism in a nutshell' InterActivist Info Exchange, http://info.interactivist.net/node/2475, date accessed: 24 September 2009.

M. Bakunin (1973) *Michael Bakunin: Selected Writings* (London: Jonathan Cape).

J. Cohn (2002) 'What is postanarchism "post"?' *Postmodern Culture*, XIII(i), http://muse.jhu.edu/journals/postmodern_culture/toc/pmc13.1.html, date accessed: 27 September 2009.

J. Cohn and S. Wilbur (2003) 'What's wrong with postanarchism?' The Institute for Anarchist Studies, http://libertarian-library.blogspot.com/2007/07/cohn-and-wilbur-whats-wrong-with.html, date accessed: 27 September 2009.

D. Dennett (1979) *Brainstorms: Philosophical Essays on Mind and Psychology* (Sussex: Harvester Press).

S. Evren, K. Kursug and E. Kosova (2005) 'Interview with Saul Newman', *Siyahi Interlocal Journal of Postanarchist Theory*, I(i), http://community.livejournal.com/siyahi/2019.html, date accessed: 28 September 2009.

R. B. Fowler (1972) 'The anarchist tradition of political thought', *Political Research Quarterly*, XXV(iv): 738–52.

H. Frankfurt (1971) 'Freedom of the will and the concept of a person', *The Journal of Philosophy*, LXVIII(i): 5–20.

B. Franks (2006) *Rebel Alliances: The Means and Ends of Contemporary British Anarchisms* (Edinburgh: AK Press).

────── (2007) 'Postanarchism: A critical assessment', *Journal of Political Ideologies*, XII(ii): 127–45.

────── (2008) 'Postanarchism and meta-ethics', *Anarchist Studies*, XVI(ii): 135–53.

M. Glavin (2004) 'Power, subjectivity, resistance: Three works on postmodern anarchism', *New Formulations*, II(ii), http://www.newformulation.org/4glavin.htm, date accessed: 27 September 2009.

W. Godwin (1971) *Enquiry Concerning Political Justice* (Oxford: Clarendon Press).

P. Hacker (2007) *Human Nature: The Categorical Framework* (Oxford: Basil Blackwell).

A. Hamilton (n.d.) 'Memory and the body: A study in self-consciousness' (in preparation).
G. W. F. Hegel (1952) *Hegel's Philosophy of Right* (Oxford: Clarendon).
R. Hursthouse (1996) 'Normative virtue ethics' in R. Crisp (ed.) *How Should One Live?* (Oxford: Clarendon Press), 19–36.
N. Jun (2009) 'Anarchist philosophy and working class struggle: A brief history and commentary', *Working USA: The Journal of Labor and Society*, XII(iii): 505–19.
D. Knowles (2002) *Routledge Philosophy Guidebook to Hegel and the Philosophy of Right* (London: Routledge).
P. Kropotkin (1970) *Anarchism: A Collection of Revolutionary Writings* (New York: Dover).
—— (2004) *Mutual Aid: A Factor of Evolution* (Whitefish, MT: Kessinger Publishing).
P. McLaughlin (2002) *Mikhail Bakunin: The Philosophical Basis of his Anarchism* (New York: Algora).
—— (2007) *Anarchism and Authority. A Philosophical Introduction to Classical Anarchism* (Aldershot: Ashgate).
E. Malatesta (1977) *Errico Malatesta: His Life and Ideas* (London: Freedom Press).
T. May (1994) *The Political Philosophy of Poststructuralist Anarchism* (University Park, PA: Pennsylvania State University Press).
S. Newman (2001) *From Bakunin to Lacan: Anti-Authoritarianism and the Dislocation of Power* (Lanham: Lexington Books).
P.-J. Proudhon (1970) *What Is property? An Inquiry into the Principle of Right and of Government* (New York: Dover).
D. Reiss and L. Marino (2001) 'Mirror self-recognition in the Bottlenose Dolphin: A case of cognitive convergence', *Proceedings of the National Academy of Sciences of the United States of America*, XCVIII(x): 5937–42.
A. Ritter (1969) *The Political Thought of Pierre-Joseph Proudhon* (Princeton, NJ: Princeton University Press).
K. Soper (1986) *Humanism and Anti-Humanism* (London: Hutchinson).
—— (2001) 'Richard Rorty: Humanist and/or anti-humanist?' in M. Festenstien and S. Thompson (eds) *Richard Rorty: Critical Dialogues* (Cambridge: Polity Press).
M. Stirner (1912) *The Ego and His Own* (London: A.C. Fifield).
P. Strawson (1959) *Individuals: An essay in Descriptive Metaphysics* (London: Routledge).
J. Tomer (2001) 'Economic man vs. heterodox men: The concepts of human nature in schools of economic thought', *Journal of Socio-Economics*, XXX(iv): 281–93.
S. Villon (2003) 'Post-anarchism or simply post-revolution?' Originally available at http://www.geocities.com/kk_ab%20acus/other/postanarc%20hism.html [Link no longer operative].
A. Wood (1990) *Hegel's Ethical Thought* (Cambridge: Cambridge University Press).

Index

activism, 1, 3–4, 8, 15, 17, 20, 31, 40, 47, 64, 114, 124–5, 127–8, 130, 135, 139, 145, 147, 169, 172, 173, 187, 194, 197, 200
Adams, Jason, 139, 141, 232
Adorno, Theodor, 167
Albert, Michael, 79
alienation, 30, 165–6, 177, 181, 190, 214
amoralism, 2, 221
Amster, Randall, 117
analytic philosophy, 3, 4, 8, 15, 22–5, 40, 41, 78, 89, 138–43, 148–50, 154, 156, 227–9, 230, 240
anarcha-feminism, 1, 50, 189, 192
anarchisms
  analytic, 3, 23–6, 136, 138–40, 145, 148–50, 151, 156
  classical, 7, 8, 13–14, 16–17, 49–50, 57, 63–4, 149, 154, 226–36, 238, 240
  class struggle, *see* anarchisms, social
  environmental, 161–83, 186
  feminist, *see* anarcha-feminism
  individualist, 2, 3, 14–15, 19–20, 50, 76–7, 88, 91, 136–9, 143
  lifestyle, 64, 189, 211, 214
  philosophical, 3–4, 5, 13–31, 37, 51, 135–9, 142, 144, 156, 230
  postanarchist, 6, 7, 8, 49, 114, 139, 141, 149, 153, 154, 155, 209, 221–2, 226–41
  practical, 135–6, 139, 141–2, 150, 154–5, 157
  social, 2, 4, 5, 6, 7, 14, 15, 18, 19–20, 23, 26, 45, 47, 49–56, 60–4, 83, 84, 86–7, 91, 98, 99, 100, 103–4, 108–9, 116, 138–9, 140, 145, 146, 149, 186, 188–9, 193, 197–9, 209–10, 210–11, *see also* social ecology; anarcho-syndicalism

Anarchist Federation, 145
anarcho-capitalism, 3, 4, 137
anarcho-syndicalism, 50, 140, 173
  See also labour unions
Anderson, Benedict, 156
animal rights, 124, 197
Anscombe, Elizabeth, 142
anti-capitalism, 1, 3, 63, 64, 125, 141, 187
Antifa, 123, 124
anti-fascism, 122–3, 124, 129, 187
anti-globalisation, *see* anti-capitalism
Aquinas, 34, 46
Aristotle, 34, 46, 103, 142, 144, 151, 153, 154, 236
authority, 3, 4, 7, 13–18, 22, 25–30, 51–4, 58, 88, 91, 97, 99, 136, 139, 141, 186–7, 192, 196, 201, 208, 211–15, 220, 221, 233
autonomy, 4, 15–17, 53, 55, 78, 80, 86, 97, 107, 117, 119, 122, 136–7, 165, 190, 198–9
Avrich, Paul, 59, 61

Bakunin, Mikhail, 2, 7, 14, 23, 49, 50, 53, 54, 55–6, 58–9, 60–2, 75, 91, 115, 116, 145, 192, 194, 208, 210–14, 215–16, 220–1, 222, 223, 226, 233, 236–8, 240
Baudrillard, Jean, 177
Benjamin, Walter, 177
Bentham, Jeremy, 40, 41
Bergson, Henri, 181
Berkman, Alexander, 54
Berlin, Isaiah, 21, 37, 145
Bey, Hakim, 191, 211
Black Flag (magazine), 145
Bookchin, Murray, 6, 55, 83, 171, 173–7, 179, 192, 210, 214–15, 221
Bové, José, 126
Bowen, James, 58, 141, 145
Brinton, Maurice, 138, 140, 149

British National Party (BNP), 122–3
Brown, L. Susan, 50, 189
Brown, Wendy, 186, 196, 201

Cafiero, Carlo, 61
Call, Lewis, 139, 149, 153
Call, The (newspaper), 2, 7
Carter, Alan, 3, 23–6, 136, 138–40, 141, 145, 149
Carter, John, 141
Chomsky, Noam, 83, 177, 186, 198
Clandestine Insurgent Rebel Clown Army (CIRCA), 147
Clark, John, 172, 173
Clark, Samuel, 1, 136, 152–3, 198
class struggle, 23, 189, 197
class struggle anarchism, *see* anarchisms, social
Class War, 4, 116
Cleyre, Voltairine de, 60, 61, 196
coercion, 2, 4, 22, 24, 35, 37, 51–4, 57–8, 71–2, 74, 78, 83, 104, 120–1, 124, 129, 136–7, 138, 140, 144, 233
Cohen, G(erry). A., 23–4, 76, 138, 141, 148
Cohn, Jesse, 154, 156, 187, 188, 202, 226, 239
Coleridge, Samuel Taylor, 40
Colson, Daniel, 188
communism, 103, 109, 210
Comte, Auguste, 5, 87–99, 104
conflict
  cultural, 15, 147, 156
  instinctual, 154, 223
  moral, 5, 99–100, 113–15, 117–22, 123, 124, 129, 147, 152, 155, 163, 223–4
  political, 15, 120, 121, 129, 141, 147, 152, 156
consensus, 115, 119, 120, 128–30
consequentialism, 59, 145–6, 151, 233–5, 238, 240
  See also utilitarianism
co-operation, *see* mutual aid
CrimethInc., 126, 200
Crowder, George, 1, 26, 50
Curran, Giorel, 117

deep ecology, 6, 161–83, 197
Deleuze, Gilles, 6, 49, 57, 188, 189, 191, 214, 221
Dennett, Daniel, 229
deontology, 35, 58, 89, 136, 143, 145–6, 150, 151, 233, 234, 235, 238, 240
Devall, Bill, 163, 173
Dissent! Network, 126
Dor or Die (magazine), 169
Douglass, Frederick, 38–42
duty, 15–17, 20, 22, 26–7, 78, 81, 93, 94, 99–100, 106, 163, 209, 235
  of rightful honour (DoRH), 77–81
  See also deontology
Dworkin, Ronald, 72, 123

Earth First, 164, 169, 174
Earth Liberation Front, 164
eco-anarchism, *see* anarchisms, environmental
ecosophy, 162
  See also Naess, Arne
egality, *see* equality
egoism, 2, 7, 14, 55, 98, 106, 144, 151, 170, 171, 227, 233, 234, 238–40
Egoist, The (newspaper), 2, 7
Emerson, Ralph, 161
emotivism, 143
environmental ethics, 5, 163, 172
  See also ecosophy
equality, 4, 26, 54–6, 59–60, 70–8, 104–5, 109, 116, 138, 140, 145, 161, 165, 167, 174, 190, 193, 194, 197, 201
essentialism, 8, 142, 144, 153–5, 157, 169, 222, 226–7, 231–3, 235, 239–41
Everett, Martyn, 156
existentialism, 143, 214

fascism, 122, 124, 171, 190
  See also anti-fascism; British National Party (BNP)
feminism, 1, 48, 50, 189, 190, 194, 196–7
Fillis, John, 166
Foot, Philippa, 33, 142
Foreman, David, 174

Foucault, Michel, 49, 55, 57, 121, 195, 198, 200, 202
Fox, Warwick, 163, 168, 173
Frankfurt, Harry, 16, 228–9, 238
Franks, Benjamin, 58, 130, 194, 202, 221, 226, 231, 232, 233, 235, 240
Freeden, Michael, 139–40
freedom
 anarchisms commitment to, 15, 26, 39, 53–6, 60, 115–16, 125–7, 136, 145, 154, 161, 197, 211, 213–14
 conflicts between, or confused, concepts of, 5, 22, 53–6, 113–30
 emergent, 55, 121, 195, 197, 214–15, 239–40
 and equality, 55, 56, 57–8, 60, 71, 74, 76, 78, 81, 116, 145, 196, 199
 external, 71, 73, 76, 79
 innate or instinctual, 2, 60, 69, 72, 75, 77, 197, 198
 internal, 71, 73
 limits on, 55, 70–2, 73–4, 113, 116–17, 122, 153, 179, 196, 211, 239
 negative, 37, 39, 53–6, 117–18, 122–4, 126, 136–8, 198
 positive, 26, 37, 54–6, 117, 122, 123–4
free will, 87, 95, 97, 197, 211, 229–30, 238–40
Freire, Paolo, 213, 220
Fromm, Erich, 53, 213

Gadamer, Hans-Georg, 169
Glavin, Michael, 239
Godwin, William, 13, 19, 23, 34, 37, 53, 69, 116, 226, 233
Goldman, Emma, 7, 53–7, 59, 60–1, 69, 135, 154, 208, 210, 212–14, 216–17, 220
Gordon, Tash, 192
Gordon, Uri, 128, 141, 145, 186, 189–91, 195
Gori, Pietro, 61
Graeber, David, 49, 58, 59, 62, 117, 125, 126, 152, 191

Graham, Robert, 74, 83, 128
Gramsci, Antonio, 61, 214
Grave, Jean, 61, 141, 149
Gray, John, 120, 121, 123
green anarchism, *see* anarchisms, environmental
Green, Leslie, 27
Green, T. H., 34, 77
Grubacic, Andrej, 117, 126
Guattari, Felix, 6, 189, 214
Guillaume, James, 145

Haar, Michel, 222–3
Hall, Constance, 90
Hamilton, A. J., 230
Hart, H. L. A., 27
Hazareesingh, Sudhir, 91
hedonism, 34
Hegel, G. W. F., 89, 91, 145, 217, 237, 238
Heinberg, Richard, 166, 168, 174, 178
Heller, Chaia, 190
Heraclitus, 210, 223
Herzen, Alexander, 109
hierarchy
 anarchisms' contestation of, 3, 4, 6, 51, 54, 56–8, 70, 113, 138, 141–2, 146–7, 152–7, 182, 187, 189, 194, 196, 198–9, 211, 214
 and essentialisms, 7, 153–4, 169, 198
 feature of capitalism, 3, 6, 7, 140–1, 147, 189, 199
 feature of Marxism, 59, 140, 149
 feature of pre-industrial societies, 175
 feature of the state, 51, 142, 149, 189
Hobbes, Thomas, 46, 152, 195
Hobsbawm, Eric, 147
Horkheimer, Max, 166–7
humanism, 114, 143, 222–3, 226–34, 238, 240
 See also essentialism
Humboldt, Wilhem, von, 14
Hurl, Chris, 125, 127
Hursthouse, Rosalind, 142, 144, 234, 236

idealism, 89, 95
Illich, Ivan, 213
Industrial Workers of the World (IWW), 64

Jensen, Derrick, 167, 193
Jews and Judaism, 50, 61, 218, 223
Joll, James, 145
Jun, Nathan, 233, 234
just distribution, 72, 102

Kaczynski, Theodor (Unabomber), 167, 174, 177
Kant, Immanuel, 4, 5, 46, 59, 69–84, 87–96, 98–100, 104, 107, 136–7, 146, 150–1, 163
See also deontology
Katz, Eric, 163, 170
Keyt, David, 136, 140, 144
Kingsnorth, Paul, 125, 187
Kinna, Ruth, 136, 138, 192
Klein, Naomi, 80
Knowles, Dudley, 2, 135, 136–7, 139, 140, 154, 237
Krishnamurti, J., 201–2
Kropotkin, Peter, 49, 50, 51, 56, 58–9, 60–1, 77, 116, 135, 140–1, 152–4, 191, 194, 214, 222, 223, 226, 233, 236–7, 240–1
Kymlicka, Will, 118, 121

labour, 20, 24, 30–1, 55, 82–3, 103, 106, 166, 167, 196
labourers, *see* working class or workers
labour theory of value
  Locke, 101
  Marx, 24, 63
  Nozick, 138
  Proudhon, 101–2, 105, 235
labour unions, 49, 50, 61, 64, 140, 152
Lamb, David, 145
Landauer, Gustav, 60, 188–9, 200
Lefebvre, Henri, 221
legitimacy, 3–4, 7, 14–20, 25–30, 35, 51, 69–70, 83, 123, 137, 139, 153
Le Guin, Ursula, 191, 193, 200
Leninism, 59, 145
Lenin, Vladimir I., 47, 56, 145, 149

liberalism, 4, 5, 14, 23, 35, 53–4, 56, 96, 100–4, 107, 113, 115, 117, 119–23, 129–30, 136–8, 143, 144, 146–7, 150, 153, 156, 193, 196, 235
libertarianism, 113, 115–16, 121, 193, 213
  left-138
  right-3, 4, 137–40, 193, *see also* Nozick, Robert
libertarian socialism, 2, 7, 56, 59, 61, 62, 140, 145, 149, 152, 193
Linebaugh, Peter, 147
Locke, John, 35, 46, 101, 139, 164, 175
love, 7, 50, 69, 194, 196, 201
Lubac, Henri de, 88–91
Lukács, Georg, 47, 61
Luxemburg, Rosa, 61
Lyotard, Jean-François, 49, 221

Machiavelli, Niccolò, 48
MacIntyre, Alasdair, 4, 35, 135, 139–44, 146–57, 220
macropolitics, 57, 189, 190
Malatesta, Errico, 55, 60, 63, 71, 77–8, 135, 141, 149, 154, 241
Marcuse, Herbert, 167, 214
Marsden, Dora, 2
Marshall, Peter, 21
Marxism, 21, 23–5, 45, 47–9, 59–63, 89, 138, 143, 145, 148–50, 208, 210–16, 221, 240
Marx, Karl, 2, 14, 23, 34, 63, 89, 92, 145, 209–12, 216
May 1968, 63, 210, 214–15, 221
May, Todd, 6, 46–9, 57, 130, 139, 141, 149–50, 153–5, 191, 201, 209, 221, 232
McDowell, John, 142
McLaughlin, Andrew, 163–4, 168, 172, 174, 178–9
McLaughlin, Paul, 1, 25, 136, 233, 235, 237–8, 241
Meltzer, Albert, 22–3
Merleau-Ponty, Maurice, 165, 181
micropolitics, 57, 189, 196, 201
Miller, David, 13, 15, 149
Mill, James, 40
Mill, John Stuart, 34, 38, 40–3, 96

Morland, David, 141, 155, 198
Morris, Brian, 51, 172, 174
Murdoch, Iris, 142
mutual aid, 6, 58, 104, 188, 194, 236
mutualism, 50, 79, 100

Naess, Arne, 6, 161–3, 169–70, 172–4
natural rights, 77–8
Nechayev, Sergei, 59, 145
New Left, 59, 64
Newman, Saul, 114, 139, 141, 149–50, 153–4, 196, 209, 221, 222, 226–7, 231–2, 234, 239–40
Nietzsche, Friedrich, 7, 34, 188, 196, 208–24
  Eternal Return, 7, 208–9, 222–3
  ressentiment, 196, 218–19
  transvaluation of values, 7, 212–13, 217
  Will to Power, 7, 208, 217, 222
nihilism, 7, 188, 209, 215–21
Nin, Anaïs, 200
Nishitani, Kieji, 216–17
No Borders, 197
Nozick, Robert, 15, 76, 79, 83, 137–8, 150
Nuer, 37, 152
Nussbaum, Martha, 142, 220

O'Neill, Onara, 136
Orwell, George, 214

Parekh, Bhikhu, 121–2
Parton, Glenn, 168
Pateman, Carole, 74, 128, 199
People's Global Action, 194
perfectionism, 4, 33–43, 223
phenomenology, 165, 181–3, 217
Plumwood, Val, 170–1, 182
Popper, Karl, 145
postanarchism, *see* anarchisms, postanarchist
postmodernism, *see* poststructuralism
poststructuralism, 4, 6, 49, 114, 139, 179–80, 209, 219, 221
Prawdin, Michael, 59
prefiguration, 58–60, 140–1, 145–9, 156, 192, 211, 230–1
primitivism, 6, 161–83, 193

property and property rights, 4–5, 53, 69–84, 86, 88, 95, 98, 100–6, 108–9, 127, 163, 165, 167, 175
possession (as opposed to property), 4, 71–7, 79–80, 101
Proudhon, Pierre-Joseph, 4–5, 14–15, 19, 21, 49–51, 53–7, 60–1, 63, 79, 86–109, 116, 187, 188, 208, 209–10, 214, 217, 220–1, 226, 233, 235
Purchase, Graham, 124, 173
Purkis, Jonathan, 58, 141

Quail, John, 59, 156

Rawls, John, 15, 34, 35, 46–7, 84, 115, 118–20, 122–3, 128–9, 150
Raz, Joseph, 15, 16, 27, 121
Read, Herbert, 116, 209, 216, 222–3
Reclus, Élisée, 60
religion, 7, 15, 21, 51, 93, 95–6, 120, 126, 156, 173, 201, 209, 211, 215–17, 222–3
republicanism, 86–8, 91, 100, 105, 107–9
revolution, 14–15, 20, 22–5, 42, 47, 49–50, 57, 59, 62, 102, 103, 106, 108, 140, 147, 149, 190, 192–3, 198, 202, 208, 210–15, 217, 234, 240
Ricoeur, Paul, 221
rights, 55, 70–5, 77–80, 82–3, 86, 106, 108, 138–9, 151, 235
  animal, 124–5
  negative, 80, 117, 138, 142
  positive, 117
  See also property and property rights
right, *see* universal principle of right
Ritter, Alan, 26, 89, 99, 115–16, 235
Rocker, Rudolf, 50, 51, 60, 84, 186, 190
Rothbard, Murray, 3
Rousseau, Jean-Jacques, 14, 87, 94, 104, 107, 167, 195
Ryder, Richard, 124

Saint-Simon Claude Henri de, 56, 91, 98, 102
Sale, Kirkpatrick, 168, 176

Sessions, George, 162, 163
sexual relationships, 50, 187–8
Shakespeare, Tom, 194
Shakespeare, William, 33
Shepard, Benjamin, 200
Shepard, Paul, 166
Sheppard, Brian Oliver, 176, 177–8
Simmons, A. John, 15, 18–21, 23, 26, 29, 51
Situationist theory, 214
Slote, Michael, 142
social ecology, 6, 173–5
socialism, 2, 6, 14, 15, 19–20, 45, 47, 50, 51, 53–4, 56, 60–1, 63, 84, 102, 103, 107, 109, 122, 140–1, 145, 209, 211, 213
See also libertarian socialism
Soper, Kate, 227–9
Spanish Civil War, 152, 187, 211, 213–14
speciesism, 124, 174
Starhawk, 193
Steiner, Hillel, 136, 138
Stirner, Max, 2, 7, 13, 14, 30, 77, 222–3, 226–7, 233, 239
Strawson, P. F., 228–9
subjectivation, 55, 57, 215
syndicalism, *see* anarcho-syndicalism; labour unions

Taylor, Bron, 172, 174, 177
Taylor, Charles, 219–20
teleology, 5, 34–5, 38, 42, 87, 91, 92, 135, 137, 142–3, 146, 150–1, 154–7, 162–3, 229–32, 234, 236, 237–8, 240
Thompson, E. P., 147
Thoreau, Henry, 143, 161
Tissot, Joseph, 90–1
Tolstoy, Leo, 143
Tomer, John, 235
Toner, Christopher, 144
Tormey, Simon, 191
Tucker, Benjamin, 2, 14, 187

Unabomber, *see* Kaczynski, Theodor (Unabomber)
universal principle of right, 70, 72–5, 79
utilitarianism, 8, 14, 19, 29, 34–5, 40, 58, 96, 100, 139, 143, 150, 161, 234
See also consequentialism

Vallentyne, Peter, 136, 138
values
 conflict, *see* conflict, moral
 transvaluation of, *see* Nietzsche, Friedrich
vanguard, 23, 25, 57, 215
Vernon, Richard, 105–8
virtue ethics, 4, 5, 8, 35–7, 42, 100, 108, 135–57, 197, 221, 227, 233, 234, 235–40

Ward, Colin, 43, 128, 191
Warren, Josiah, 14
Watson, David, 168
Weber, Max, 167
Weil, Simone, 191
Whitefield, Patrick, 194
Wilbur, Shawn, 154, 226
Wilde, Oscar, 213
Williams, Bernard, 142
Williams, Leonard, 186
Wittgenstein, Ludwig, 33, 178
Wolff, Jonathan, 4, 135, 154
Wolff, Robert Paul, 3, 13, 15–18, 30, 51, 135, 136–7, 139
Woodcock, George, 145, 156, 209, 210–13, 216
working class or workers, 2, 20, 30–1, 49, 60–4, 82, 86–7, 106, 108, 173, 234

Young, Iris Marion, 118, 121, 122

Zapatismo, 193
Zerzan, John, 6, 164–70, 174, 176, 179–80, 182